Martin Crean.
51 Caiystone A
Edinburgh EH 1c --, .

CW00807452

Soviet Oil Exports:
Trade Adjustments, Refining
Constraints and Market Behaviour

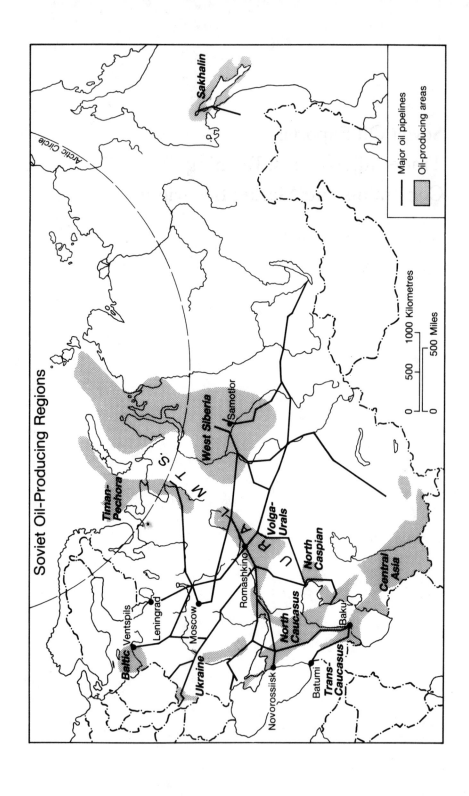

Soviet Oil-Producing Regions

Major oil pipelines
Oil-producing areas

1000 Kilometres
500 Miles

Arctic Circle

Sakhalin

Timan-
Pechora

West Siberia

Samotlor

U R A L S   M T S.

Volga-
Urals

North
Caspian

Romashkino

North
Caucasus

Baku

Central
Asia

Batumi

Trans-
Caucasus

Novorossiisk

Ukraine

Moscow

Leningrad

Ventspils

Baltic

Soviet Oil Exports: Trade Adjustments, Refining Constraints and Market Behaviour

MARGARET CHADWICK
DAVID LONG
MACHIKO NISSANKE

Published by Oxford University Press
for the Oxford Institute for Energy Studies
1987

Oxford University Press, Walton Street, Oxford OX2 6DP
Oxford New York Toronto
Delhi Bombay Calcutta Madras Karachi
Petaling Jaya Singapore Hong Kong Tokyo
Nairobi Dar es Salaam Cape Town
Melbourne Auckland
and associated companies in
Beirut Berlin Ibadan Nicosia

Oxford is a trade mark of Oxford University Press

OIES books are distributed in the United
States and Canada by PennWell Books, Tulsa, Oklahoma

© Oxford Institute for Energy Studies,
1987

British Library Cataloguing in Publication Data
Chadwick, Margaret
    Soviet oil exports: trade adjustments,
    refining constraints and market behaviour.
    1. Gas industry—Soviet Union
    2. Petroleum industry and trade—Soviet
    Union   3. Soviet Union—Commerce
    I. Title   II. Long, David   III. Nissanke,
    Machiko   IV. Oxford Institute for Energy
    Studies
    382'.4228'0947   HD9581.S652
    ISBN 0-19-730006-5

Typeset by Joshua Associates Limited, Oxford
Printed in Great Britain
at the University Printing House, Oxford
by David Stanford
Printer to the University

PREFACE

Since its establishment in 1983, the Oxford Institute for Energy Studies has been engaged in a large research programme on the world petroleum market. This programme involves the study of the configuration of particular markets where different varieties of crude oil and petroleum products are traded; the assessment of market structures and of economic performance; the analysis of oil prices, their behaviour, their relationships with one another, and their determinants; and the role and policies of major actors, mainly the exporting countries and the oil firms. Different parts of this programme of studies have been published in OIES working papers and books. This book presents work done on the oil trade and policies of one of these important actors, the Soviet Union, at present the largest oil producer and one of the top-ranking countries in the world league of petroleum exporting countries.

This book is about: (a) the patterns of Soviet oil production and trade and the constraints that affect these patterns, particularly the rigidities of the Soviet refining system; (b) the Soviet oil export policy, studied as an economic problem of balance-of-payments adjustment measures; and (c) the trading and marketing of Soviet oil exports with an emphasis on the Russian gas oil market, a market which offers one of the few opportunities available in the petroleum world for forward physical dealings.

Because of its coverage this book should be of interest to economists concerned with balance-of-payments and trade adjustment issues, to students of the Soviet economy and all those who puzzle over the apparent mysteries of Soviet economic policy, and of course to the members of the oil and energy community.

This book is divided into three parts according to the topics mentioned above. The three authors have divided the research and writing task between themselves according to their professional competence and their interests. Machiko Nissanke is an economist educated at Moscow and London Universities and now a Research Fellow of the Institute, and of Nuffield College, Oxford. She is the author of Part II where the oil export policy issue is studied in the economic framework of trade adjustments analysis. Margaret Chadwick and David Long, both Research Fellows of the Institute, have direct experience of the oil industry. Their work (Chadwick's in Part I and Long's in Part III) covers the oil issues: the features of the Soviet oil industry upstream and downstream, the behaviour of oil trade aggregates, the trading strategies and the channels through which Soviet oil exports reach the world petroleum market and transmit their impact.

The distinctive feature of this book, indeed of the Institute's approach to the study of energy issues, is the attempt to research the subject matter from different standpoints: those of academic economists and of professionals with knowledge and experience of the technical and structural aspects of the industry. The Institute believes that there is merit in this approach because the economic and technical aspects of any issue in the energy field are complementary, and the study of these various aspects requires the application of different skills. Authors do not share the same academic or professional background, do not use the same methods and do not write in the same style; but the lack of formal homogeneity is, in our judgement, more than compensated for by the information and insights gained from the pluralistic approach.

Although consisting of three different parts, the book follows a logical progression. The Introduction relates the different topics of the study to central themes of oil export performance and policies affected by severe constraints. The first chapters provide an indispensable factual background and focus on the domestic aspects of the Soviet oil industry that are relevant to the study of exports. The book then proceeds from structural features to issues of policy and this completes the study of the internal aspects of the Soviet oil exports problem. The next and final step is concerned with the relationship of Soviet oil to the world petroleum market which may be construed as the international aspect of the subject.

The preface of a book provides the authors, and the Institute to which they belong, with an opportunity to thank those who helped them in their work. Thanks are due to the directors of PlanEcon, Inc., who granted permission to use their invaluable data base on Soviet oil for the purpose of this research. Ed Hewett, of the Brookings Institution, and Jonathan Stern, of Chatham House, encouraged the authors in their endeavours and provided helpful criticism. The refinery model used by Chadwick for her analysis in Chapter 4 was made available by Bob High and David Edwards of High and Watt Associates. Peter Havlik of the Vienna Institute for Comparative Economic Studies supplied useful data published by the First Austrian Bank. We are grateful for the permission to use these data.

Chadwick and Long, with help from Brian Haskell-Thomas, interviewed many traders of Soviet oil and oil professionals in a number of oil companies. They respect their wish for anonymity but would like nevertheless to express to them collectively and individually their gratitude for their time and thoughtful responses to questions. *Petroleum Argus* kindly provided access to their data on the Russian gas oil market without which Chapter 11 could not have been written.

The authors benefited from discussions within the Institute with Peter Beck who subjected some of their writings to his incisive criticism, Robert Bacon who discussed the econometrics and many analytical issues, Ali Khadr and others. Jayne Dexter produced the figures; Margaret Ko and Susan Millar typed successive drafts with professional competence and a cheerful smile; and David Guthrie removed warts from the copy through a patient exercise of the healer's art. Thanks are also due to Jim Cane for producing the map and to Gordon Davies for designing the jacket.

Robert Mabro

CONTENTS

Part IV: Appendices

TABLES

FIGURES

ABBREVIATIONS

API	American Petroleum Institute
ARA	Amsterdam, Rotterdam, Antwerp area
ASSR	Autonomous Soviet Socialist Republic
bcm	billion cubic metres
b/d	barrels per day
BIS	Bank for International Settlements (Basle)
BNOC	British National Oil Corporation
BP	British Petroleum
CDU	Crude distillation unit
CIA	Central Intelligence Agency (USA)
c.i.f.	Cost, insurance and freight
CMEA	Council for Mutual Economic Assistance (Comecon)
CPEs	Centrally planned economies
EEC	European Economic Community
EIU	Economic Intelligence Unit
FAO	Food and Agriculture Organization (UN)
f.o.b.	Free on board
FTOs	Foreign Trade Organizations
GDP	Gross domestic product
GNP	Gross national product
IEA	International Energy Agency (OECD)
IMF	International Monetary Fund
IPE	International Petroleum Exchange (London)
km	kilometres
LDCs	Less developed countries
LNG	Liquefied natural gas
LPG	Liquefied petroleum gas
mb/d	million barrels per day
MDCs	More developed countries
MON	Motor octane number
mtpa	million tonnes per annum
MW	megawatts
n.a.	not available
NATO	North Atlantic Treaty Organisation
NGLs	Natural gas liquids

NMP   Net material product
NYMEX   New York Mercantile Exchange
OCPEs   Other centrally planned economies
OCS   Oil company source
OECD   Organisation for Economic Co-operation and
              Development
OPEC   Organization of the Petroleum Exporting Countries
PIW   *Petroleum Intelligence Weekly*
PWR   Pressurized water reactor
RON   Research octane number
RVP   Reid vapour pressure
SEB   Soviet Export Blend
UNCTAD   United Nations Conference on Trade and Development
              (Geneva)
UNECE   United Nations Economic Commission for Europe
VTSS   *Vneshnyaya torgovlya SSSR* (Foreign Trade of the USSR)
WIIW   Wiener Internationale Institut für Wirtschaftsvergleiche
              (Vienna Institute for Comparative Economic Studies)
WTI   West Texas Intermediate

1 INTRODUCTION

The Soviet Union is the world's largest oil producer: Soviet output of crude oil and natural gas liquids was 12.5 mb/d in 1986, when it exceeded US production by 22 per cent and was 2.4 times larger than Saudi Arabia's output (BP, 1987). The Soviet Union is also a major participant in international oil trade. Since the beginning of the 1980s, the Soviet Union has consistently been one of the two largest exporters of oil in the world; in certain years it ranked first just ahead of Saudi Arabia; and in other years it ranked second, lagging slightly behind the giant Gulf producer.

The main destinations of Soviet oil exports are: (a) Western Europe, where Soviet crude and petroleum products are sold under flexible contractual arrangements; and (b) the CMEA countries where Soviet oil is delivered under long-term and fairly rigid bilateral agreements. Although Soviet oil exports to Western Europe usually account for less than half the total volume exported, their volume is significant (some 78 million tonnes or approximately 1.56 mb/d in 1986), and the Soviet Union is, like Mexico and the North Sea, a principal source of non-OPEC oil for international trade in the non-Communist world.

These characteristics of Soviet oil production and trade define the important place occupied by the Soviet Union in world petroleum. The volumes involved are large, and questions about the role, influence and policies of such a major oil producer and exporter naturally arise. The authors' concern with these issues constitutes one of the motivations of their research for this book.

Soviet oil is not only important from a world perspective. It is first and foremost a national resource and a major domestic industry. Oil provides the Soviet economy with a sizeable proportion of its energy requirements. It also makes a considerable contribution to the Soviet balance of payments as the main source of hard currency earnings. In this respect oil exports to the West (the main hard currency area) play an important role in the management of the Soviet balance of payments, and by implication, of other parts of the macroeconomy. On the negative side, it must be recalled that oil suffers from the many problems that beset the Soviet economy. There are supply constraints and chronic shortages of essential commodities, goods and services.

The Soviet economy operates under a system of 'taut' planning which sets production, investment and consumption targets very close to, if not above, the levels that are attainable under the most favourable conditions likely to obtain. There is not enough slack or flexibility in the system to cope with the consequences of planning errors, with unanticipated supply difficulties or higher than expected demand in some important sector, or with accidents or emergencies.

This study will naturally be concerned with both the international and the domestic aspects of the Soviet oil industry. This is partly because export behaviour depends on internal factors such as production, costs, domestic demand, planning and policies, and on the economic conditions of world markets, such as demand for the commodity in question, prices, competing supplies, foreign trade regimes and the like. Furthermore, any question raised about the international significance of Soviet oil refers us back to internal issues of industrial performance, allocation of oil output between alternative uses and economic policies.

Our research on Soviet oil exports was initially motivated by a broader interest in the operation of the world petroleum market and particularly in the role played by major participants. As mentioned earlier, the Soviet Union is a large exporter, and this simple observation suggests that it may exercise an influence on the international oil market through volume and/or pricing policies.

On *volumes*, our starting-point is the observation that the quantities and composition (crude and products) of Soviet oil exports to the West fluctuate during the year and from year to year. The annual pattern of variations involves seasonality, but this factor by itself does not explain all short-term fluctuations. The behaviour of oil export volumes over time, say in the past twenty years, involves a rising trend but there are significant deviations from the trend line in certain years. There are also changes in the composition of petroleum products exports both within years and from year to year, and changes in the shares of crude oil and products in total petroleum exports to the West.

A question immediately arises: are these variations and changes the result of policy or of factors and conditions beyond the control of planners or policy-makers? It is useful to take stock, at this juncture, of two extreme hypotheses which we shall formulate here in an extreme form in order to provide reference-points for the analysis. The first hypothesis focuses on the economic, organizational and technological difficulties faced by the Soviet Union. It emphasizes the facts that the Soviet Union is supply constrained; that Soviet oil production upstream suffers from technical malpractices, dependence on obsolete technology and shortages of labour and capital; and that the processing of petroleum products is adversely affected by the rigidities and the age structure of the refining system. It recognizes the existence of severe constraints on the allocation of oil output because certain targets for domestic consumption and deliveries to the CMEA countries must be met in priority. On these bases, the following hypothesis is formulated: that Soviet oil exports to the West are a mere residual, the unplanned difference between (a) a variable and incorrectly anticipated output and (b) rigid consumption requirements in the Soviet Union and rigid export commitments to the CMEA countries. In its extreme form this hypothesis leaves little or no room for the planning of Soviet oil exports to the West. It implies that there is no significant link between any Soviet export policy and the behaviour of oil exports to the West.

The second hypothesis, which we never found explicitly formulated by recognized authorities, but which is implicit in comments on Soviet oil in trade journals and in questions asked by outsiders about Soviet oil policy, suggests that variations in the volume of exports to the West are for the purpose of market intervention. This hypothesis reflects a suspicion that the Soviet Union seeks to influence prices or to improve its bargaining position *vis-à-vis* customers by withholding exports in certain circumstances, and to take advantage of favourable market conditions by increasing export volumes in other circumstances. A more general formulation of this hypothesis is that autonomous policy decisions, whether for the purpose of market intervention or for *other* economic objectives, determine variations in export volumes.

The first hypothesis states that, because of a variety of adverse domestic factors, the Soviet Union is a passive agent that exports any amount of oil that *happens* to be available; while the second hypothesis expresses the view that the Soviet Union has an *effective* oil export policy, a view which must logically imply that supply constraints and other structural rigidities leave policy-makers with significant room for manoeuvre.

It is difficult to agree with either hypothesis as expressed in these extreme forms. Their only merit is to bring into sharp focus two factors that influence Soviet oil export behaviour: economic policy and the constraints that the economy, and perhaps politics, place on the making of policy decisions. Our view is that it is wrong to emphasize the role of one of these factors at the expense of the other. There is always a role for policy in any country however small, poor or crippled with economic difficulties, *a fortiori* in a country as important as the Soviet Union. And everywhere policy-makers face restricted choices. The interesting question for the analyst is about the relationship between policy and constraints in the particular situation he or she purports to study. The task is to assess the nature of these two factors, their interaction, and the role that constrained policy actually plays.

In short, our own hypothesis is that the variations in the volume of Soviet oil exports to the West and the changes in their composition partly reflect production problems (both in the upstream and in the downstream of the Soviet oil industry) and constraints on the allocation of Soviet oil output, and partly reflect planning and policy decisions. We shall argue in this book, however, that the relevant policies are related to the management of the Soviet balance of payments. Oil exports are used by the Soviet authorities, together with other instruments, for the purpose of *trade adjustments* on a year-to-year basis. The policy aim is not systematic intervention on the world petroleum market; the oil export policy should rather be viewed as a response in any year to the balance-of-payments surplus or deficit that emerged in the preceding year, partly as a result of oil export performance in given world market conditions.

But are the oil export *pricing policies* of the Soviet Union the instrument of intervention on the world petroleum market? And what is the impact of these pricing policies on world oil? We can dispose of these questions in this Introduction by referring to the previous arguments about volumes. An effective policy on prices is necessarily dependent on the use of the volumes exported as an instrument for intervention. Our argument in this book, that volume targets are set year on year in the context of trade adjustment policies, and the further argument that short-term variations in export volumes reflect binding constraints (which planners are able to relax to a greater extent in the medium and long term than in the short period) both suggest that there is little scope for manipulating oil export volumes for the purpose of intervention on the world petroleum market. This does not preclude altogether the possibility of tactical moves, undertaken occasionally, to secure a better bargain with a customer, or to improve the trading position in particular circumstances. But production, refining, storage, logistical and other constraints, together with the economic and political factors that predetermine the allocation of a year's oil output, may severely limit the scope of these tactical moves and the ability of the Soviet authorities to sustain them over a significant period of time. To recognize that the Soviet Union is occasionally able to play some commercial games of limited scope and duration is not sufficient to establish a case for significant intervention. An oil exporter with restricted room for manoeuvre on volumes cannot operate as a price maker in normal circumstances, even if his share of the world export market is large. However, a distinction must be made between *incidental* and *desired* price effects. Movements in Soviet oil exports may, and undoubtedly sometimes do, have some impact on the behaviour of world oil prices at least in the short term. But unless the changes in the volume of oil exports are specifically geared to move world oil prices in a desired direction or towards a target level, their impact on price is just an occurrence which may or may not correspond to the economic interests of the oil exporter. They are what they happen to be, the result of factors outside its control, not the desired effects of a conscious exercise of market power.

The impact of Soviet oil on world petroleum prices in recent years is better understood in the context of the relationship between OPEC and non-OPEC exporters. Between 1980 and 1985, and again in 1987, OPEC has attempted to set the international price of oil in adverse market conditions. The success of these attempts depended essentially on OPEC's willingness to meet the residual world demand for oil that corresponded to the OPEC price. Non-OPEC producers took these prices as given, and each of them acting as a typical price taker put on to the market whatever volume of oil it was able or willing to supply. In these years (1980–85), however, there were: (a) an expansion of non-OPEC production and exports; (b) a decline in world oil demand; and (c) a significant drawdown of oil stocks.[1] The combined effect of these factors was to reduce OPEC production by 10.2 mb/d from 27.4 mb/d in 1980 to 17.2 mb/d in 1985, a drop of 37 per cent (BP, 1987). Their more significant impact was to weaken OPEC's ability to administer the oil price, a weakening which led to price reductions in 1983 and 1984, and eventually to the oil price collapse of 1986. The growth of Soviet oil exports during this period was part of the expansion of non-OPEC supplies in a shrinking market, and to that extent a contributing factor to the fall in the oil price.

However, we can not infer from this analysis that the oil price decline was an objective of Soviet oil policy nor that it was welcomed by the Soviet Union as a desired or beneficial occurrence. The Soviet Union being, despite its large share of world oil production and exports, on the competitive fringe of the oil market and not in the cartelized core, must always prefer to take high rather than low oil prices. The reason, simply, is that the export volumes of a price taker are not influenced by the price level. Thus, higher oil prices either yield higher oil revenues for the Soviet Union or enable any chosen revenue target to be met with a lower volume of exports, and this releases oil either for domestic use

[1] According to BP, 1987, world oil consumption declined from 61.5 mb/d in 1980 to 58.5 mb/d in 1985, a reduction of 3 mb/d (5 per cent). In the same period non-OPEC production increased from 35.3 mb/d in 1980 to 40.4 mb/d in 1985, an increment of 5.1 mb/d. Between these two years OPEC production declined by 10.2 mb/d. The fall in OPEC output was greater than the sum of the decline in world consumption and the increase in non-OPEC production because of an inventory drawdown which, according to these figures, seems to have been very significant.

or for delivery to CMEA countries. To sum up, Soviet oil may have some adverse impact (though this is impossible to measure) on oil prices, but it can not be said that the Soviet Union has an interest in, nor that it actively seeks, low oil prices.

All this brings us back to the issue of export volumes and explains the central place it occupies in the book. The issue is important because the Soviet Union is a very large exporter and it supersedes the pricing issue because the Soviet Union is not a price maker on the world petroleum market in the usual meaning of this concept.[2]

In this book the issue is approached from three angles. In Part I, the focus is mainly on the features of Soviet crude oil production and the refining system, the constraints and the problems that affect both the volume and the composition of oil exports to the West. Part I also serves the necessary purpose of providing the factual background and the data on Soviet oil output, the supply and consumption balance and foreign trade. Chadwick describes the upstream side of the Soviet oil industry in Chapter 2: oilfields, reserves, crudes and the behaviour of oil output over time, that is growth, year-to-year fluctuations and seasonality. She discusses the oil production problems of the Soviet Union, relying mainly on the scholarly literature available on this subject. She then presents estimates of the Soviet oil balance which update work done by others and introduces new assumptions and a modified methodology.

In Chapter 3, she describes and analyses the main statistical features of Soviet oil trade: the growth of exports and imports, their composition, the destination of exports and their seasonality. This chapter also includes a discussion of the statistical sources and of the important problem of the valuation of Soviet oil exports to CMEA and OECD countries in Soviet statistical publications. Chapter 4 is concerned with the Soviet refining system and with the problems that the age structure of refineries and the limited amount of upgrading capacity available to them can cause. This chapter and the section in Chapter 2 on the causes of production difficulties upstream reveal some of the important constraints that restrict planners' choices in matters of oil export policy.

The analysis in Chapter 4 uses a small refinery model to assess the flexibility of the Soviet refining system and to determine the impact of limited flexibility, in the face of changing demand patterns for oil products, on the volume and composition of products exports. The main findings are that the operational flexibility of the Soviet refining system is limited on the volume side by capacity and technology while the freedom to vary product qualities is effectively restricted to the

---

[2] There is a sense in which an exporter in the competitive fringe makes the price. This happens when the market is in disequilibrium (Arrow, 1959; Roberts, 1984).

sulphur content of gas oil. Further, the refining system may run into difficulties in the medium term if the demand barrel changes significantly towards middle distillates and away from fuel oil.

Part II deals with the Soviet oil export policy. In Chapters 5 and 6, Nissanke addresses the issues of whether and how oil, being a well-traded commodity and a swing fuel, has been used for balance-of-payments adjustment purposes. Her argument is that the role of oil exports to the West in the Soviet economy is that of a flexible export commodity and a core source for financing long-term planned import needs. To assess this role, oil is compared with the other major export commodities of the Soviet Union; and the use of oil exports as an instrument for trade adjustment in conjunction with other instruments – borrowing in the international capital market and gold sales – is examined.

In Chapter 7, the focus is on both policy and constraints, and the question raised is how Soviet planners allocate oil output between domestic consumption, CMEA and Western export markets in the face of severe physical and economic constraints on increasing oil production. Nissanke then evaluates the flexibility of their responses to changing conditions and requirements in these three 'destination' areas, and identifies both the factors that limit the planners' ability to respond and the policies pursued to relax these constraints and release oil for export to the hard currency area. These policies include gas-for-oil substitution and energy conservation in the Soviet economy, measures to increase imports of non-OPEC oil in barter exchange for military and other goods, and decisions relating the volume of oil deliveries to CMEA countries.

Chapter 8 updates the discussion on the Soviet oil export policy to cover the most recent situation (1985–6), which is significantly different from the period covered by earlier chapters (1970–84). The two main changes are the 1986 collapse in oil prices and the 1985 decline in Soviet oil production. The implications of these changes for the conclusions reached for the earlier period are traced.

Having examined the planners' need to use oil exports for trade adjustments purposes and the constraints they encounter in designing and implementing this oil export policy, Nissanke undertakes an econometric analysis to test her arguments (Chapter 9). Oil export functions construed as a planners' behaviourial equation are estimated. The results show that the 'balance-of- payments adjustment' model, which expresses the volume of oil exports as a function of the one-year lagged hard currency trade balance and the current world oil price, can explain to a large extent the annual fluctuations in Soviet *crude oil* shipments to the West. Thus, Soviet planners appear to have succeeded in using crude oil exports as a key instrument for the annual adjustments of the external trade balance, despite the constraints restricting their allocation decisions. In contrast, the export pattern of *refined products* is not explained by the balance-of-payments adjustment model. This latter result confirms Chadwick's findings in Chapter 4 on the rigidities of the refining system which were arrived at through a totally different approach. These two separate parts of the analysis reinforce each other. An important conclusion, therefore, is that the crude oil production difficulties and constraints are less binding for Soviet oil export policy in the short run (here defined as the period allowing for a year-to-year adjustment) than the rigid and partly obsolete refining system.

In Parts I and II the authors studied both the internal and the economic policy aspects of Soviet oil exports. But Soviet oil leaves at some point the borders of the Soviet Union and enters the world petroleum market. This leads us to a third aspect of the export issue: the trading arrangements and the particular market structures through which Soviet oil is disposed of in Western markets. This is the subject matter of Part III. The analysis of the trading and marketing aspects of Soviet oil exports is of interest for three main reasons. First, as a price taker the Soviet Union needs to adopt a flexible marketing approach, and this is reflected in the types of contracts entered upon with buyers and the pricing formulae adopted. Secondly, the crude oil production and refining problems faced by the Soviet Union do not enable it to enter into very firm commitments on the exact volume and timing of deliveries. The ability to set a volume target for crude oil exports on a year-to-year basis for balance-of-payments purposes (see above) is not necessarily associated with the ability to perform on quantities, quality specifications and time schedules in an efficient and absolutely reliable manner. The inability to ensure a high standard of performance on supplies has a bearing on both contracts and marketing methods. Thirdly, for a complex set of reasons relating both to the nature of a particular petroleum product exported by the Soviet Union, gas oil, and the conditions of the West European market, a forward physical market for Russian gas oil has developed. This market is one of the few in oil where economic agents can perform hedging and speculative operations.[3] A finding of particular interest is that the forward price of Russian gas oil was the best predictor of future spot prices, a result that is consistent with the 'Efficient Markets Hypothesis'. This hypothesis was rejected by the data used in previous studies undertaken at the Oxford Institute for Energy Studies on the Brent market and the

[3] The other oil markets that provide opportunities to deal in futures or forward contracts are the NYMEX in New York, the IPE in London, and the informal forward markets in Brent and Dubai.

NYMEX (Mabro et al, 1986; Chassard and Halliwell, 1986), and Long's results in this book suggest significant differences between the operations of the Russian gas oil market and other futures and forward petroleum markets. Long's work indicates that an oil product exported by the Soviet Union plays an important functional role in the world petroleum market. The trading and marketing arrangements for Soviet oil exports are studied in Chapter 10, and the Russian gas oil market is described, and its role and performance assessed, in Chapter 11.

PART I

PRODUCTION AND REFINING CONSTRAINTS

Margaret Chadwick

2 PRODUCTION, CONSUMPTION AND THE SOVIET OIL BALANCE

2.1 Producing Areas ·

Oil deposits are widely scattered throughout the Soviet Union, and oil is thus produced in several regions (see frontispiece); the relative importance of these petroleum producing regions has changed over the 100 years since the industry was initially developed. Until World War II the fields in the Caucasus and Caspian areas were predominant, but these declined in importance when further significant discoveries and developments were made, first in the Volga–Urals region and then in West Siberia. Today, 60 per cent of Soviet oil production comes from West Siberia, and this proportion may rise even further as new fields in Tyumen province are brought on stream. The six regions (a)–(f) detailed below now account for over 95 per cent of Soviet oil production.

(a) *West Siberia*. The main oilfields are situated in the basin of the rivers Ob and Irtysh, south of the Arctic Circle. Exploration drilling is being extended northwards into the Kara Sea but no significant discoveries have yet been made there. Oil was first found in West Siberia at Shaim in 1960. Gradually, exploration was extended eastwards into Tyumen province where the giant Samotlor field was discovered in 1965. This huge field was originally estimated to have reserves of 13 billion barrels, a figure which is now believed to be nearer 25 billion. Development began in 1968 and production increased rapidly from 90,000 b/d in 1970 to a peak of 3.1 mb/d in 1980.[1] There are 4,700 production wells in operation on Samotlor, which accounted for 25 per cent of total Soviet production in 1980. Other large fields in the region include

[1] The production figures quoted in this section include condensate from both associated and non-associated gas. West Siberia is believed to contain two-thirds of all the Soviet Union's condensate resources. Other condensate sources are the gas fields of Central Asia, Orenburg in the southern Urals and Vuktyl in the Komi ASSR. No separate figures are published by the Soviet Union for condensate production. Published Western sources estimate that, of the 12.3 mb/d crude plus condensate produced in 1983, around 600,000 b/d was condensate (CIA, 1985) and that condensate production was 1 million tonnes (23,000 b/d) in 1965, rising to 9 million tonnes (210,000 b/d) in 1975 and 23 million tonnes (535,000 b/d) in 1982 (Sagers, 1984). The production figures quoted in this section for individual fields are drawn from Yuasa, 1985, and from 'Country profile: USSR', Part 1, printed in the *OPEC Bulletin*, Vol. XVI, No. 8, October 1985, pp. 38–48, 86.

Fedorovo, the third-largest field in the Soviet Union, which produced 725,000 b/d in 1984, and Mamontovo, which produced around 590,000 b/d in 1985. Total production in West Siberia in 1984 was around 7.5 mb/d, 60 per cent of the Soviet Union's production.

(*b*) *Volga–Urals*. This region covers 500,000 km² between the Volga and the Urals (CIA, 1985, p. 20). Production began on a small scale in the 1930s but the region only became important in the 1950s when output from the older fields around the Caspian Sea began to decline seriously.

Romashkino, at one time thought to be the largest field in the world, was discovered in 1948 and began production in the early 1950s. This giant field had estimated recoverable reserves of over 14 billion barrels and production peaked at around 1.65 mb/d in 1970. North of Romashkino, the Arlan field was found in 1955 with estimated reserves of 3.2 billion barrels.

Output from the Volga–Urals region increased rapidly during the 1950s, reaching 2.2 mb/d in 1960 (almost 75 per cent of total Soviet production). Production peaked at 4.5 mb/d in 1975–6 and has now declined to less than 3 mb/d.

(*c*) *Timan–Pechora (Komi ASSR)*. The Timan–Pechora basin lies in the Komi ASSR, which is in the north-eastern part of the European USSR, to the west of the Urals and bordering the Barents Sea. Small deposits were developed from the 1930s to the 1950s, and two fairly large fields, Vozei and Usinsk, were brought on stream in the late 1960s/early 1970s. Production for this region is currently just below 400,000 b/d.

(*d*) *North Caucasus*. The North Caucasus region lies to the west of the Caspian Sea and has been an area of oil production for over sixty years. The large Groznyi fields were developed in the early 1900s when output from the Baku region to the south began to decline. Production was interrupted first during the Revolution and then during World War II. Output eventually peaked in 1971 at 740,000 b/d and fell rapidly to 260,000 b/d by 1983 (CIA, *International Energy Statistical Review*).

(*e*) *Trans-Caucasus*. Oilfields around Baku in Azerbaidzhan are reported to have been producing small quantities of oil early in the nineteenth century. Output took off in the 1870s and by 1883 exceeded 20,000 b/d. Since World War II production has been sustained by developments in Georgia, to the west of Baku, which produced 60,000 b/d in 1980, and by offshore wells in the Caspian Sea, which now account for over 70 per cent of Azerbaidzhan's output (CIA, 1985, p. 21). Production from Azerbaidzhanian fields declined from 400,000 b/d in 1970 to 280,000 b/d in 1983 (CIA, *International Energy Statistical Review*).

(*f*) *Central Asia*. This is primarily a gas-producing region but substantial oil deposits have also been developed in west Turkmenistan on the eastern shore of the Caspian Sea. Production from these fields peaked in 1975 at 830,000 b/d and has declined to just over 500,000 b/d in 1985.

(*g*) *Other Regions*. Other oil-producing regions include the Ukraine, Belorussia, and Sakhalin Island in the Far East. These areas produced 450–500,000 b/d in the mid-1970s but output subsequently fell to around 350,000 b/d in the early 1980s. Table 2.1 lists Soviet production by region for 1970–85.

Table 2.1: Soviet Oil Production by Region. 1970–85. Thousand Barrels per Day.

	West Siberia	Volga–Urals	Trans-Caucasus	North Caucasus	Central Asia	Komi	Others	Total
1970	630	4,170	400	700	600	150	410	7,060
1971	900	4,230	380	740	680	160	450	7,540
1972	1,250	4,300	370	710	730	170	460	7,990
1973	1,750	4,430	360	610	780	180	470	8,580
1974	2,330	4,460	350	560	800	200	480	9,180
1975	2,960	4,520	350	470	830	220	470	9,820
1976	3,620	4,500	350	440	800	260	400	10,370
1977	4,370	4,420	340	440	710	290	350	10,920
1978	5,080	4,290	350	430	630	340	310	11,430
1979	5,660	4,030	340	420	600	380	280	11,710
1980	6,250	3,820	340	400	570	370	280	12,030
1981	6,690	n.a.	n.a.	n.a.	n.a.	n.a.	n.a.	12,180
1982	7,060	3,350	n.a.	n.a.	n.a.	410	n.a.	12,250
1983	7,380	3,130	340	260	550	380	290	12,330
1984	7,580	2,900	n.a.	n.a.	n.a.	n.a.	n.a.	12,260
1985	7,610	2,720	n.a.	n.a.	n.a.	n.a.	n.a.	11,980

Note: The figures quoted include production of gas condensate.
Sources: CIA, *International Energy Statistical Review*, various issues
         Wilson, 1986 (for 1985 only)

2.2 Reserves

No precise figures for the size and location of Soviet reserves exist since this information is a state secret (CIA, 1985, p. 14). The 1986 *BP*

Statistical Review of World Energy reports 'explored' reserves at end 1985 as 61 billion barrels (8.6 per cent of total world proved reserves), and the 1985 *OPEC Annual Statistical Bulletin* reports proven reserves at end 1985 as 75 billion barrels (10 per cent of the world total).

In 1985, Petroconsultants downgraded their estimates of remaining recoverable Soviet reserves from 61 billion to 50 billion barrels (*Petroleum Economist*, Vol. LII, No. 12, December 1985, p. 460). This revision was based on Soviet reports of a significant decline in reserves in the Komi ASSR and a decreasing reserves/production ratio in West Siberia.

Given current production of around 12 mb/d, the overall reserves/ production ratio in the Soviet Union is probably 14 years. However, it may be as low as 11.5 years if the computation is made on the basis of the lower reserves estimates. Table 2.2 lists the main oil-producing fields of the Soviet Union grouped by estimated size of their reserves.

2.3 Crude Oil Production

Production of petroleum (i.e. crude oil plus NGLs) in the Soviet Union has increased from 147.9 million tonnes in 1960 to 615.0 million tonnes in 1986. Soviet sources publish only the combined volume of crude oil and NGLs output, but PlanEcon provide an estimated disaggregation of the figures (see Table 2.3). Their data show that crude oil production rose from 147.2 million tonnes in 1960 to 571.5 million in 1985. Considering that their estimate of NGLs output has remained roughly constant for the last four years of the series, we may assume that production of NGLs in 1986 was 22–23 million tonnes, indicating that crude oil output was around 592–593 million tonnes in 1986.

The highest production level so far was attained in 1983 (crude, 594.6 million tonnes; crude and NGLs, 616.3 million tonnes). It would be rash to infer that Soviet oil production has already passed its peak. The significant drop (22.3 million tonnes) that occured between 1983 and 1985 has been largely offset by a production increase of 21.0 million tonnes in 1986. A more accurate description of the output profile is that production reached a plateau in the early 1980s. There was considerable growth in the 1960s owing to the discovery and development of super-giant fields; continuing growth but at a reduced rate in the 1970s; and, allowing for minor fluctuations of plus or minus 2 per cent around an average level of 605 million tonnes,[2] a levelling off in the period 1980–86. The reduction in the rate of growth of production in the 1960s and 1970s is apparent from Table 2.4.

[2] Crude oil plus NGLs.

Table 2.2: Main Oil-producing Fields of the Soviet Union.

(a) Super-giant Fields (Reserves of over 5 billion barrels)

Region	Field	Date of Discovery
West Siberia	Samotlor	1966
	Fedorovo	1971
Volga–Urals	Romashkino	1948
	Arlan	1955
Central Asia	Kotur-Tepe	1956

(b) Giant Fields (Reserves of 500 million to 5 billion barrels)

Region	Field	Date of Discovery
West Siberia	Agan	1966
	Kholmogory	1973
	Mamontovo	1965
	Megion	1961
	Pokachi	1970
	Pravdinsk	1964
	Severnyi Pokur	1971
	Severo-Varegan	1971
	Sovetskoe	1962
	Ust-Balyk	1961
	Varegan	1970
	Vata	1961
	Vategan	1971
Volga–Urals	Bavly	1946
	Mukhanovo	1945
	Novoelkhovo	1955
	Shkapovo	1953
	Tuimazy	1937
Central Asia	Barsa-Gelmes	1962
	Nebit-Dag	1934
Trans-Caucasus	Neftyanye Kamni	1949
	Ostrov Bulla	1959
	Samgori	1974
North Caspian	Uzen	1961
	Zhetybai	1960
North Caucasus	Yuzhno-Sukhokumskoe	1963
Timan–Pechora	Usinsk	1963
	Vozei	1972

Source: CIA, 1985, p. 66

Table 2.3: Soviet Oil Production. 1960–86. Million Tonnes.

	Crude Oil	NGLs	Combined
1960	147.2	0.7	147.9
1965	241.7	1.2	242.8
1970	348.8	4.2	353.0
1971	371.8	5.3	377.1
1972	393.8	6.7	400.4
1973	421.4	7.7	429.0
1974	450.6	8.3	458.9
1975	481.8	9.0	490.8
1976	509.3	10.4	519.7
1977	533.8	12.0	545.8
1978	557.7	13.8	571.5
1979	569.7	15.9	585.6
1980	584.5	18.7	603.2
1981	587.8	21.0	608.8
1982	591.1	21.5	612.6
1983	594.6	21.7	616.3
1984	590.7	22.0	612.7
1985	571.5	22.5	594.0
1986	n.a.	n.a.	615.0

Note: The combined totals may not add up exactly because of rounding.
Sources: PlanEcon, 1986; *Ekonomicheskaya gazeta* (for 1986 only)

Table 2.4: Average Percentage Growth Rates of Soviet and US Crude Oil
Production. 1960–86.

	Soviet Union	USA
1960–65	10.4	2.6
1965–70	7.8	4.6
1970–75	6.8	−1.3
1975–80	4.2	−0.6
1980–86	0.2	0.0

Sources: Figures calculated from Table 2.3 and from API, various issues

A comparison of the Soviet and the US oil production profiles is of
interest. Both countries can legitimately claim to be the oldest oil
producers in the world, and today they rank first and second in the
international league of oil-producing nations. Yet, the Soviet production profile in the 1960s and early 1970s has the typical growth feature
of a newcomer, while the USA's profile for the same period displays the
characteristic decline of a mature oil producer. The contrast is
illustrated by the data presented in Table 2.4.

Another interesting aspect of Soviet petroleum production is its seasonality. The annual output profile is characterized by a summer peak (third quarter) and a winter trough (first quarter) (see Figure 2.1). The fluctuations are regular but not very dramatic. The weather is undoubtedly the cause of this particular seasonal pattern. Severe conditions in winter have adverse effects on the production of oil. It is interesting to note that North Sea output peaks in winter and tends to decline in summer (Mabro et al, 1986). The same seasons have opposite effects on the output pattern in the two cases. The reason is that maintenance work in the North Sea, where all installations are in a hostile environment off shore, is performed more easily in favourable weather conditions and is therefore usually scheduled for the summer and spring. Some production is then shut in. In the winter months workovers and repairs cannot be conveniently carried out and are only undertaken when circumstances make them inevitable. Production therefore suffers no hindrance or delay and tends to rise to a seasonal peak.

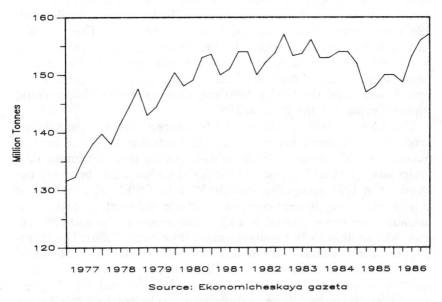

Source: Ekonomicheskaya gazeta

Figure 2.1 Soviet Oil Production: Quarterly Data. 4Q76–4Q86.

However, as we shall see in Chapter 7, output seasonality aggravates the effects of consumption seasonality on the export pattern. In the Soviet Union the need for heating increases oil consumption in winter, which is when production tends to decline. Higher domestic demand

and lower production in the first quarter significantly reduce the amounts available for export during that quarter.

2.4 Production Problems

The extent and nature of the problems faced by the Soviet Union in its oil production industry have been the focus of debate amongst Soviet experts in the West since the mid-1970s. Although oil production was still growing rapidly in the 1970s, the failure to meet planned targets during the early 1970s awoke many people both inside and outside the Soviet Union to the fact that the industry had underlying problems which could seriously affect its ability to meet production targets in the 1980s.

Campbell, 1976, was the first to point out the Soviet Union's increasing depletion rates and poor drilling record. However, the issue was brought to the forefront of the debate by two reports published by the CIA (CIA, 1977a and 1977b). These highly publicized reports forecast that Soviet oil production would peak at a maximum of 12 mb/d in 1980 (or at the latest in the early 1980s), and that by the mid-1980s the Soviet Union would be a net importer of oil. This view was flatly contradicted by a report by PetroStudies, which claimed that Soviet oilfields were actually under-producing by up to 30 per cent below their potential capacity. PetroStudies went on to predict that production could double by 1990 and that the Soviet Union would triple oil exports to the West by 1985.[3]

The CIA reports turned out to be correct about a peak in oil production, although this occurred at 12.4 mb/d in 1983, and not at a maximum of 12 mb/d in 1980 as indicated by the most pessimistic CIA projection. The CIA forecast that the Soviet Union would become a net importer by 1985, competing with the West for OPEC oil, proved to be completely wrong. Soviet net exports of crude and products to the non-Socialist countries increased by 25 per cent between 1978 and 1984, i.e. from 63.5 million to 79.1 million tonnes (PlanEcon, 1986). The Petro-Studies report, which made sensational counter-claims on Soviet oil production in order to refute the CIA's equally sensational conclusions, was based on a mistaken view of the Soviet oil industry. Exports to the West did indeed increase during the first half of the 1980s but the increase was modest relative to the projected tripling. However, at the time of its publication the prevailing wisdom still tended to be that the Soviet Union would meet or come close to its production targets well into the 1980s.

---

[3] See 'Russia "poised to triple oil exports"', *Financial Times*, 13 September 1978.

Neither the CIA analysts nor the PetroStudies team were objective and impartial students of the issue. The former were motivated in part by political aims and the latter seem to have been more concerned with apologia and polemics than with establishing reliable facts.

The CIA's contention that the Soviet Union would be a net importer of oil by 1985 had clear implications for security in the Middle East and may have erred towards the pessimistic view in order to raise political awareness of the problem. The timing of the CIA report also suggests that it aimed at creating a sense of emergency to facilitate the adoption of President Carter's new plan for greater US self-sufficiency in energy.

Nevertheless the main part of the CIA report, which focused on the Soviet Union's upstream difficulties, was an accurate analysis and has stood the test of time. According to Hewett, 1984a, the weakness of its conclusions was due to its poor analysis of the trends in consumption, its failure to take into account substitution of other fuels, particularly gas, and the lack of an overall energy supply and demand analysis.

(*a*) *The Causes of the Production Problem*. The Soviet Union failed to meet oil production targets in the early 1970s.[4] This led planners to set lower targets for later years, but despite these adjustments they proved to be over-ambitious. The problem faced by planners was in the allocation of resources between developing new fields and stemming the decline of old ones. During the 1970s the ratio of the decline in output from existing fields to the increase in new productive capacity, which we define as the 'depletion rate', was rising. Had the planners diverted more resources to investment in new fields, the depletion rate would probably have risen further in the short and medium term; yet such a reallocation might have been economically beneficial in the long term.

It seems that, in the 1950s and 1960s, Soviet planners concentrated more on the older fields, mainly those in the Volga–Urals region which received the most resources. The resulting fall in the depletion rate, which was naturally associated with an under-fulfilment of output targets, forced them to turn their attention to new developments. There was a massive shift of resources to West Siberia in the late 1970s. Since these reallocations of resources always involve a trade-off, the opportunity cost of the shift was a more rapid production decline in the Volga–Urals field.

In short, the main cause of the production problem is the scarcity of resources – skilled labour, technology and capital – which limits investment growth and forces Soviet planners to cope with problems by changing the allocation of these resources between new and old fields. The depletion rate increases when the development of new capacity is

---

[4] This section draws heavily on Hewett, 1984a, Chapter 2.

neglected in favour of maintenance and workovers in old fields; and the rate of the output decline of the older fields falls rapidly when resources are transferred to new oil regions. Furthermore, Soviet planners tend to delay necessary infrastructural investment until it becomes necessary in order to build up production. This is the cause of many of the problems encountered today in West Siberia.

Besides this general issue there are specific problems faced by the oil industry which can be classified as technical and administrative.

(*b*) *Technical Problems.* The CIA reports (CIA, 1977a and 1977b) analysed the technical problems in some depth and their conclusions are still valid to a large extent in the mid-1980s. In the 1950s the Soviet Union began the practice of waterflooding fields in the Volga–Urals region to prevent a decline in production. In the West, when wells stop flowing naturally, pumps are installed at the well-head to maintain the flow. However, pumping equipment was scarce in the Soviet Union at this time and a cheap alternative was to inject water along the edges of each field to raise the pressure and keep the oil flowing. Waterflooding is still common practice today and has been used extensively in the fields of West Siberia. In 1976 water-injected fields accounted for 80 per cent of production. This system differs from the secondary recovery techniques used in the West in that it increases pressure in the field rather than merely maintaining it.

Although the technique can boost production for a few years, in the longer term it damages the reservoir and limits the eventual recovery rate. Water seeps into the oil-producing channels, leaving pockets of oil trapped in less permeable parts of the rock. Once the oil begins to show significant amounts of water, the field has to be pumped with special electric submersible pumps which have a large fluid-lifting capacity. Fields may have to be redrilled if the water content becomes too high. The CIA reported that Romashkino had been redrilled four times by 1977. The Soviet Union claimed for many years that its water injection system enabled it to achieve a higher recovery rate than Western oil producers. However, it is now recognized that waterflooding, while boosting front-end production in a field, has caused many unforeseen problems which tend to reduce the expected recovery rate. These problems appear to be particularly severe in West Siberia where growth in production began to decline much sooner than was expected.

The accelerating depletion rate in the 1970s increased the requirement for additional drilling to add to reserves. Again, technical problems obstructed the achievement of drilling targets. The widespread use of the turbo drill (preferred to the more efficient rotary drill

since the latter requires high-strength steel pipe), which had been successful in developing the Volga–Urals fields in the 1960s, slowed down
the rate of drilling and the difficulties were compounded by the poor-
quality rock bits produced by Soviet manufacturers. Indeed almost all
domestically produced machinery was of inferior quality, and there
were frequent supply bottlenecks, causing delays in drilling programmes.

Similar problems dogged the producing fields, which experienced
delays due to shortages of pumps and secondary recovery machinery.
Only in 1986, after Gorbachev's visit to West Siberia, did there appear
to be any sign that these difficulties were being tackled.

(c) *Administrative Problems*. Gustafson, 1985a, argues that Soviet production problems of the last decade have been compounded by bad
decision-making which has led to planning under shorter and shorter
time horizons.[5] The most serious results of this policy have been the
concentration of resources on boosting short-term output and the
neglect of exploration.

According to Gustafson the exploration process itself can be roughly
divided into two categories: 'upstream' exploration which covers
geophysical surveys and mapping new structures, and 'downstream'
exploration which consists of identifying new reserves by prospective
drilling. Investment must be carefully balanced between these two
phases in order to ensure that neither long-term prospects nor
medium-term development is neglected.

Exploratory drilling in the Soviet Union slumped in the 1970s and
did not regain its 1967 level until 1980. In the mid-1970s West Siberia
held two-thirds of the additions to reserves (proved plus probable) but
only 15 per cent of exploratory drilling was carried out there. This
puzzling state of affairs may be explained by the Government's concern
over the rapidly decreasing output from older fields; priority was given
to trying to arrest the decline elsewhere. Also, the incentive system for
drilling programmes was in terms of metres drilled rather than reserves
proved or wells opened. This mitigated against exploratory drilling,
particularly in costly, remote regions with difficult rock formations,
such as West Siberia.

In 1976 and 1977 the growth in production began to decline; and this
coincided with a failure to meet planned additions to reserves and a
decrease in the flow rate of new wells. The Government's response was
almost immediate: resources were diverted from west of the Urals into
increased activity in Siberia. However, the immediate requirement to
boost output meant that investment was poured into development and

---

[5] This section is based on Gustafson, 1985a.

the supporting 'downstream' exploratory activity rather than prospect-ive exploration. Even in the 1980s the share of 'downstream' explora-tion has continued to grow at the expense of the 'upstream'.

The Soviet response to production problems is akin to emergency 'fire-fighting' measures, which stem the decline in output in the short term but fail to solve the industry's underlying problems. The 'fire-fighting' response to the crisis of the late 1970s did not prevent the immediate emergence of new problems. Thus, in 1982, for the first time, Tyumen province failed to meet its production target and in 1984 the shortfall was 9 million tonnes.

The most recent 'fire-fighting' measures were applied, with some degree of success, in 1986. Local management was replaced, teams of skilled workers were flown in from fields west of the Urals, and investment increased by 31 per cent over the 1985 level. Most of this investment was allocated to production and development in West Siberia, once again concentrating on short-term rather than long-term horizons. The generally held view is that the increase in production in 1986 is not sustainable, first because the neglect of upstream explora-tion will limit the prospects for new developments, and secondly because Gorbachev's plans to modernize Soviet industry will compete with the oil sector for investment (Hewett, 1987 forthcoming). If the long-term problems of the oil industry are to be solved, resources must be diverted away from production and development into prospective activity with the inevitable result that output must be allowed to fall. Whether or not the planning system can meet this challenge is a fascinating subject for the future.

2.5 The Soviet Oil Balance

The purpose of this section is to provide estimates of the crude oil production/oil products consumption balance and to discuss some aspects of oil planning in the Soviet Union. The construction of oil balances brings together existing data on production and trade, and informed estimates, based on technical assumptions, of other oil flows. The aims are as follows. First, to derive plausible and internally consistent estimates of important aggregates, namely the refinery crude oil throughput and the apparent consumption of petroleum products. There are no complete, or for that matter reliable, statistics on the amounts of oil used every year by the Soviet refining system nor on the volumes of refined products consumed internally, and this deficiency can only be remedied by indirect calculations. Secondly, to provide a statistical bird's-eye view on the disposition of crude oil production between domestic refineries and export markets and the further disposition of the refinery output between internal and external markets, allowing for volumes used up by both the transmission and the transformation systems.

(a) *Methodology*. The methodology followed to estimate the Soviet oil balances was pioneered by Campbell, 1968 and 1976. This methodology has the merit of being both sound and practicable and we applied it with some modifications to the period 1976–85 which had not been covered in this way by previous studies. Campbell's approach distinguishes crude flows and oil products flows and the balance is built up in the following way:

A. Crude Oil Flows
Total oil production (crude plus condensates)
minus field losses
minus new pipeline fill
minus crude oil exports
plus crude oil imports
equals refinery throughput.

B. Oil Products Flows
Refinery throughput
minus refinery losses
minus refinery fuel
minus products exports
plus products imports
equals consumption of petroleum products plus (minus) any increase (decrease) in stocks.

Unfortunately, there are no data on stocks and no method for estimating directly or indirectly changes in their volumes. Thus, the final result of this accounting exercise should be interpreted as an estimate of the domestic disposition, rather than consumption, of petroleum products, disposition being defined as the aggregate of total consumption and inventory changes.

The Campbell methodology does not account for the production and processing of gas condensate, probably because these factors were not important in the 1960s when the method was developed.[6] This situation has now changed: the production of condensate from both associated and non-associated gas increased from 4.2 million tonnes in 1970 to 22.5 million in 1985; and though crude oil production

---

[6] Further, as noted in Section 2.3 above, the Soviet Union publishes only the aggregate production of crude oil plus NGLs, so the disaggregated figures used in this section are the estimates provided in PlanEcon, 1986.

increased during the same period, from 348.8 million to 571.5 million tonnes, the proportion of condensate in the total production still rose from about 1 per cent in 1970 to almost 4 per cent in 1984. Condensates therefore cannot be ignored, and we introduce slight modifications to the Campbell methodology to take this aspect into account. This is done by *adding* to the crude oil flows an element consisting of part of condensate production: the unstabilized condensate that is not burnt directly in the field. This particular flow of condensates reaches the oil refineries where it is processed, adding therefore to the petroleum throughput. It is also necessary to *add* to the products flows the liquids obtained from the recovery, stabilization and refining of condensates in natural gas plants.

Sagers, 1984, estimates that in 1980 approximately 50 per cent of the condensate produced in the Soviet Union was stabilized. The remainder was lost, used *in situ* at the field or transferred unstabilized (by mixing it with crude oil) to refineries. Losses incurred during the extraction, transportation and processing of condensates are high owing to their light hydrocarbon content. The percentage lost varies from field to field. There is also extensive use of condensates for internal fuel needs at the field, and this use is thought to account for between 7 and 20 per cent of total production depending on the region.

We have assumed that the production of condensates divides into three components as follows: 20 per cent is accounted for by losses and direct use at the field, 30 per cent is unstabilized condensates transferred to oil refineries where it is used as an input, and 50 per cent is stabilized condensates processed in natural gas plants yielding an output of liquid products equivalent to 95 per cent of the input volume.

Finally, it is necessary to make a number of assumptions about the percentage of oil production used up in the fields, in filling new pipelines, and in the refineries. In the absence of direct information, we have made these assumptions on judgements based on the experience of the oil industry in the West, with due allowances for differences in the age and the efficiency of Western and Soviet technology. Our assumptions are as follows:

(a) Field losses: 4 per cent of crude oil production in 1976–9 and 3.5 per cent in 1980–85;
(b) Pipeline fill: estimates of the quantities of current production required to fill new pipelines coming on stream are calculated from reports in various journals;
(c) Refinery losses: 2 per cent of refinery throughput in 1976–81 and 1.5 per cent in 1982–5;

(d) Refinery fuel: 5 per cent of refinery throughput in 1976–81 and 4.5 per cent in 1982–5.

As can be seen, it is assumed that new investments and improved technology have slightly reduced input losses in the 1980s compared with earlier years.

Taking these modifications and assumptions into account, the oil balances were constructed as follows:

A. Crude Oil Flows
Crude oil production (excluding condensates)
minus field losses
minus new pipeline fill
minus crude oil exports
plus crude oil imports
plus unstabilized condensates
equals refinery throughput.

B. Oil Products Flows
Refinery throughput
minus refinery losses
minus refinery fuel
minus products exports
plus products imports
plus natural gas plants' liquid output
equals consumption of petroleum products plus (minus) any increase (decrease) in stocks.

In spite of the modifications made to the original Campbell methodology, this accounting framework remains incomplete in some respects. Ideally, an oil balance should include a number of additional components which are listed below. Though their quantitative significance may be small, their inclusion improves the description of the global picture. These are:

(a) the production of non-conventional oil and oil from tar sands and shale;
(b) backflows from industry, specifically oil returned from chemical and petrochemical plant;
(c) other transfers of products back to refineries for further processing;
(d) flows of crude oil and condensates used directly, that is without processing in oil refineries, for example crude oil used in its raw form for electricity generation;
(e) refinery inputs of non-oil origin;

(f) international marine bunkers which include fuels supplied to ships of all flags (this item, however, may not be very relevant to the Soviet oil balance);

(g) changes in the stocks of crude oil and oil products, a significant component of the balance, as mentioned above; the inclusion of this element is essential for the correct estimation of consumption and for the economic interpretation of the movements of the main aggregates.

The lack of data precludes us from building up oil balances with these additional features. Although there are no reasons for regretting too much the exclusion of components (a)–(f), the absence of information on stock changes either in total or by crude oil and products is a serious weakness of the statistical base available to analysts for the study of the Soviet oil industry.

(*b*) *Annual Oil Balances: 1976–85*. By applying our simple methodology to the PlanEcon data on oil production and trade, we constructed annual oil balances for the period 1976–85. The results are presented in Table 2.5 and the main trends depicted in Figure 2.2. The broad picture is one of closely correlated growth in crude oil production, refinery throughput and 'apparent' internal consumption between 1976 and 1980, followed by a plateau in the volume of refinery throughput between 1981 and 1985. In this latter period the annual deviations of refinery throughput from the average of the five years are

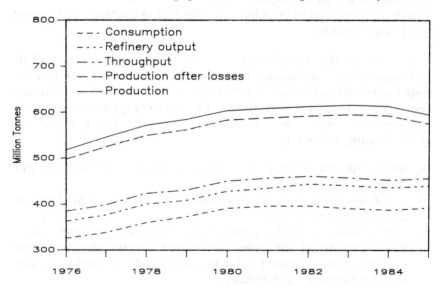

Figure 2.2 Soviet Oil Balance: Annual Data. 1976–85.

Table 2.5: Soviet Oil Balance: Annual Data. 1976–85. Million Tonnes.

	1976	1977	1978	1979	1980	1981	1982	1983	1984	1985
Crude Oil Production	509.3	533.8	557.7	569.7	584.5	587.8	591.1	594.6	590.7	571.5
(NGLs Production)	(10.4)	(12.0)	(13.8)	(15.9)	(18.7)	(21.0)	(21.5)	(21.7)	(22.0)	(22.5)
minus										
Field Losses	−20.4	−21.4	−22.3	−22.8	−20.5	−20.6	−20.7	−20.8	−20.7	−20.0
Pipeline Fill	−1.6	−1.6	−1.6	−1.7	−1.7	−0.7	−1.3	−2.1	−0.3	−2.3
Net Crude Exports	−104.4	−115.9	−114.4	−118.2	−117.5	−115.7	−114.2	−120.3	−124.2	−99.7
plus										
Unstable Condensate	3.1	3.6	4.1	4.8	5.6	6.3	6.5	6.5	6.6	6.8
equals										
Refinery Throughput	386.1	398.6	423.5	431.7	450.5	457.1	461.3	457.9	452.2	456.3
minus										
Refinery Losses	−7.7	−8.0	−8.5	−8.6	−9.0	−9.1	−6.9	−6.9	−6.8	−6.8
Refinery Fuel	−19.3	−19.9	−21.2	−21.6	−22.5	−22.9	−20.8	−20.6	−20.3	−20.5
equals										
Oil Refinery Output	359.0	370.7	393.9	401.5	418.9	425.1	433.6	430.4	425.0	428.9
plus										
Gas Refinery Output	4.9	5.7	6.6	7.6	8.9	10.0	10.2	10.3	10.5	10.7
minus										
Net Products Exports	−36.9	−38.1	−40.9	−35.7	−36.7	−38.8	−47.5	−49.4	−47.9	−47.1
equals										
Apparent Consumption	327.0	338.2	359.6	373.4	391.1	396.3	396.4	391.3	387.6	392.5

Note: Figures may not add exactly because of rounding. 1985 figures on production and exports are preliminary estimates.
Sources: Figures calculated from PlanEcon, 1986, and author's own estimates of pipeline fill

always less than 1 per cent. However, both crude oil production and apparent consumption seem to fluctuate within a slightly wider margin.

It is important, however, to stress the difference between this accounting exercise and the planning process. The former aggregates series of historical data, only some of which are available from published sources. Certain figures are therefore necessarily calculated as residuals. Planning, in contrast, is concerned with target-setting and decision-making. The variables chosen as planning targets may well be residuals in the oil balance, and figures that provide the basis for the oil balance computation may be treated by planners as subsidiary or residual variables in the planning process.

3 THE GROWTH AND PATTERN OF SOVIET OIL TRADE

3.1 Main Features of Total Soviet Oil Trade

The Soviet Union is a significant exporter of both crude and products. Oil is exported to Western Europe, to most CMEA countries, to other centrally planned economies and to a number of developing countries. However, total Soviet petroleum exports do not consist exclusively of oil produced in the Soviet Union; they include re-exports of oil obtained from the Middle East in exchange for military equipment and other goods. It is therefore important to distinguish from the outset between *gross* and *net* exports, and to define the contexts in which each of these concepts has particular relevance. In general, the gross concept is relevant to the analysis of the balance of payments and to an assessment of hard currency earnings because oil imported for re-export is paid for by the Soviet Union in goods which cannot normally be traded in the hard currency area. The gross concept is also useful in the discussion of the issue of oil allocation between various destinations because oil imports for re-export introduce an element of flexibility in the allocation. The net concept is relevant to the study of the impact of Soviet oil supplies on the world petroleum market.

A further distinction between net oil exports from the Soviet Union to the rest of the world and net exports to the world outside Communist (or centrally planned) countries is also in order. The former concept enables us to assess the role of the Soviet Union in international oil trade and its significance as an oil exporter. The latter is much more restrictive as it usually accounts for only 40–50 per cent of total Soviet oil exports. Most analysts of the world oil industry usually publish and use this smaller aggregate, which understates the significance of the Soviet Union as an oil exporter. But Western analysts in the petroleum industry are mainly concerned with the Soviet contribution to the oil supply/demand balance of the non-Communist world, which is measured by the net exports of the Soviet Union to the world outside Communist countries: hence their interest in this latter concept, and their apparent neglect of other export aggregates.

Before proceeding to an analysis of the development of Soviet oil trade in further detail, it is worth while to make some remarks about the original data sources and the information problems that beset research on the Soviet oil industry. As noted previously, the Soviet Union does not publish disaggregated data on oil production distinguishing between crude oil and condensates. Worse, after 1976 the Soviet Union stopped publishing information on the volume of its oil exports and imports. The only official information available on Soviet oil trade for the years from 1977 onwards is about the aggregate value (in foreign trade roubles) of imports and exports of crude oil and refined products taken together. Indirect and rather complex methods are used by PlanEcon to derive estimates of the quantities of Soviet exports (and imports) of crude and products. These methods involve subtractions from Soviet aggregate energy balances of estimated non-oil exports from reported total energy exports, the use of 'mirror' quantities and unit value statistics from the statistical publications of trading partners and educated guesses.

On the basis of the data given in PlanEcon, 1986, total net oil exports from the Soviet Union to all destinations reached a peak of 172.0 million tonnes in 1984, having increased, at first rapidly and then at a declining rate, from a mere 28.8 million in 1960 (see Table 3.1). In 1984 gross oil exports reached 187.2 million tonnes. The deceleration of oil export growth from an impressive average annual rate of 16 per cent in 1960–65 to 3 per cent in 1980–84 (see Table 3.2) raises the interesting

Table 3.1: Soviet Trade in Crude Oil and Products. 1960–85. Million Tonnes.

	Total Exports	Crude		Products		Total Imports	Net Exports
1960	33.2	17.8	(54)	15.4	(46)	4.4	28.8
1965	64.4	43.4	(67)	21.0	(33)	1.9	62.5
1970	95.8	66.8	(70)	29.0	(30)	4.6	91.2
1975	130.4	93.1	(71)	37.3	(29)	7.5	122.9
1976	148.5	110.8	(75)	37.7	(25)	7.2	141.3
1977	161.0	122.1	(76)	38.9	(24)	7.0	154.0
1978	164.9	123.4	(75)	41.4	(25)	9.5	155.4
1979	161.4	124.7	(77)	36.7	(23)	7.6	153.8
1980	158.6	121.1	(76)	37.5	(24)	4.4	154.2
1981	160.2	119.9	(75)	40.3	(25)	5.7	154.5
1982	170.5	121.8	(71)	48.7	(29)	8.8	161.7
1983	183.4	132.8	(72)	50.6	(28)	13.6	169.8
1984	187.2	138.3	(74)	49.0	(26)	15.2	172.0
1985	162.1	114.0	(70)	48.2	(30)	15.3	146.8

Note: The figures in brackets represent the shares in total Soviet oil exports held by crude oil and refined products. 1985 figures are preliminary estimates.
Source: PlanEcon, 1986

Table 3.2: Average Annual Percentage Growth Rates of Soviet Oil Export Volumes (Crude plus Products). 1960–84.

	Gross Exports	Net Exports
1960–65	14	16
1965–70	9	8
1970–75	6	6
1975–80	4	5
1980–84	4	3

Source: Figures calculated from PlanEcon, 1986 (see Table 3.1)

question of whether the Soviet Union will now enter a period of stagnant, or even declining, exports.

Despite this decline, the Soviet Union is now, after Saudi Arabia, the second-largest net oil exporter in the world: a position reached in 1980 when Iran and Iraq lost their lead because of the Gulf war. Furthermore, the Soviet Union moved to the first place in 1984: in that year Saudi Arabia's exports slumped because of its attempts to defend the OPEC system of administered prices. Even if the narrow definition of oil exports to the world outside Communist countries is used, it still appears that the Soviet Union achieved the rank of second-largest oil exporter in 1983 and 1984.

Soviet oil exports can be disaggregated according to composition (crude and products). Table 3.1 shows total oil exports and the breakdown into crude oil and petroleum products. For all years in the period 1970–85, crude oil accounted for at least 70 per cent of total Soviet oil exports. There are interesting contrasts between the growth profiles of crude oil and products exports. As shown in Table 3.3, the average annual rate of increase of crude exports was a very high 19.5 per cent in 1960–65 and then declined from period to period down to 3.4 per cent in 1980–84. The rates of growth of products exports were

Table 3.3: Average Annual Percentage Growth Rates of Soviet Crude and Products Exports. 1960–84.

	Crude	Products
1960–65	19.5	6.4
1965–70	9.0	6.6
1970–75	6.8	5.2
1975–80	5.3	0.1
1980–84	3.4	6.9

Source: Figures calculated from PlanEcon, 1986 (see Table 3.1)

initially more modest but remained fairly stable at around 5.0–6.5 per cent per annum except for a dip in 1975–80.

3.2 Oil Exports by Destination: The Case for Disaggregation

It is important to make sharp distinctions between Soviet oil trade with the CPEs and with the rest of the world and to study the behaviour of Soviet oil exports to countries of the various blocs separately. The main reason for this distinction is *not* the conventional argument that net Soviet oil exports to the world outside Communist areas is the only aggregate that matters in analysing the role of the Soviet Union in the world petroleum market. This argument is invalid because it ignores the important fact that the volume of Soviet net oil exports to the non-Communist bloc depends in part on Soviet decisions about oil allocation to the CPEs.

The real case for treating Soviet oil exports to the CPEs and to the West separately, other than the broad methodological case for a sensible disaggregation of data in applied economic analysis, is that Soviet trade with the rest of the Communist bloc is inherently a different type of economic activity from trade with other areas because different rules, pricing principles, planning decisions and allocation policies apply in the two cases. To begin with, different ministries and organizations are in charge of trade with the CPEs and trade with other countries. More importantly, the transaction prices and the relative price structure of traded commodities are not determined in the same way. Trade with the West follows market principles and the prices of imports and exports relate closely to world market prices; but the prices of the same commodities in intra-CMEA trade are administratively determined by applying a five-year moving average formula to the relevant world market prices. These differences in procedure can result in considerable divergences between the price of a barrel of Soviet oil exported to the CPEs and the price obtained for a shipment to the West. Furthermore, the five-year moving average method dampens price fluctuations and delays the transmission of price shocks. Thanks to this pricing principle the CPEs did not feel immediately the impact of the sudden and significant oil price increases of 1973–4 and 1979–80.

Another major difference between Soviet trade with the CPEs and the West relates to the currencies used. In one instance trade is carried out in 'transferable roubles', mostly under bilateral clearing agreements. One main exception is that 'above-quota' deliveries of oil to CMEA countries are valued at world market prices and settled in convertible currencies. In the other instance (trade with the West), most transactions are settled in convertible currencies. There are some exceptions, however: in particular, trade with Finland is carried out under a long-standing bilateral agreement.

These differences in trading methods and pricing principles have two important implications for the study of Soviet foreign trade. First, the aggregate data on the *values* of exports and imports, as published by the Soviet Union, are not useful for purposes of economic analysis because they combine together quantities that are not comparable. The aggregate values of exports and imports in Soviet statistical sources are expressed in 'foreign trade roubles' by applying official (and largely arbitrary) conversion rates for the 'transferable roubles' used for intra-CMEA trade and the convertible currencies used for settling transactions with the West. Secondly, the differences in trading and pricing practices mean that, in any given period, the *volumes* of exports to or imports from the CPEs and the West respond to different sets of economic factors and are subject to different allocation policies. For this reason, an analysis of time-series of trade volume aggregates is of limited value.

3.3 Oil Exports to the CPEs and the Market Economies: A Comparison of Trends

There are important differences in the pattern and movements over time of Soviet oil exports to the CPEs and to the non-Communist area, which are concealed by the aggregates.

Table 3.4 shows that the share of exports to the world outside CPEs, i.e. to the MDCs and LDCs combined, though above 50 per cent in the earlier years, never exceeded half the volume of total Soviet oil exports in the period 1970–85.[1] This share dropped to 38–39 per cent in 1979–81 for reasons explained later. The impact of the 1985 decline in oil production, which was associated with a reduction in exports of some 25 million tonnes, was borne almost entirely by exports to the MDCs. The broad picture, however, is that in most years the CPEs as a group took the larger share of Soviet oil exports. It can also be seen that total Soviet oil exports to the CPEs and to the MDCs both grew rapidly between 1960 and 1978. In 1979, however, the behaviour of the two time-series began to diverge because the Soviet Union's responses to the second oil price shock had different effects on oil trade with the CPEs and the MDCs. The nature of these responses and the policies

[1] Throughout the discussion of statistics based on Soviet sources (including the PlanEcon estimates), the four main trading areas are as follows. The CMEA-6 consists of Bulgaria, Czechoslovakia, East Germany, Hungary, Poland and Romania; OCPEs include Albania, China, Cuba, Mongolia, North Korea, Vietnam and Yugoslavia; MDCs include Western Europe, North America, South Africa, Japan, Australia and New Zealand; and LDCs include all other countries.

Table 3.4: Gross Oil Exports (Crude plus Products) by Main Destination. 1960–85. Million Tonnes and Percentage Shares.

	MDCs		LDCs		World outside CPEs		CMEA-6		OCPEs		Total CPEs	
	Volume	*% Share*	*Volume*	*% Share*	*Volume*	*% Share*	*Volume*	*% Share*	*Volume*	*% Share*	*Volume*	*% Share*
1960	15.9	48	2.2	6	18.1	54	9.2	28	6.0	18	15.2	46
1965	27.7	43	7.8	12	35.5	55	22.4	35	6.5	10	28.9	45
1970	41.5	43	3.7	4	45.2	47	40.3	42	10.2	11	50.5	53
1975	47.8	37	4.7	4	52.5	41	63.5	49	14.4	11	77.9	60
1976	59.9	40	4.6	3	64.5	43	68.4	46	15.6	10	84.0	57
1977	65.2	40	6.0	4	71.2	44	73.4	46	16.4	10	89.8	56
1978	67.1	41	5.1	3	72.2	44	75.4	46	17.3	10	92.7	56
1979	56.5	35	6.8	4	63.3	39	78.1	48	20.0	12	98.1	60
1980	53.5	34	6.7	4	60.2	38	80.3	51	18.1	11	98.4	62
1981	55.0	34	7.0	4	62.0	38	79.7	50	18.5	12	98.2	62
1982	71.0	42	7.5	4	78.5	46	72.5	43	19.5	11	92.0	54
1983	82.6	45	9.1	5	91.7	50	70.6	38	21.1	12	91.7	50
1984	85.2	46	8.6	5	93.8	50	71.1	38	22.3	12	93.4	50
1985	63.9	39	6.9	4	70.8	44	69.0	43	22.3	14	91.3	56

Note: Total shares may not add to 100 per cent because of rounding. 1985 figures are preliminary estimates.
Source: PlanEcon, 1986

that determined them are analysed in detail in Chapter 7. It will suffice here to note that Soviet oil exports to the MDCs were reduced in 1979, while exports to the CPEs continued to increase. There was a further reduction in the volume of exports to the MDCs in 1980 when they fell to a level of 53.5 million tonnes, but after that year growth resumed until 1984.

The behaviour of oil exports to the CPEs during these years was markedly different: they remained at a peak level of slightly more than 98 million tonnes until 1981 and then declined by 5–6 million to a new plateau at around the 92 million tonne level with small variations of about 1 million. In 1985, when oil exports to the MDCs were severely reduced, from 85.2 million tonnes in the previous year to 63.9 million, exports to the CPEs, though slightly reduced, remained very close to the plateau attained in the previous years.

3.4 Oil Exports to the CPEs:
The CMEA–6 and Other Centrally Planned Economies

A further disaggregation of Soviet oil exports to the CPEs which separates the CMEA–6 and the OCPEs reveals some interesting differences in behaviour. The share of Soviet oil exports to the CMEA–6 tended to fluctuate in 1970–85 within a wide range (between 38 and 51 per cent), while the share of Soviet oil exports to the OCPEs remained remarkably stable during the same period at around 10–12 per cent (with the exception of 1985). Furthermore, the volume of exports to the CMEA–6 varied more erratically from year to year than exports to the OCPEs which grew throughout the period in a fairly steady manner.

A feature of Soviet oil policy that deserves notice is the difference in the treatment of the CMEA–6 and the OCPEs in the 1980s in response to the second oil crisis. Oil exports to the CMEA–6 were reduced from a peak of 80.3 million tonnes in 1980 to 69.0 million in 1985; this reduction was not gradual, since most of it occurred in 1982. In sharp contrast, oil exports to the OCPEs increased from 18.1 million to 22.3 million tonnes in the respective years.

The CMEA–6 suffered therefore a double squeeze in 1982–5, first because of a reduction of the oil allocation to the CPEs in general and secondly because of an increase in the allocation to the OCPEs. Furthermore, the European members of the CMEA were not made to share the burden of this significant reduction in their oil supplies equally, as shown in some detail in Chapter 7.

3.5 Oil Exports to the MDCs: Growth and Fluctuations

A detailed analysis of oil exports to MDCs cannot be made on the basis of Soviet data (see Section 3.1 above). One way round the difficulty is to concentrate instead on exports to the OECD area, since this enables us to use OECD statistical sources and other Western data. In fact we shall have recourse to OECD data from 1974, and to the *BP Statistical Review of World Energy* for earlier years. Although the sets of countries covered by the MDCs and the OECD are not strictly identical, the differences are minor and can be disregarded for the purposes of this analysis.

The growth and fluctuations of Soviet oil exports to the OECD between 1962 and 1986 are shown in Figure 3.1. Three main features of these long time-series are of interest. First, there is a very marked upward trend in the volume of exports to the OECD throughout the period. A statistical fit of the trend line indicates that the *average* (compound) rate of growth was of the order of 5.7 per cent per annum between 1962 and 1985. Secondly, the trend line shows that the rate of growth has been declining. Thirdly, the significant drop in the volume of exports in 1985 cannot be taken as evidence that the trend now displays negative growth, since this drop represents just a single observation and follows a very steep rise in the preceding years. Furthermore, the statistics for 1986 show that exports to the OECD

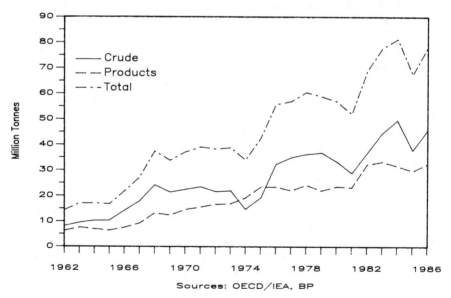

Figure 3.1 Soviet Oil Exports to the OECD: Annual Data. 1962–86.

have increased again and may have reached a new peak. Fourthly, there are marked fluctuations around the trend line. These include very sharp increases in certain periods (1965–8, 1974–6 and 1981–4) followed by episodes of slower growth or decline. Finally, the time-series for crude oil and products exports have some contrasting features. Figure 3.1 clearly shows that, although both crude oil and products exports to the West were on a rising trend during the period considered, crude oil exports were subject to more significant fluctuations than products exports.

3.6 Oil Exports to the OECD: Crude and Products

The Soviet Union generally exports more crude than products to the OECD. Only in 1974 and 1975 did the share of crude oil in total exports fall below 50 per cent. In all the other years between 1970 and 1986, the share of crude oil exports varied between 53 and 62 per cent (see Table 3.5). There is no clear trend in the export structure. As mentioned earlier, fluctuations are more marked, on average, in crude than in products exports, which means that the year-to-year changes in the demand structure are attributable to a large extent to the significant

Table 3.5: Soviet Oil Exports to the OECD. 1962–86. Million Tonnes.

	Total Oil Exports	Crude		Products	
		Volume	% Share	Volume	% Share
1962	14.3	8.1	56.6	6.2	44.4
1965	16.7	10.4	62.3	6.3	37.7
1970	38.3	22.9	58.9	16.0	38.9
1975	42.6	19.2	45.1	23.4	54.9
1976	55.8	32.3	57.9	23.5	42.1
1977	57.0	35.0	61.4	22.0	38.6
1978	60.5	36.3	60.0	24.2	40.0
1979	58.9	36.9	62.6	22.0	37.4
1980	57.0	33.4	58.6	23.6	41.4
1981	53.5	29.4	54.9	24.1	45.1
1982	69.0	36.8	53.3	32.2	46.7
1983	77.9	44.6	57.3	33.3	42.7
1984	81.2	49.6	61.1	31.6	38.9
1985	67.4	37.8	55.9	29.7	44.1
1986	78.1	45.7	58.5	32.4	41.5

Note: Data for crude exports up until 1969 are only available in Western sources as a total for the Soviet Union and Eastern Europe. Figures for 1962 and 1965 in this table have been adjusted by 1 million tonnes which represents the highest estimate of exports from Eastern Europe in those years.

Sources: OECD/IEA, BP

deviations from the trend line of crude oil exports. As we shall argue later, changes in the volume of crude oil exports to the West are one of the main instruments used by Soviet planners in adjusting the foreign trade balance. It seems that products exports are not used in the same way, partly because of constraints on the refining system and partly because products imports, being small, do not play the same role as crude imports in providing additional flexibility.

There is no strong evidence from the data to suggest that the Soviet Union has fulfilled its intention, repeatedly expressed in many statements, of increasing the proportion of products in the total volume of its oil exports to the OECD. There was a marked increase to 32 million tonnes in 1982 after a long period (1975–81) during which the products volume was virtually stagnant at 22–24 million. As this rise to a new level of 32–33 million tonnes was associated in 1982–4 with an increase in the volume of crude exports, however, the favourable change in the proportion of products was not sustained.

Soviet exports of products to the OECD consist largely of gas oil (which accounted for 52–62 per cent of total products exports in 1979–86). Fuel oil and naphtha come next, and there are also small volumes of gasoline and other products. In most years since 1979, the share of light distillates (naphtha and gasoline) remained stable at around 21 per cent of total products exports. The shares of gas oil and fuel oil have tended to vary from year to year within a fairly wide range as is apparent from Table 3.6, but these changes are inversely correlated. The share of fuel oil rises when gas oil declines and vice versa. There may be a technical explanation for this apparent relationship. The Soviet Union exports a high-quality fuel oil known as F10 which almost certainly contains a proportion of the gas oil refining cut. Thus, an increase in the share of fuel oil in the export barrel requires a reduction in the share of gas oil.

3.7 Oil Exports to the OECD: Seasonality

The quarterly time-series of crude and products exports to the OECD display a regular seasonal pattern. As is readily apparent from Figure 3.2, exports of both crude and products are at their lowest during the first quarter of each year. Exports usually reach a seasonal peak in the third quarter, except in odd years such as 1982 when the highest level occurred in the second quarter.

Econometric analysis provides us with another quantitative description of the seasonal pattern. Crude oil exports CO_t and refined products exports RP_t to the West were regressed on seasonal dummies and a time trend. The dummies *1Q*, *2Q* and *4Q* refer to the first, second and

Table 3.6: Soviet Exports of Refined Products to the OECD by Product. 1979–86. Thousand Tonnes.

	Total	Gasoline		Naphtha		Gas Oil		Fuel Oil		Others
		Volume	% Share	Volume	% Share	Volume	% Share	Volume	% Share	% Share
1979	22,019	495	2	2,941	13	12,557	57	5,354	24	4
1980	23,584	608	3	3,783	16	14,209	60	4,048	17	4
1981	24,124	1,167	5	3,668	15	15,010	62	3,936	16	2
1982	32,189	1,490	5	5,316	17	17,001	53	7,631	24	1
1983	33,304	1,375	4	5,729	17	18,461	55	7,066	21	3
1984	31,565	991	3	4,606	15	18,419	58	6,749	21	3
1985	29,692	1,074	4	4,790	16	15,633	53	7,434	25	2
1986	32,372	1,108	3	5,463	17	16,859	52	8,219	25	3

Source: OECD/IEA

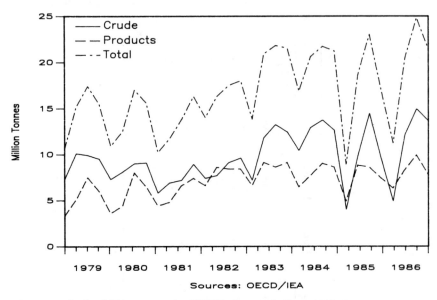

Figure 3.2 Soviet Oil Exports to the OECD: Quarterly Data. 1979–86.

fourth quarters respectively; and therefore the intercept indicates the export volume for the third quarter.

The results are shown in Table 3.7, and indicate, other things being equal, that the volume of crude exports in the first quarter falls on average by 2.23 million tonnes from the peak level of the third quarter. Seasonal variations in the second and fourth quarters relative to the third (which, in this analysis, is the bench-mark) are not very significant. Similarly, the volume of products exports in the first quarter falls on average by 1.95 million tonnes from the third quarter

Table 3.7: Regression of Volumes of Crude Oil and Products Exports to the OECD (excluding Finland). 4Q76–4Q84 (33 Observations). Million Tonnes per Quarter.

Dependent Variable	Constant	1Q	2Q	4Q	Trend	R^2	DWS	Mean of Dependent Variable
CO_t	6.25 (8.67)	−2.23 (−2.99)	−0.18 (−0.24)	−0.46 (−0.63)	0.11 (4.05)	0.52	0.62	7.43
RP_t	4.58 (11.12)	−1.95 (−4.56)	−0.74 (−1.74)	−0.05 (−0.12)	0.12 (7.46)	0.76	1.09	5.85

Source: Figures calculated from OECD/IEA

level. The variations in products exports are explained by the seasonal dummies and the time trend with greater statistical significance than the variations in crude exports. A further difference between the crude and products export patterns is that the seasonal decline in products exports continues in the second quarter.

A breakdown of total products exports by product reveals some interesting differences in seasonality (see Figure 3.3). In the period 1979–86, fuel oil exports fell sharply in the first quarter to less than 1 million tonnes and peaked regularly in the third quarter at around 2.0–2.5 million. The difference between seasonal trough and peak is thus considerable; it has, however, tended to decrease to some extent in recent years. In the same period, the seasonal behaviour of gas oil changed in an important respect. Although gas oil exports always fell in the first quarter and peaked in either the third or the fourth quarter of each year, the magnitude of the seasonal variation, which was considerable in 1979–81, became much smaller in 1982–6.

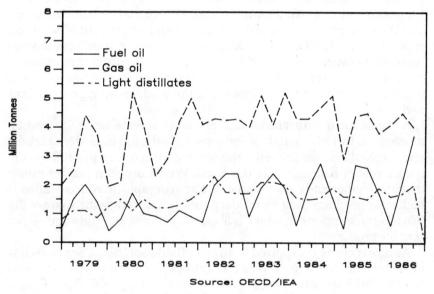

Figure 3.3 Soviet Products Exports to the OECD: Quarterly Data. 1979–86.

The inverse correlation between the shares of gas oil and fuel oil observed in the annual data (see Section 3.6 above) is also apparent in the quarterly time-series. Rises in the fuel oil share correspond to falls in the gas oil share and vice versa. This contrasts with the seasonal behaviour of light-distillate exports, which is not very pronounced and displays no regularities. An econometric analysis of the seasonality of gas oil, fuel oil and light-distillate exports is given in Appendix 1. The effect of these seasonal patterns is that the shape of the product export barrel varies significantly throughout the year.

3.8 Oil Exports to the OECD: Destination

The purpose of this section is to identify which OECD countries are the major importers of Soviet crude oil and products. The analysis of trade data by destination will enable us to delineate the geographical boundaries of the Western market for Soviet oil and to assess the dependence of OECD importers on the Soviet Union.

The geographical distribution of Soviet oil exports to the OECD is shown in Table 3.8. First of all, we note that more than 95 per cent of these exports go to destinations in Western Europe and that only minimal amounts reach Japan and the USA. The degree of geographical concentration is high: for all years from 1983 to 1986, six European countries (Belgium, Finland, France, Italy, the Netherlands and West Germany) absorbed between 75 and 78 per cent of Soviet oil exports to the OECD. The ranking varied, however, from year to year. All in all, between sixteen and eighteen OECD countries import Soviet oil each year; and the ten or twelve that rank below the top six, taken together, absorb less than a quarter of the total, on average 2 per cent each.

A breakdown into crude and products reveals some interesting differences. In 1983–6, Italy was consistently the top importer of crude, and the Netherlands the top importer of products, but this reflects the special role of Rotterdam in the North West European market rather than the Netherlands' own demand. The geographical concentration is higher for products than for crude: a simple indicator is the share of the two top-rank importers, which is about 40 per cent for crude and 50 per cent for products.

As Soviet crude is exported from both Baltic and Black Sea ports it is in direct competition in Western Europe both with Atlantic basin crudes and with Middle East oil coming through the Suez Canal. Table 3.9 shows the sources of crude oil imports of the six main West European importers of Soviet oil in 1986. It appears that Finland is the only country that is heavily dependent on the Soviet Union, and Finland is indeed a special case. West Germany, France and the Netherlands, which are among the top importers of Soviet crude, depend very little on this source, their import shares being between 2 and 9 per cent; and the dependence of Italy, the largest importer of Soviet crude, is just over 12 per cent. Belgium stands out with a better

Table 3.8: Main OECD Importing Countries of Soviet Oil. 1983–6. Thousand Tonnes.

	Total Imports	% Share	Rank	Crude Imports	% Share	Rank	Products Imports	% Share	Rank
1983									
Netherlands	13,490	17.3	1	2,282	5.1	7	11,208	33.7	1
Finland	11,636	14.9	2	8,872	19.9	2	2,764	8.3	3
West Germany	10,561	13.6	3	4,424	9.9	4	6,137	18.4	2
Italy	9,774	12.5	4	9,187	20.6	1	587	1.8	11
France	8,399	10.8	5	6,076	13.6	3	2,323	7.0	4
Belgium	5,723	7.3	6	3,458	7.7	5	2,265	6.8	5
1984									
Netherlands	13,519	16.7	1	4,004	8.1	6	9,515	30.1	1
Italy	12,098	14.9	2	11,184	22.5	1	914	2.9	9
West Germany	11,960	14.7	3	5,765	11.6	3	6,195	19.6	2
Finland	10,324	12.7	4	7,542	15.2	2	2,782	8.8	3
France	7,975	9.8	5	5,523	11.1	5	2,452	7.8	4
Belgium	7,264	8.9	6	5,689	11.5	4	1,575	5.0	6
1985									
Netherlands	11,742	17.4	1	2,178	5.8	7	9,564	32.2	1
West Germany	10,543	15.6	2	3,885	10.3	4	6,658	22.4	2
Finland	9,900	14.7	3	7,216	19.1	2	2,684	9.0	3
Italy	8,706	12.9	4	8,410	22.3	1	296	1.0	12
France	6,344	9.4	5	4,083	10.8	3	2,261	7.6	4
Belgium	4,922	7.3	6	3,518	9.3	5	1,404	4.7	6
1986									
Netherlands	10,719	13.7	3	955	2.1	9	9,764	30.2	1
West Germany	10,645	13.6	4	3,785	8.3	5	6,860	21.2	2
Finland	12,440	15.9	1	8,917	19.5	2	3,523	10.9	3
Italy	10,861	13.9	2	10,030	21.9	1	831	2.6	9
France	8,661	11.1	5	6,173	13.5	3	2,488	7.7	4
Belgium	5,653	7.2	6	4,659	10.2	4	994	3.1	8

Source: OECD/IEA

spread of sources. The share of its imports from the OPEC region is smaller and the share of its oil imports from the Soviet Union, though not excessively high (17.5 per cent), is significantly higher than those of Italy and the other major West European countries.

The import dependence of OECD Europe on the Soviet Union is relatively greater for products than for crude. Dependence increases significantly if products imports from Eastern Europe are also taken

Table 3.9: Sources of Crude Oil Imports of the Major West European Importers of Soviet Oil. 1986. Percentage Shares of Total Crude Oil Imports.

Source	Italy	Finland	West Germany	Belgium	France	Netherlands
Soviet Union	12.2	86.2	5.7	17.5	8.7	2.0
OPEC	72.4	10.3	55.9	51.5	58.6	61.3
Others	15.4	3.5	38.4	31.0	32.7	36.7

Source: OECD/IEA

into account. In 1986, for example, the Soviet Union supplied 42 per cent, and Eastern Europe 21 per cent, of OECD Europe's gas oil imports. The Soviet Union and CMEA–6 supplied 50 per cent of all products imports. Of course, Finland is the most dependent country in this respect (94 per cent). Still, the Soviet Union is the second-largest exporter of products to West Germany, France and Belgium and the largest single source of products imports for Switzerland and the Netherlands. However, as imports of refined products are not a major component of total petroleum availabilities in Western Europe (excluding Finland in this context) the strategic significance of West European reliance on oil products from the CPEs should not be exaggerated.

4 THE SOVIET REFINING SYSTEM AND PRODUCTS EXPORTS

4.1 Introduction

In the previous chapters we have provided the reader with a quantitative description of the Soviet oil industry and of Soviet foreign trade in crude oil and refined products. We now turn to an analysis of substantive questions. We begin this chapter with a brief overview of the Soviet refining system and then consider the constraints the Soviet refining system imposes on the volume, quality and pattern of oil products output, and by implication exports. The flexibility of the refinery system is assessed with the aid of a small model. This is done in two stages: first, to discover the likely specifications of refined products, such as gasoline and kerosine, for which no precise information exists; secondly, using these results and data on the quality of other products, to assess the Soviet refiner's ability to operate a trade-off between reduced products quality and increased production. We then turn to the issue of seasonality of products exports and explain it in relation to the seasonality of internal consumption. A recent change in the seasonal export pattern of gas oil and fuel oil (F10) is shown to be a by-product of programmes of gas-for-oil substitution in the Soviet Union. Finally, possible future trends in Soviet exports of refined products are examined in the light of both refinery constraints and plans for investment in new plant with upgrading facilities.

4.2 The Refining System

The Soviet refining system consists of around forty refining complexes which together can process almost 12 mb/d of crude oil. A number of detailed descriptions of individual refineries and analyses of the structural problems confronting the industry are available (Sagers, 1984; Sagers and Tretyakova, 1985 and 1986; Wilson, 1983). Data were also made available on a confidential basis from an oil company source (referred to as OCS) and the figures presented in this section and in Appendix 2 are collated from all the above sources. The main characteristics of the Soviet refining system are described briefly.

For purposes of analysis the refineries have been grouped into eight regions:

(a) Caucasus/Caspian – the region lying between the Black and Caspian Seas plus the northern and eastern shores of the Caspian;
(b) Central – the region around Moscow;
(c) Volga–Urals;
(d) North West – the regions lying to the north and west of Moscow, including Belorussia, Lithuania and Komi;
(e) The Ukraine;
(f) Central Asia/Kazakhstan – the large region to the east of the Caspian and south of Siberia, but excluding the Caspian Sea coast in (a) above;
(g) Siberia;
(h) The Far East.

The regional distribution of refinery capacity is summarized in Table 4.1. (A complete list of the refineries in each region, their capacities and dates of commissioning is given in Table A2.1.) Some 9.5 mb/d out of the total Soviet refining capacity of 11.7 mb/d is situated west of the Urals, and almost half is still concentrated in the older producing regions of the Caucasus and Volga–Urals. Until the 1960s, Soviet refineries were built near the main producing fields. However, the construction of the crude pipeline network reduced the cost of transporting crude over long distances, and most of the newer capacity has been constructed close to areas of high consumption such as the Central region, the North West and the Ukraine. A large share (45 per cent) of the capacity built since 1970 is in these three regions.

Table 4.1: Refinery Capacity by Region. 1986. Thousand Barrels per Day.

	Capacity	% of Total	Number of Refineries
Caucasus/Caspian	1,880	16	6
Central	1,500	13	4
Volga–Urals	3,580	31	9
North West	1,360	12	5
Ukraine	1,140	10	6
Central Asia/Kazakhstan	660	6	4
Siberia	1,320	11	3
Far East	240	2	2
Total	11,680	100	39

Sources: see Appendix 2

The Soviet refining industry dates from the nineteenth century and twelve of its existing refineries were in operation before World War II. Pre-war refineries tended to be rather small, however, and most have been extended and modernized. Thus the actual proportion of distillation capacity that pre-dates 1945 is around 9 per cent, or 1.1 mb/d (see Table 4.2). (The age distribution of capacity in each refinery is detailed in Table A2.2.) The age structure varies considerably from region to region. The Caucasus/Caspian region, the original centre of the oil industry, still contains some 680,000 b/d of pre-1945 capacity, 36 per cent of its total. However, considerable reconstruction of these refineries has taken place and 28 per cent of the plant is now less than fifteen years old.

Table 4.2: Age Distribution of Soviet Refining Capacity. Thousand Barrels per Day.

	Pre-1945	*1945–59*	*1960–69*	*1970–79*	*1980–86*	*Total 1986*
Caucasus/ Caspian	680	420	260	360	160	1,880
Central	60	80	880	480	–	1,500
Volga–Urals	240	1,420	1,320	600	–	3,580
North West	–	120	400	600	240	1,360
Ukraine	60	120	440	400	120	1,140
Central Asia/ Kazakhstan	20	100	–	180	360	660
Siberia	–	320	420	420	160	1,320
Far East	40	160	–	40	–	240
Total	1,100	2,740	3,720	3,080	1,040	11,680

Sources: see Appendix 2

More than 4 mb/d of capacity has been added since 1970, including seven new refineries built on green-field sites. The main beneficiaries of this expansion were Central Asia/Kazakhstan and the North West, which each gained two refineries and now contain the most modern regional refining systems in the Soviet Union. This is reflected in the estimates of refinery utilization shown in Table 4.3. There is a fairly clear link between the newness of the plant and the rate of utilization: regions with above-average proportions of modern capacity also run above-average throughputs. (Data on throughput by refinery are shown in Table A2.3.)

Total throughput in 1980 was around 82 per cent of capacity and in 1985 this figure was still around 80 per cent. With internal Soviet consumption of 8.5–9.0 mb/d, well over 70 per cent of capacity is

Table 4.3: Refinery Throughputs and Utilization Rates by Region. 1980. Thousand Barrels per Day.

	Capacity	Throughput	% Share of 1980 Capacity Built 1970–79	Apparent Utilization Rate (%)
Caucasus/Caspian	1,720	1,280	21	74
Central	1,500	1,320	32	88
Volga–Urals	3,580	2,630	17	73
North West	1,240	1,280	58	103[a]
Ukraine	1,020	900	39	88
Central Asia/ Kazakhstan	300	340	60	113[a]
Siberia	1,160	980	36	84
Far East	240	100	17	42
Total	10,760	8,830	29	82

Note: (a) These figures suggest either that the capacity data is underestimated or that throughput is overstated.

required just to meet the domestic requirements of the Soviet Union. A large proportion of the 1 mb/d of capacity that is more than fifty years old may be inoperable and the rest is likely to be extremely inefficient. The amount of spare capacity in the system is therefore in practice rather small.

Compared with refining systems in Western industrialized countries, the Soviet system has very little upgrading capacity and is short of the more technologically complex processes such as hydrocracking and the manufacture of lubricating oils. Total upgrading capacity is shown in Table 4.4.[1] As a proportion of distillation capacity, upgrading amounts to only 12.6 per cent, and cracking capacity is a tiny 3.7 per cent. Figures published in the *Oil & Gas Journal* indicate that cracking capacity alone was 39 per cent of distillation capacity in the USA in 1986 while in the twelve EEC countries, taken as a whole, this figure was 25 per cent.

The regional distribution of reforming and cracking capacity in the Soviet Union is not uniform, as can be seen from Table 4.5. Reforming capacity is only 7.4 per cent of distillation capacity for the Soviet Union as a whole, while an average barrel of Soviet Export Blend yields 12–13

[1] Catalytic reforming is a process that converts naphtha into higher-octane gasoline components. It is also used in the petrochemical industry for the production of benzene. Cracking is a term used to encompass all processes that convert residue into varying yields of distillates. These range from straightforward thermal cracking (visbreaking) to more complex catalytic processes such as catalytic cracking, hydrocracking and combination cracking. Coking destroys residue altogether, producing a mixture of distillates and coke.

Table 4.4: Upgrading Capacity in the Soviet Union. 1986. Thousand Barrels per Day. Percentage Shares of Distillation Capacity.

	Capacity	% Share
Catalytic Reforming	860	7.4
Cracking	425	3.7
Coking	200	1.7
Total	1,485	12.8

Sources: Sagers and Tretyakova, 1985; OCS

Table 4.5: Upgrading Capacity by Region. 1986. Thousand Barrels per Day.

	CDU	Reforming	% Share of CDU	Cracking	% Share of CDU
Caucasus/Caspian	1,880	202	10.7	85	4.5
Central	1,500	75	5.0	80	5.3
Volga–Urals	3,580	200	5.6	141	3.9
North West	1,360	145	10.7	20	1.5
Ukraine	1,020	70	6.9	20	2.0
Siberia	1,320	95	7.2	40	3.0
Central Asia/ Kazakhstan	660	60	9.1	40	6.1
Far East	240	12	5.0	–	–
Total	11,560	859	7.4	426	3.7

Sources: Sagers and Tretyakova, 1985; OCS

per cent of heavy naphtha (reformer feedstock). It can thus be seen that in only two regions, the Caucasus/Caspian and the North West, does reforming capacity even approach the level that would permit the whole of the naphtha yield to be converted into lighter products (see Table 4.5). Thus, although most refineries contain reformers, they appear, by Western standards, to be small in relation to their distillation capacity.

Only eighteen of the thirty-nine refineries are believed to have any cracking capacity at all and some units are between twenty and thirty years old. Central Asia/Kazakhstan and the Central region have the highest proportion of cracking to distillation, but even in these areas the cracking capacities are tiny compared with those of an average Western refinery. Rough calculations based on the capacities in Table 4.5 show that the proportion of motor gasoline in the output mix of regions such as the Caucasus/Caspian and Central Asia/Kazakhstan may be 5–6 per cent higher than in the Far East, where there is no cracking and only a small amount of reforming. Regions with an above-average share of cracking, i.e. the Caucasus/Caspian, the Central region and Central Asia/Kazakhstan, will produce 4–5 per cent less residue than those such as the Far East and the North West which have very little.

The large distances between refineries and the discrepancies in output of regions with different amounts of upgrading capacity lead to the transportation of significant volumes of products across the Soviet Union, with surpluses from one area filling shortages in another. Few product pipelines yet exist and 80 per cent of oil products movement is by rail (Sagers and Tretyakova, 1986).

Until the large-scale development of gas reserves in the late 1970s, the pattern of Soviet demand for oil matched the refinery output mix reasonably well since consumption was dominated by the use of fuel oil (or *mazut*) in power stations and industrial boilers. Demand for motor gasoline, which is highly significant to Western refiners, accounted for less than 20 per cent of demand in 1980 (Wilson, 1983; Sagers and Tretyakova, 1985). The steady increase in demand that occurred in the 1960s and 1970s was met by the construction of more distillation capacity. However, the gas-for-oil substitution programme that is now under way will seriously change the pattern of consumption, even if demand for distillates does not increase.

Refineries with small upgrading capacity have very little flexibility to change their output pattern when demand varies. This poses both a seasonal and a long-term problem for the Soviet refining system unless significant investment is made in cracking capacity within the next few years. Successful gas-for-oil substitution will leave refineries with large volumes of virtually un-exportable heavy fuel oil. This problem will be compounded if, as expected, consumption of light and middle distillates increases. The seasonal differences in consumption are already becoming more severe. Gas storage capacity is currently not sufficient for peak demand on power stations to be met, which leads to a significant switch back to *mazut* during the winter months. An increase in the proportion of lighter products in domestic Soviet consumption will exacerbate the seasonal differences and increase the pressure on the refining system to upgrade and improve its operational flexibility.

4.3 The Operation of the Refining System

It is instructive to compare the Soviet refining system with systems in Western Europe operated by majors, independents and national oil companies. Let us note, first, that no refining system can be completely self-contained; there will always be shortages or surpluses of product at the margin as refiners attempt to balance output with demand. Western refineries effectively have two degrees of freedom in this balancing operation: choice of feedstock, both in type and volume, and trading opportunities for products. Most of them run on a flexible, short-term basis, taking advantage of feedstock and product price movements. This flexibility manifests itself in such operations as:

(a) reducing crude throughput and buying feedstock to run upgrading plant;
(b) increasing throughput and selling output on the spot market when refining margins are high;
(c) buying products to cover demand when refining margins are low;
(d) swapping product surpluses with other refiners.

Thus, the Western refiner generally takes advantage of the market to optimize the use of inputs (the amounts and the quality of feedstock purchased), the pattern of capacity utilization (which units to run in his refinery), and the sales of his output.

The Soviet refiner seems able to exercise some of these options since the Soviet Union purchases crude from OPEC countries and imports small quantities of products from time to time. In practice, however, the system limits him to a single degree of freedom, namely the volume of products exports. This is because Soviet crude 'imports' do not, as a rule, physically enter the Soviet Union. The refinery crude slate is therefore restricted to domestic crude, which is delivered to most refineries through the pipeline network from the major fields of Siberia and the Volga–Urals region.

A Soviet refinery is thus constrained at the input end of the operation. As we shall see below, this effectively dictates the output yield of refineries, largely because the technological flexibility of Soviet plants is small. The one factor that prevents the system becoming completely closed is the opportunity to export products both to the West and to other CPEs. This is allowed for by the planning process, which sets the level of throughput on an annual basis and determines the allocation to the domestic market and to exports. The Soviet Union has a well-developed organization for moving products into Western markets. It is indeed in their interests to do this efficiently for both balance-of-payments and logistical reasons. The need to earn hard currency is obvious; but the logistical problem requires some elaboration. It seems that the Soviet Union is short of storage facilities for oil products and faces transport constraints on products movements from export terminals back to domestic markets. Furthermore, products exports are the only safety valve of the refining system.

The Soviet refiner's actions are further limited by the targets imposed on him by the planners. These targets are set in relation to several conflicting objectives: the needs to meet certain minimum domestic requirements, to fulfil commitments to the CMEA countries, and to adjust imbalances in the external accounts. Changing circumstances alter the possible trade-off between these objectives and targets are subject to revisions within the various time-frames of the plans.

4.4 Constraints on the Refining System

The principal task of any refining system is to match output to a set of fixed demands with given volume and quality specifications. The constraints on the refinery itself are capacity, technology and feedstock quality. In general each refinery will operate at the limit of at least one constraint, these being the 'balancing' factors in the running of the refinery.

The Soviet refining system operates under several constraints which we investigated quantitively with the aid of a small linear programming model.[2] A general description of the model along with the data assumptions can be found in Appendix 3. Data from Sagers and Tretyakova, 1986, and information kindly supplied by an oil company (OCS) were used to construct models of the Soviet refining system in 1980 and 1983. The aims were: (a) to provide estimates for certain factors on which information is not available and (b) to identify points of constraint.

The following exercises were performed with the model. We assumed that crude input to the refining system was equal to the levels calculated in the oil balance (see Table 2.5), and we varied estimates of internal demand until the resulting volume of oil products available for export corresponded to the recorded export figures for the appropriate year. We assumed that the capacities of the different refinery plants were equal to the estimates given in Section 4.2 and used these numbers in the exercises. The model was then used: first to provide estimates for the unknown variables, and secondly to analyse the flexibility of the refining system.

(*a*) *Unknown Variables*. The broad quality specifications of oil products used for internal consumption in the Soviet Union are known, but there is no information on the precise specifications of certain products (see, for example, Campbell, 1968 and 1976; Sagers and Tretyakova,

---

[2] The model was developed by High and Watt Associates.

1985). For example, much is known about the quality of gas oil from the investigations and discussions of experts. It is thus thought that the quality of Soviet gas oil is equivalent, if not better, than that of gas oil used in Western Europe. This is supported by the fact that Soviet gas oil exported to Western Europe is of both high and reliable quality. In contrast, much less is known about gasoline and kerosine, two major products in the refinery's slate.

The model was used to attempt an estimate of the characteristics of gasoline which the Soviet refineries could produce given the other parameters and the output and capacity constraints of the system. We found, on the basis of 1980 data, that the system then could produce only 5 per cent of gasoline with a high octane number (more precisely 94 RON),[3] the remainder being a low-quality product with a low number (averaging 74 RON). After 1983 the picture improved because Soviet reforming capacity increased by 100,000 b/d. This allowed the production of high-octane gasoline of up to 10 per cent of the total output and for a slightly higher average octane number (77 RON instead of 74 RON) for the remainder. These results are consistent with Sagers and Tretyakova, 1985, who report that in 1980 only around 65 per cent of Soviet gasoline was higher than 75 octane whereas by mid-1984 80 per cent was at least 76 octane.[4]

The rise in average octane was made possible by the stagnation of the share of gasoline in total oil products demand (16–17 per cent) since the late 1970s. In other words, gasoline consumption in the Soviet Union, though rising, increased at a slower rate than total oil consumption, and thus enabled the Soviet refiner to use new reforming capacity to improve the quality of the product. Problems will arise, therefore, if the market share of gasoline rises significantly in the future. Such an increase will result in an octane shortage unless the Soviet Union takes measures that are already overdue, and invests in additional reforming capacity.

We also used the model to identify the likely characteristics of Soviet aviation kerosine. Western refiners find this product one of the most difficult to make because safety standards impose stringent quality requirements on the fuel. These requirements mean that aviation fuel can only be manufactured from a narrow straight-run cut (no components from upgrading can be blended in). Assuming Soviet demand for kerosine of around 8 per cent of the total product barrel, we found that

---

[3] Research Octane Number.

[4] Sagers and Tretyakova, 1985, do not specify whether this is Research Octane Number (RON) or Motor Octane Number (MON). For the purposes of this calculation we have assumed that their figures refer to the RON which is generally around ten points higher than the MON. The quality of premium leaded gasoline in North West Europe is 97 RON.

the best-quality aviation fuel the system could produce was one containing 30 per cent naphtha. By comparison the fuel burnt by international civil airlines in the West (Jet A-1) has a maximum naphtha content of 20 per cent. Soviet aviation kerosine appears close in quality to the fuel currently used by NATO military aircraft (JP-4).[5] The higher distillate content of this variety implies greater volatility and greater likelihood of carbonaceous deposits in aircraft fuel systems.

(*b*) *Flexibility*. There are two main areas of flexibility open to the refiner: volume and quality. A complex refinery with highly sophisticated plant and distillation capacity generally in excess of local demand can be run in an extremely flexible way to produce varying patterns of output. The Soviet refiner's degrees of freedom are much more limited, however, for reasons summarized below.

Distillation capacity on the ground is 11.6 mb/d. Crude throughput in the 1980s has averaged around 9.3 mb/d, or 80 per cent of capacity. Allowing for maintenance and repairs, a Western refiner would not expect to run his plant at more than 90 per cent utilization over the course of a year. Soviet distillation capacity is generally believed to be much less efficient than its Western counterpart and is on average significantly older. One-third of primary capacity is more than twenty-five years old (see Section 4.2) and is unlikely to be capable of sustaining high levels of utilization. The age distribution of the plant suggests that 10 mb/d is probably the maximum operable capacity.[6] Planning targets, quite rationally, aim at maximizing the use of this effective capacity. Planners cannot afford to leave operational capacity idle, which in a sense is efficient. The drawback, however, is the lack of flexibility on volumes in the short term. Refinery flexibility is also a function of the complexity of the upgrading plant, which allows varying output yields to be produced by changing throughputs in different units. As we saw in Section 4.2, the capacity of upgrading units in the Soviet Union is small by Western standards compared with distillation capacity. Increasing or decreasing throughput by 425,000 b/d of cracking capacity makes very little impact on a total throughput of over 9 mb/d. Similarly, reforming capacity is only just large enough to support gasoline demand, and even this is of very poor quality by Western standards. Overall, Soviet refiners have little in the way of volume flexibility.

Flexibility may also be attained by varying the qualities of final

---

[5] NATO aircraft will in future be fuelled by JP-8, a product close in quality to Jet-A1. This decision was apparently due in part to concerns over fuel quality (*Petroleum Economist*, Vol. LIV, No. 5, May 1987, p. 161).

[6] This assumes 100 per cent utilization from 1980s plant, 90 per cent utilization for 1970s plant, etc.

products. Relaxing specifications generally allows the refiner to increase output. However, the quality of the products coming from Soviet refineries is already very poor, with the exception of gas oil. To seek a reduction in the quality of products that are already sub-standard for the purpose of a quantitative increase is unlikely. Even if Soviet planners contemplated such a course, the gains in terms of additional volumes would be very small. The model shows that a fall of five points in the octane number of gasoline would be needed to obtain additional amounts of 3 mtpa of naphtha, and 6 mtpa of F10. Such a significant reduction in the quality of gasoline would entail costs in terms of the inefficiency of its use that would probably be much greater than the quantitative gain. Similarly, easing the quality restriction on aviation kerosine, by increasing the naphtha content from 30 to 35 per cent, a significant deterioration of the product, would add only 1.5 mtpa of middle distillates to the output stream. Finally, little can be done with fuel oil despite the absence of serious quality restrictions on its production. A major qualitative feature of fuel oil is sulphur content, but since Soviet fuel oil is not usually desulphurized (because Soviet crude is fairly low in sulphur), there is no room for a trade-off between increased quantity and lower quality.

Gas oil is the one exception in terms of quality. The quality of domestically consumed gas oil was improved by reducing its sulphur content from 1 per cent in the early 1970s to about 0.2 per cent in 1985 (Sagers and Tretyakova, 1985). The production of such a low-sulphur gas oil was apparently made necessary by the inability of the refining system to manufacture high-quality lubricants suitable for use in diesel engines. Lubricants production requires expensive, high-technology plant which the Soviets appear unable to manufacture for themselves. Reducing the sulphur content in diesel fuels compensates for this failing to some extent by lowering contamination in engines, thereby prolonging their lives.

This policy has the drawback that a large proportion of the gas oil must be desulphurized to meet the specification, and this results in a volume loss of 2–3 per cent. Information from industry sources indicates that Soviet refiners maximize their gas oil yield by widening the gas oil cut from the distillation column to include some light residue. The quantity gain of around 4 per cent by weight is balanced by a loss in quality since the deeper cuts contain more sulphur. Substantial desulphurization capacity is therefore required by the refining system to produce this high-quality diesel fuel. Our analysis shows that more than 1.6 mb/d of desulphurization capacity would be needed to meet a specification of 0.2 per cent sulphur on a demand of 95–100 mtpa.

It is the view of some Western industry analysts that the Soviets are being too cautious in keeping gas oil sulphur levels as low as 0.2 per cent. To investigate the implications of raising this limit, we used the refinery model to calculate the effect of setting the maximum sulphur content at 0.3 per cent, the normal specification for gas oil traded in Western Europe. An increase in gas oil exports of a little under 1 mtpa resulted, and the requirement for desulphurization capacity fell to 1.4 mb/d. A relaxation on gas oil sulphur content could therefore yield only a small increase in gas oil output and, presumably, in exports.

None of the other quality constraints on gas oil such as cetane number and pour point, which affect its engine and cold weather performance, was found to be a restrictive factor in the system. Tightening the constraints while keeping within feasible limits had no effect on the overall output.

The operational flexibility of the Soviet refining system is limited on the volume side by capacity and technology, while its freedom to vary product qualities is limited to gas oil sulphur content. The only method by which the system can be made truly flexible is investment in substantial amounts of upgrading and secondary processing plant to improve product quality.

4.5 Seasonality

The pattern of Soviet products exports to the West displays a pronounced seasonal pattern which differs from product to product (see Chapter 3). This seasonality is most pronounced in the volumes of gas oil and F10, which peak in the third or fourth quarter and are typically 2–3 million tonnes lower in the first quarter. Quarterly refinery throughput can be estimated from production and export statistics. On average, it varies by no more than 5 million tonnes between the first and third quarters – too small a change in throughput to account for the seasonal effects observed in export volumes. These are therefore principally due to the seasonal pattern of internal demand in the Soviet Union.

The large variation in temperature between summer and winter in the Soviet Union results not only in seasonal changes in the level of demand but also in a varying demand pattern. Consumption of fuel burnt in furnaces and boilers (principally *mazut* with small quantities of gas oil) rises considerably during the winter months, while the use of transport fuels declines. Refinery throughput is raised slightly to meet the extra winter demand; however, the output pattern is unlikely to change since upgrading capacity is relatively small and fuel oil demand can easily be met without backing off cracking. A constant refinery yield combined with a seasonally changing demand barrel clearly affects the seasonal pattern of exports.

The lower level of demand in summer coupled with a drop in the share of fuel oil in total demand results in proportionately more residue being available for export. Although additional gas oil is also available, a substantial amount is required as a blending component for F10 (around 500,000 and 700,000 tonnes in the third quarters of 1985 and 1986 respectively). The proportion of gas oil in total exports is therefore lower in the third quarter of the year.

More interestingly, it can be observed that the seasonal variations in gas oil and F10 exports have changed since the early 1980s (see Figure 4.1). Since 1982 exports of F10 have fluctuated seasonally more than those of gas oil, whereas in previous years the opposite was true.

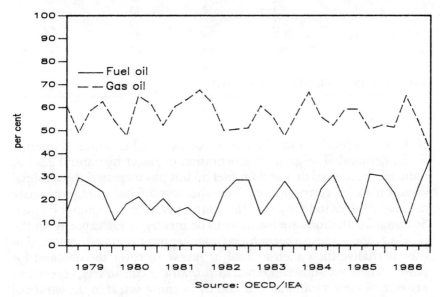

Figure 4.1 Shares of Fuel Oil and Gas Oil in Total Soviet Products Exports to the OECD: Quarterly Data. 1979–86.

Further, the percentage of gas oil in third quarter products exports was around 41 per cent in 1986 whereas in 1982 it was 51 per cent. At the same time the share of F10 fuel oil in third quarter products exports rose from 29 per cent in 1982 to 41 per cent in 1986. The reverse pattern can be seen in first quarter exports where the share of gas oil has increased and that of F10 has declined (see Table 4.6).

Output volumes of gas oil and F10 are related since F10 contains around 20 per cent gas oil. The change in seasonal variation of exports

Table 4.6: Percentage Shares of Gas Oil and Fuel Oil in First and Third Quarter Products Exports. 1979–86.

		Gas Oil	Fuel Oil
1979	1Q	58	14
	3Q	58	27
1980	1Q	54	12
	3Q	65	21
1981	1Q	52	21
	3Q	64	16
1982	1Q	62	11
	3Q	51	29
1983	1Q	61	14
	3Q	48	28
1984	1Q	67	10
	3Q	52	30
1985	1Q	59	9
	3Q	53	31
1986	1Q	65	12
	3Q	41	41

Source: Figures calculated from OECD/IEA

of these two products can be traced back to the behaviour of internal Soviet demand. The gradual substitution of *mazut* by natural gas has reduced the annual demand for fuel oil but has increased the seasonal variation in its consumption. The shortage of gas storage capacity means that demand for gas in the winter peak periods cannot be met. Seasonal fluctuations are too large to be met by 'surge capacity' in the pipeline, and some gas consumers (mainly power stations) are forced to use alternative fuels such as coal or *mazut* to cover the demand for power. These consumers, known as *bufernii* gas consumers, covered 53 per cent of their additional demand by burning *mazut* in the winter of 1980 (Sagers and Tretyakova, 1986).

The influence of *bufernii* users on seasonal demand can also explain the change in the export pattern. During the summer when there is no *bufernii* demand, more fuel oil is becoming available for export as gas substitution increases and refinery throughput remains stable. However, this is most easily exported in the form of F10 which requires the blending in of a proportion of the gas oil pool, reducing the volume of gas oil for export. Further substitution of natural gas for *mazut* without investment in the necessary storage facilities will exaggerate the seasonal variation in demand and confirm the shift towards a larger proportion of F10 in the summer export pattern.

4.6 Future Trends in Products Exports

The volume and pattern of products exports are basically determined by two factors – Soviet internal demand and the refinery structure. In the short term the output pattern is inflexible since changing the refinery configuration involves lead times of at least three years. In the medium and longer term, however, the opportunity exists for the Soviet Union to invest in its refining system and give it the flexibility to meet changing demand without sacrificing valuable products exports.

The increase in natural gas production gave the Soviet Union the chance to reduce its economy's heavy dependence on oil. The eleventh and twelfth five year plans contained loose objectives for industry to make more efficient use of oil products. This was quantified in the eleventh plan which set a target for a 25 mtpa reduction in the consumption of *mazut* by power stations during the period 1980–85 (Sagers and Tretyakova, 1985). This target was almost certainly too ambitious: nevertheless a significant amount of substitution has now taken place. A longer-term objective, as gas production increases, is to halve total fuel oil consumption, which in 1985 was around 160 million tonnes, or 40 per cent of demand.

A major shift in fuel oil demand clearly has implications for the future level and pattern of products exports. The total level of domestic demand in the Soviet Union is expected either to decline (Hewett, 1984a) or to remain at around the current figure of 393 mtpa (OCS). Many industrial sectors that are heavy users of oil are likely to grow over the next ten years, compensating for the planned contraction of oil consumption in boilers and furnaces. These growth sectors include transport (road, rail and air), agriculture, petrochemicals and construction. The domestic sector has potential for growth but also great scope for conservation. For example, hot water and space heating are largely unmetered in residential areas (Campbell, 1983). The overall effect will probably be stable demand in this area.

The long-term implications of these growth assumptions for the levels of demand for individual products are that diesel fuel consumption could rise significantly (in the transport, agricultural and construction sectors) while the use of naphtha, gasoline and kerosine will grow but more slowly. Consumption of bitumen and lubricants may also rise slightly. Clearly, if total demand is to be kept at or below the current level, any growth in distillate demand must be balanced by substitution or conservation in other sectors.

Fuel oil substitution accompanied by growth in middle-distillate consumption would substantially change the shape of the Soviet demand barrel. The result would be a mismatch between refinery output yield and final demand. Were the objective of halving fuel oil consumption to be achieved with overall demand unchanged, fuel oil would constitute an astonishingly low 20 per cent of the demand barrel. Assuming that this objective is a genuine one, what are the options open to the Soviet Union that will enable it to be met?

Since the refining system yields 46 per cent residue on average, a fuel oil surplus could be avoided by reducing refinery throughput and increasing crude exports. However, this course would result in short-falls of lighter products, particularly gasoline, naphtha and kerosine, even if demand for distillates were to remain stable (see Table 4.7).

Table 4.7: Estimates of Demand and Refinery Output in the Soviet Union. 1984–5. Million Tonnes.

Product	Demand		Output	
	1984	*1985*	*1984*	*1985*
Gasoline	66	67	70	72
Naphtha	16	16	21	21
Kerosine	31	31	31	31
Gas Oil	93	94	113	114
Residue	182[a]	185[a]	200	202
Total	388	393	435	440

Note: (a) Includes around 30 million tonnes of bitumen and lubricants.
Sources: Aggregate figures from the oil balance (Table 2.5); breakdown by product from the refinery model (Appendix 3)

This problem could be overcome if light and middle distillates were imported to meet demand. This course seems unlikely, however, since it would lead to the Soviet Union being dependent on external sources to fulfil its oil products requirements.

A second option is to continue running the same volume of crude through the same refinery configuration. It is clear from Table 4.7 that this would simply produce increasingly large surpluses of fuel oil which would have to be diluted with gas oil to make an easily saleable product. A one-third reduction in fuel oil demand (50 mtpa) would require around 12 mtpa of gas oil to blend to F10. This would result in a 60–70 per cent drop in gas oil exports, even assuming that there were no rise in internal demand. Increasing middle-distillate demand combined with falling fuel oil demand could wipe out gas oil exports altogether, making this option an unattractive one for the Soviets.

The economic benefits of making F10 for the export market rather than selling heavy fuel oil and some extra gas oil will depend on their relative export prices. The condition for blending to F10 can be simply formulated by the following inequality:

$$P_{go} + 4P_{hfo} \leqslant 5P_{f10}$$

where P_{go} is the export price of gas oil;
P_{hfo} is the export price of heavy fuel oil;
P_{f10} is the export price of F10.

Assuming that F10 is priced at a certain premium m over heavy fuel oil, where $m \geqslant 0$, then:

$$P_{go} + 4P_{hfo} \leqslant 5(P_{hfo} + m)$$

so that:

$$P_{go} \leqslant P_{hfo} + 5m$$

This tells us that, if the price of gas oil is less than the export price of heavy fuel oil plus five times the F10 premium, it is more valuable to blend all the residue to F10, assuming enough gas oil is available.

It is not clear what price the Soviets could expect to fetch for unblended residue in the West European market. If it matched the specification for West European heavy fuel oil and the quantities were not large enough to swamp the market, a spot-related price could be achieved. If, however, quality were unreliable and the volumes large, the residue could become a 'distress' product.

A substantial reduction in fuel oil consumption is not a feasible option for the Soviet Union unless it invests in upgrading its refining system. Substitution of an exportable commodity, natural gas, for fuel oil only makes sense if the fuel oil can be converted to more valuable products, i.e. F10 or distillates. Doubling cracking capacity to 1 mb/d would absorb 25–30 mtpa of waxy distillate (the top 60 per cent of the straight-run residue) while increasing distillate production by 20–25 mtpa.

A side-effect of increasing cracking capacity is the deterioration in the quality of the fuel oil pool due to the inclusion of residue from vacuum distillation, visbreaking and catalytic cracking. Residue can be almost completely destroyed by a process known as coking which produces only distillates and solid coke. There is some evidence that the Soviet Union intends to include coking in its refinery configuration: 200,000 b/d is already in operation.

A well-planned programme of refinery investment synchronized with steady gas-for-oil substitution could, in the long run, allow the Soviet Union to maintain, or even increase, the amount of oil available for export. Higher upgrading capacity will reduce the crude through-put necessary to meet internal demand if fuel oil consumption is cut.[7]

[7] The total export volume will also depend, of course, on the level of crude oil and condensate production.

PART II

SOVIET OIL TRADE AND THE BALANCE OF PAYMENTS

Machiko Nissanke

5 OIL EXPORTS AND THE SOVIET ECONOMY

5.1 Introduction

Oil is a major export commodity and a significant earner of foreign exchange in the Soviet economy. It is a core source of finance for long-term planned imports. Our purposes in this part of the book are first to examine whether Soviet oil exports to the West, i.e. to the hard currency area, can be construed as a decision variable used by planners in the management of the foreign trade sector, and by implication of the entire Soviet economy, and secondly to assess the extent of this role. The central issue is one of trade adjustments in response to the imbalances – both surpluses and deficits – that regularly affect the external account.

For these purposes we begin this chapter with a discussion of the functions of foreign trade in the Soviet planned economy (Section 5.2). This is followed by a review of the development of Soviet trade with the West (Section 5.3): the motivations that caused a shift from autarky to open trade with OECD and other non-Socialist countries in the 1970s, and the problems of balance-of-payments adjustments that naturally arose. We then examine the possible roles of main exports, such as natural gas, military equipment and certain primary commodities, and of other instruments, namely gold sales and capital borrowing from the West, in balance-of-payments adjustments, comparing them with oil exports (Sections 5.4 and 5.5).

This analysis provides the context for Chapter 6 where we attempt to identify the episodes in the period 1970–84 during which oil exports were used, in conjunction with other instruments, for balance-of-payments adjustments. Because of constraints on oil production, whenever increases in the volume of oil exports to the hard currency area are required for trade adjustment purposes, they involve a reallocation between the different markets served by the Soviet Union or an increase in oil imports for re-export. Similarly, a reduction in the oil export volumes, in response to an amelioration of the external balance with the West, leads to reallocation in favour of other areas. These issues are examined in Chapters 7 and 8. Finally Chapter 9 presents econometric tests of our proposition that Soviet oil exports to the West are adjusted in response to changes in the state of the external balance.

5.2 Foreign Trade and the Soviet Economy

In Soviet-type centrally planned economies, planners are accorded control over the allocation and use of virtually all resources.[1] Market forces do play a limited role, but only in the household sector, where decisions over labour supply and personal consumption are left to the individual's discretion.

One of the major principles of the direct centralized allocation of resources is the use of detailed material balances covering the supply and utilization of every product and factor of production in physical units.

However, it is well known that a physical allocation system of this nature is heavily supply based, and that Soviet plans are made deliberately 'taut' throughout the processes of planning and plan-implementation. This initial 'taut planning' aims to elicit maximum output, but the optimistic underestimates of input requirements exert enormous pressure from the start on the entire supply system. This pressure is multiplied further throughout the implementation stage, as the whole system of material incentives in the economy is traditionally geared to encourage the over-fulfilment of physical output targets.

Inevitably, this practice results in generalized excess demand in the productive sectors, and the development of a severely supply-constrained economy. Furthermore, prices are set administratively and remain rigidly fixed. All these factors lead to disequilibria at the micro and macro levels in the form of chronic shortage and quantity rationing, and excess supplies of various kinds of unwanted goods (Portes, 1983; Neuberger and Tyson, 1980).

These features of the centrally planned economies, i.e. the central-ization of decisions on resource allocation and the system of constraints on supply, have given foreign trade a crucial role to play in the management of the national economy.

The first important point to be noted is that the levels of exports and imports are set as an integrated part of the national economic plan, and that the actual performance of foreign trade is closely monitored subsequently in the course of the implementation of this overall plan. As the foreign trade sector has increasingly become a critical deter-minant of Soviet economic growth in recent decades, so the medium-

[1] The new economic reforms discussed and implemented under Gorbachev, calling for greater democracy and decentralization of decision-making, may bring substantial changes to the planning system discussed in this chapter.

and long-term planning of the foreign trade sector has become more prominent in the formulation of strategies for the development of the Soviet economy. At the same time, the greater dependence of the economy on the foreign trade sector has inevitably made it more vulnerable to external shocks. In these circumstances, short-run deviations from the planned trade level require careful attention on the part of planners and constant revisions to the plan to ensure that the economy remains on its planned course.[2] Therefore, *ex ante*, the 'net exports' of any product, and especially those of such strategic export commodities as oil, gas and gold, are not a mere 'surplus' left over from domestic production that remains unused after domestic needs have been satisfied. Rather, depending on the choice of development strategy and the extent of the imbalance in the external account at the time, these 'net exports' serve as one of the major decision-making variables at planners' disposal. Hence, the levels of 'net exports', both as originally planned and as adjusted in the course of the plan's implementation, are treated by planners as decision variables in their own right, along with production and domestic consumption (Jensen et al, 1983).

The actual quantity of exports is, in this sense, a manifestation of planners' behaviour. Hence, the analysis of net exports (i.e. export supply and import demand) of Soviet main traded commodities should always incorporate an examination of this behaviour.

The second characteristic of Soviet foreign trade is the planners' use of foreign trade as a means by which to alleviate the supply bottlenecks and excess real demand generated by 'taut' planning in the domestic sector. This explains immediately the well-established planning sequence of the Soviet foreign trade sector: planning starts with the calculation of essential import needs and then proceeds to determine the level of export earnings needed to finance the required imports. The economic growth of centrally planned economies thus follows an 'import-fed' path, in contrast with the export-led path of market economies. As Portes describes, 'Western countries are typically *neomercantilist*, seeking to loosen the balance-of-payments constraint on domestic stabilization policy. Soviet planners are *antimercantilist*, viewing exports as a necessary evil to pay for required imports.' (Portes, 1983, p. 30, *our italics*.)

The two key elements of planners' decision-making on exports can be seen here. On the one hand, planners operating in an economy dominated by real excess demand are unlikely to expand exports purely for exports' sake or primarily in response to changes in relative

---

[2] Throughout this discussion, 'short-run' refers to a period of duration up to eighteen months, 'medium-term' up to five years, and 'long-run' beyond five years.

prices in the world market. On the other hand, Soviet planners, in correcting short-term fluctuations of the trade balance, will pay more attention to 'supply multiplier effects' than to 'demand multiplier effects', since the macroeconomic impacts of foreign trade on the domestic sector in the 'overfull employed economy' are transmitted through 'supply' rather than through 'demand' as is the case for market economies (Neuberger and Tyson, 1980).

For all these reasons, it is not uncommon in the literature for Soviet planners' short-run export behaviour to be described as a balance-of-payments adjustment mechanism (Jensen et al, 1983; Neuberger and Tyson, 1980).

Naturally, political considerations can sometimes dominate purely economic factors, especially in the cases of exports to the Socialist countries or arms sales and other concessional trade with LDCs. In fact, a distinctive feature of Soviet foreign economic policy is that trade with these regions is treated separately from trade with the West, and is governed by different principles. Therefore, in the following section, our discussion will concentrate on Soviet trade with the West.

5.3 Soviet Trade with the West

The overall level of Soviet trade with the West and its medium- to long-term trend is planned by *Gosplan* as a part of its long-term economic development strategy, and as such, it is heavily influenced by the political climate of global East–West relationships.[3]

Historically, the Soviet Union embarked on a heavy industrialization programme on an autarkic basis for two reasons: first on account of its preference for self-sufficiency over reliance on the West, and secondly in response to the restrictions imposed on the expansion of external trade by the hostile political environment in the inter-war period. During the early post-war years, however, this policy of complete autarky was ameliorated to some extent with the development of intra-CMEA trade.

However, with the gradual exhaustion of readily available domestic resources, the scope for further advance on the traditional pattern, by

[3] The Ministry of Foreign Trade with its numerous Foreign Trade Organizations (FTOs), including *Soyuznefteksport* and *Soyuzgazeksport*, is in practice subordinate to *Gosplan* (the State Planning Committee). Its main function is to provide information to *Gosplan* concerning export and import possibilities. The central role of *Gosplan* in making actual export decisions is clear; it is supported by the Council of Ministers (which includes the Ministers of the Oil Industry and the Gas Industry) and the central administration of the Ministry of Foreign Trade. In accordance with decisions made by *Gosplan* concerning planned and unplanned flows, export commodities are delivered by enterprises through *Gossnab* (the State Committee on Material-Technical Supply) to the FTOs. For details of the organizational structure of Soviet foreign trade, see Hewett, 1983a, p. 648).

means of 'extensive' industrialization, had diminished. Almost all the indicators of Soviet economic performance presented in Table 5.1 unequivocally show a downward long-term trend. It also became apparent to Soviet policy-makers and planners that autarky entailed heavy costs to the economy because of inefficiencies in the allocation and utilization of resources.

Table 5.1: Trends in Soviet Economic Performance. Average Annual Percentage Growth Rates. 1951–85.

	1951–5	1956–60	1961–5	1966–70	1971–5	1976–80	1981–5
Net Material Product[1]	11.4	9.2	6.5	7.7	5.6	4.2	3.4
Industrial Production	13.1	10.4	8.6	8.5	7.4	4.5	3.7
Agricultural Production	4.0	5.9	2.4	4.2	0.8	1.6	2.0
Gross Investment[1]	12.3	13.0	6.2	7.6	6.9	3.4	3.5
Employment[1]	4.1	4.4	4.4	3.2	2.5	1.9	1.0
Labour Productivity[1] in Industry	8.2	6.5	4.6	5.8	6.0	3.2	3.1
Real Per Capita Income[2]	7.2	5.7	3.5	5.9	4.4	3.4	2.2
GNP[2]	6.0	5.8	5.0	5.5	3.8	2.7	2.7

Sources: 1. *Narodnoe khozyaistvo SSSR*, various issues
2. CIA, *Handbook*, various issues

The recognition of these costs and the desire to reap the potential benefits from participation in international trade, especially the acquisition of advanced technology, led to a pronounced shift of Soviet foreign trade policy towards the West in the early 1970s (Hewett, 1983b; Wolf, 1983). The shift was also clearly related to a change in Soviet agricultural policy. Planners now sought to increase imports of feed grain in order to increase the meat content of the average diet of the population. As a result, around this time the Soviet Union ceased to be a net grain-exporting country and became a net grain-importing country, and it is now the second-largest grain importer in the world (Kostecki, 1984). Data on production, imports and exports of grain are shown in Table 5.2.

The shift in Soviet trade policy coincided with changes in the attitudes of the Western countries, in keeping with the general spirit of *détente*, who now began to regard the Soviet Union positively as a new and growing market and a secure supply source of essential raw materials and energy.

This recognition of mutual interests and the political will on both sides to further the advancement of East–West trade were supported materially by a marked augmentation of Soviet hard currency purchasing power associated with the quadrupling of oil prices in the world

Table 5.2: Domestic Production, Imports and Exports of Grain. 1970–84. Volumes in Million Tonnes. Values in Million Dollars.

	Production	Imports		Exports	
	Volume	*Volume*	*Value*	*Volume*	*Value*
1970	186.6	2.8	207	6.9	493
1971	181.2	4.0	278	9.6	670
1972	168.2	16.2	955	5.1	380
1973	222.5	24.4	1,607	5.8	571
1974	195.7	7.8	827	8.5	999
1975	140.1	16.7	2,857	4.4	632
1976	223.8	21.4	3,139	2.4	342
1977	195.7	11.8	1,632	4.7	651
1978	237.4	23.5	2,642	2.5	328
1979	179.3	26.9	3,823	3.9	715
1980	189.1	31.2	5,680	2.3	497
1981	160.0	43.7	8,306	2.6	589
1982	179.0	40.1	6,735	2.2	480
1983	200.0	32.1	5,442	2.3	404
1984	170.0	43.2	6,929	2.1	369

Source: FAO yearbooks, various issues

market. Indeed, as discussed below, Soviet planners embarked on a major expansion of hard currency imports at this time, apparently under the assumption that the terms-of-trade improvement following the sharp oil price increases of 1973–4 would last for the foreseeable future.

These developments are easily seen in the volume and value indices of Soviet foreign trade presented in Tables 5.3 and 5.4.[4] Imports from all areas increased at phenomenal rates in both value and volume terms, but it was clearly the volume of imports from the non-Socialist countries that showed the most dynamic growth – three- and fourfold increases – and the more conspicuous volatility.

The volume of exports registered a lower growth rate than the volume of imports to all regions, but particularly to non-Socialist countries. The growth of exports also lagged behind that of imports, partly reflecting the large improvement in the Soviet terms of trade as shown in Table 5.5. The faster growth of imports was also facilitated by the increased use of Western credits from the highly liquid international capital markets in the 1970s as discussed below. The trade

[4] The volume indices reported in the tables differ from the Soviet official series, which are chain-linked Laspeyres indices. The total trade volume indices reported in the official foreign trade yearbook *VTSS* are subject to substantial annual revisions, and do not agree with the volume indices for the trade blocs taken separately.

Table 5.3: Soviet Import Index. 1970–84 (1970 = 100).

	Total			Socialist Countries			Non-Socialist Countries		
	Value	Volume	Unit Value	Value	Volume	Unit Value	Value	Volume	Unit Value
1970	100.0	100.0	100.0	100.0	100.0	100.0	100.0	100.0	100.0
1971	106.3	106.3	100.0	107.0	105.5	101.4	105.0	107.5	97.7
1972	125.9	123.5	101.9	123.8	119.2	103.9	129.8	129.6	100.2
1973	147.1	134.8	109.1	134.0	128.3	104.4	171.6	143.9	119.2
1974	178.3	141.9	125.7	149.8	142.1	105.4	231.4	141.6	163.4
1975	252.4	186.3	135.5	203.1	166.9	121.7	344.6	213.7	161.3
1976	272.4	186.4	146.1	219.6	161.5	136.0	370.4	221.6	167.1
1977	284.8	189.3	150.4	249.6	178.5	139.8	350.5	204.5	171.4
1978	327.1	211.3	154.8	301.6	203.3	148.4	374.7	222.6	168.3
1979	358.6	217.8	164.6	311.7	202.6	153.8	445.9	239.2	186.4
1980	420.9	236.4	178.0	343.8	207.2	165.9	564.7	277.5	203.5
1981	498.2	257.4	193.6	388.7	212.7	182.7	702.4	320.4	219.2
1982	533.9	264.4	201.9	448.0	227.2	197.2	694.4	316.8	219.2
1983	564.0	277.1	203.5	489.8	236.4	207.2	702.5	334.3	210.1
1984	618.3	288.3	214.5	555.6	256.7	216.4	735.4	332.8	221.0

Sources: Value indices are calculated from the values in foreign trade roubles reported in various issues of the *VTSS* yearbook. Volume indices are calculated from data on Soviet foreign trade in constant price series, as reported in the UNECE *Economic Bulletin*, Vol. 37, 1985. The deflators used in the UN data, given in million 1975 US dollars, are Hungarian foreign trade indices, with statistical adjustments for certain commodities.

Table 5.4: Soviet Export Index. 1970–84 (1970 = 100).

	Total			Socialist Countries			Non-Socialist Countries		
	Value	Volume	Unit Value	Value	Volume	Unit Value	Value	Volume	Unit Value
1970	100.0	100.0	100.0	100.0	100.0	100.0	100.0	100.0	100.0
1971	107.9	108.4	99.5	107.8	106.9	100.8	108.0	110.6	97.6
1972	110.5	109.2	101.2	110.0	107.4	102.4	111.5	111.9	99.6
1973	137.2	132.4	103.6	121.1	118.6	102.1	167.6	152.8	109.7
1974	180.0	143.7	125.3	147.3	144.2	102.1	241.8	143.1	169.0
1975	208.6	144.0	144.9	193.7	146.5	132.2	236.8	140.3	168.8
1976	243.2	153.7	158.2	218.3	150.3	145.2	290.0	158.9	182.5
1977	288.7	172.0	167.8	253.7	162.2	156.4	354.7	186.5	190.2
1978	309.6	176.3	175.6	282.3	166.0	170.1	361.3	191.5	188.7
1979	368.4	186.7	197.3	314.0	173.4	181.1	472.5	206.4	228.9
1980	430.9	184.7	233.3	357.3	178.0	200.7	569.7	194.5	292.9
1981	495.7	185.1	267.8	414.2	178.9	231.5	649.5	194.3	334.3
1982	548.3	193.2	283.8	453.3	171.1	264.9	727.5	225.9	322.0
1983	589.3	202.2	291.4	500.8	171.2	292.5	756.3	248.1	304.8
1984	645.7	208.8	309.2	559.2	179.9	310.8	808.9	251.6	321.5

Sources: as for Table 5.3

Table 5.5: Soviet Terms-of-Trade Index. 1970–84 (1970 = 100).

	Total	*Socialist*	*Non-Socialist*
1970	100.0	100.0	100.0
1971	99.5	99.4	100.0
1972	99.3	98.6	99.5
1973	95.0	97.8	92.0
1974	99.7	96.9	103.4
1975	106.9	108.7	104.7
1976	108.3	106.8	109.2
1977	111.6	111.9	111.0
1978	113.4	114.6	112.1
1979	119.8	117.7	122.8
1980	131.0	121.0	143.9
1981	138.4	126.7	152.5
1982	140.5	134.4	146.9
1983	143.2	141.2	145.1
1984	144.2	143.6	145.5

Note: The terms-of-trade indices are calculated by dividing the export unit value indices by the import value indices reported in Tables 5.3 and 5.4.

indices show clearly that both exports and imports grew much more quickly than the domestic economy (see Table 5.1).

The noticeable shift in Soviet trade policy towards the West in the 1970s is also clearly seen in the geographical distribution of foreign trade (see Table 5.6).[5] A marked move away from the Socialist countries to the MDCs, i.e. the Western industrialized countries, is evident.

However, it can be seen in retrospect that the Soviet Union had to pay a price for its decision to use foreign trade with the West as a spur to its economic performance. First of all, there was a loss of stability – a critically important factor for any planned economy. In the past, the autarky strategy, though with its own costs, had successfully insulated the domestic economic planning system from the volatile fluctuations of international markets and the impact of political and strategic embargoes imposed by the West. The decision to open up the Soviet economy to world trade has exposed it to unpredictable external forces on a greater scale. The growth of foreign trade has increased the vulnerability of the economy to these external disturbances. The decision was taken at the time when the world economy lost the secular growth trend of the post-war era, and when the international markets lost their stability and began to experience more frequent upheavals.

[5] As foreign trade roubles are used for these computations, the interpretation of the figures must be qualified (see Chapter 3 above).

Table 5.6: Geographical Distribution of Soviet Foreign Trade. 1960–84. Percentage Shares by Value in Foreign Trade Roubles.

	Socialist	(CMEA)	MDCs	LDCs
(a) Imports				
1960	70.7	(50.1)	19.8	9.5
1970	65.1	(57.0)	24.1	10.8
1975	52.4	(48.3)	36.4	11.2
1980	53.2	(48.2)	35.4	11.4
1981	50.8	(44.9)	34.4	14.8
1982	54.6	(48.8)	33.5	11.9
1983	56.5	(51.7)	31.4	12.1
1984	58.5	(52.9)	30.0	11.5
(b) Exports				
1960	75.7	(56.0)	18.2	6.1
1970	65.4	(54.3)	18.7	15.9
1975	60.7	(55.6)	25.5	13.8
1980	54.2	(49.0)	32.0	13.8
1981	54.6	(50.0)	30.2	15.2
1982	54.0	(49.3)	29.8	16.1
1983	55.6	(50.7)	28.9	15.5
1984	56.6	(51.3)	28.7	14.7

Source: *Narodnoe khozyaistvo SSSR*, various issues

It is true that the actual performance of the Soviet economy had never followed the planned path exactly even *before* the shift in trade policy. The oscillations of the actual growth rates around the planned targets before the mid-1970s may be seen in Figure 5.1.

These were largely the result of fluctuations in the agricultural sector, where output is subject to wide variations (see Figure 5.2). The variability of domestic agricultural production translates into significant fluctuations in grain import requirements, and therefore in total import requirements, because of the large share of food in the import bill with non-Socialist countries (see Figure 5.3).

Two further interrelated external forces add to the domestic factors and multiply the unanticipated fluctuations in the external account: the world demand effect, and the terms-of-trade effect.

As discussed in the next section, the Soviet Union's exports to the hard currency trade area consist mainly of primary commodities. The demand for these commodities is known to be subject to large fluctuations in the level of world economic activity, especially that of the industrialized countries. An unforeseen large drop in demand for

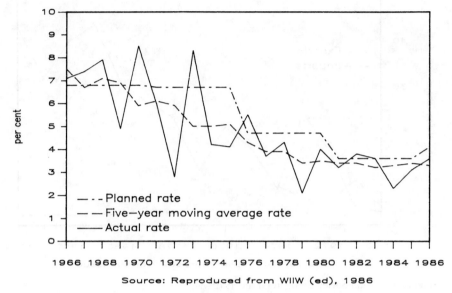

Figure 5.1 Actual and Planned Percentage Growth Rates of NMP. 1966–86.

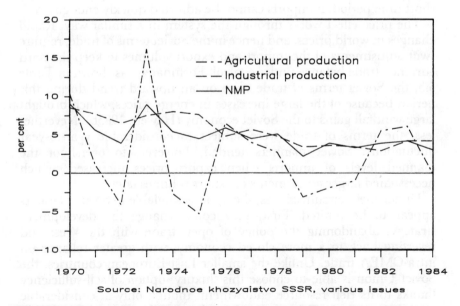

Figure 5.2 Annual Growth Rates of Key Indicators of the Soviet Economy. 1970–84.

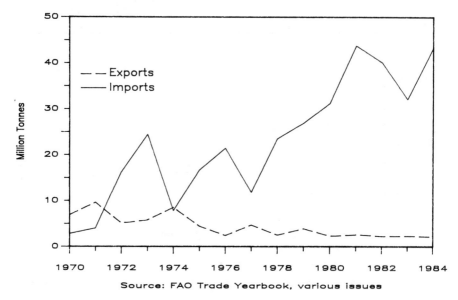

Source: FAO Trade Yearbook, various issues

Figure 5.3 Total Soviet Trade in Grain. 1970–84.

exports can worsen the Soviet trade balance significantly within a very short time period, if imports cannot be adjusted quickly enough.

The price effect works through the system in a similar way. Rapid changes in world prices, and hence in the Soviet terms of trade, require swift adjustments of the import and export volumes to keep the hard currency trade balance under control. Fortunately, as shown in Table 5.5, the Soviet terms of trade were on an upward trend during this period because of the large increases in energy prices, which brought large windfall gains to the Soviet economy (Hewett, 1983b). Nevertheless, the terms of trade were subject to considerable year-to-year fluctuations. Soviet planners tended, however, to overshoot the planned levels of imports when export prices increased, which necessitated larger adjustments of export volumes later.

Under these circumstances, the options available to Soviet planners appear to be limited. First, they could change the development strategy, abandoning the policy of open trade with the West and reverting back to a more closed economy, with greater reliance on intra-CMEA trade. Unlike the smaller East European countries, the Soviet Union is able to choose this 'luxury' option of self-sufficiency thanks to its rich resource endowment, though only at considerable costs in terms of efficiency. In fact, the deterioration of East–West political relations in the late 1970s and the Soviet economy's problems in absorbing imported technology efficiently put the brake on further expansion of trade with the West, as can be seen clearly from Table 5.6.

The second option is to try to expand the share of trade with the West conducted under government-to-government, long-term, bi-lateral export agreements encompassing countertrade and credit agreements (e.g. gas-for-pipe deals, ammonia plant deals, etc.), which enable the Soviet Union to obtain Western technology without the immediate need for hard currency.

However, these two measures are medium- and long-term solutions, which can not alleviate Soviet hard currency problems in the short run. Besides these long-run 'planned' changes, Soviet planners need to have short-run adjustment mechanisms and instruments to enable them to deal with unforeseen shocks encountered in the implementation of the plan. Because of this, any plan must contain implicit flexibility to allow for unplanned physical transactions in hard currency.

Naturally, the planned economy finds it relatively easy to accommo-date long-term *planned* changes, while it is not necessarily suited to short-run adjustments. Although the domestic sector is in large measure shielded from the immediate impact of changes in inter-national market prices by the 'tax-subsidy' scheme, and the state budget can comfortably absorb these external disturbances and contain their impact within the foreign trade sector,[6] beyond a certain critical point, the planners must start to adjust real trade flows, and these adjustments have repercussions on resource allocation within the domestic economy. As discussed in Section 5.2, the Soviet economy is, in essence, a full (or rather overfull) employment economy with generalized excess demand, in which real trade flow adjustments involving increased output are not easily managed. Furthermore, if the adjustments needed to restore unforeseen trade deficits are to be effective and successful in the short term, it is essential that those export commodities that *can* be allocated very flexibly are at the planners' disposal, and also highly tradable in Western markets.

5.4 Oil and Other Export Commodities

To address this issue, we now turn to examine the commodity structure of Soviet exports to the hard currency area. The share of energy exports in Soviet hard currency earnings had increased to

[6] The link between the domestic and foreign prices of tradables is very feint, and they are divorced from one another by a system of variable taxes and subsidies (the price equalization subsidy system) (Neuberger and Tyson, 1980). This 'insulation layer' is said to have weakened in recent years (Treml, 1983), but domestic prices are still altered in response to world market price changes only with considerable time-lags and at infrequent intervals.

Table 5.7: Commodity Structure of Soviet Imports. 1975–84. Percentage Shares by Value in Foreign Trade Roubles.

	Machinery and Transport Equipment	Fuels, Electrical Energy	Ores, Metals and Metal Goods	Food	Industrial Consumer Goods	Others
(a) Socialist Countries						
1975	38.7	3.0	6.7	21.2	19.4	11.0
1976	40.0	2.7	6.7	19.3	19.1	12.2
1977	40.8	2.4	5.8	19.8	18.5	12.7
1978	46.6	2.4	4.5	17.9	17.0	11.6
1979	45.8	2.2	5.6	18.6	16.9	10.9
1980	43.8	1.7	6.1	18.6	17.7	12.1
1981	42.9	1.5	6.5	17.8	18.6	12.7
1982	43.0	1.9	5.9	18.8	17.9	12.5
1983	47.0	2.2	5.9	16.4	15.7	12.8
1984	46.7	2.3	5.3	17.4	15.6	12.7
(b) Non-Socialist Countries						
1975	28.6	4.9	17.0	25.0	5.8	18.7
1976	32.2	4.6	15.3	26.7	5.4	15.8
1977	34.5	5.2	14.0	22.1	5.5	18.7
1978	35.0	5.7	17.5	21.2	4.0	16.6
1979	27.8	5.9	18.5	26.2	4.2	17.4
1980	22.7	4.5	16.1	30.6	5.7	20.4
1981	17.1	5.8	13.6	37.9	7.0	18.6
1982	24.0	7.9	14.7	29.6	6.4	17.4
1983	26.7	10.0	12.6	25.8	6.0	18.9
1984	22.6	11.5	12.5	29.7	6.2	17.5

Source: *VTSS* yearbook, various issues

almost 80 per cent by the early 1980s, with the share of oil being not less than 60 per cent (see Table 5.9). Fuels also account for a large share of exports to Socialist countries (now about 50 per cent) and oil is known to be the main commodity within this category (see Tables 5.7 and 5.8).

There is therefore no doubt that oil is a leading export commodity for the Soviet economy today. Its share in hard currency exports increased from 22 per cent in 1970 to over 60 per cent in 1984. Furthermore, the annual compound growth rate of oil exports in value terms was a phenomenal 29.8 per cent on average over this fifteen-year period although this growth rate was subject to large annual fluctuations (see Table 5.9). Though this growth was in large part accounted for by the more than twentyfold increase of oil prices in the world

Table 5.8: Commodity Structure of Soviet Exports. 1975–84. Percentage Shares by
Value in Foreign Trade Roubles.

	Machinery and Transport Equipment	Fuels, Electrical Energy	Ores, Metals and Metal Goods	Food	Industrial Consumer Goods	Others
(a) Socialist Countries						
1975	23.5	26.0	19.6	5.6	3.3	22.0
1976	25.6	27.3	18.4	3.6	3.3	21.8
1977	25.9	29.8	16.3	4.2	2.8	21.0
1978	25.8	31.8	14.9	2.6	2.9	22.0
1979	24.2	36.0	13.5	3.4	2.6	20.3
1980	22.8	39.7	13.1	2.4	2.6	19.4
1981	18.8	44.3	12.5	2.8	2.2	19.4
1982	17.5	47.9	11.3	2.1	2.3	18.9
1983	16.2	50.1	11.0	1.7	2.2	18.8
1984	16.0	51.2	10.4	1.6	2.2	18.6
(b) Non-Socialist Countries						
1975	11.3	39.7	6.1	3.6	2.8	36.5
1976	10.6	44.2	5.8	2.1	2.6	34.7
1977	9.2	42.3	4.1	1.6	2.6	40.2
1978	10.5	41.2	3.5	1.6	3.4	39.8
1979	9.1	50.0	3.6	1.6	1.9	33.8
1980	7.5	55.4	3.7	1.3	2.4	29.7
1981	7.6	57.3	2.6	1.0	1.3	30.2
1982	7.5	57.5	2.8	1.0	1.4	29.8
1983	7.9	58.2	3.1	1.3	1.3	28.2
1984	7.9	58.6	3.0	1.4	1.4	27.7

Source: *VTSS* yearbook, various issues

market, the contribution of volume growth was not negligible: exports
of crude and products to the West rose from 45 million tonnes in 1970
to 94 million in 1984 (PlanEcon, 1986). This demonstrates how the
rapid growth of oil exports, prompted by large price increases, was
instrumental in the massive expansion of Soviet imports from the West
during this period (see Table 5.3).

At the same time, by choosing this option rather than diversifying
the export trade structure, Soviet planners increased the economy's
vulnerability to the external forces governing the world oil market. In
fact, since the early 1970s, the Soviet economy has developed gradually
into a 'one-crop economy', heavily dependent on oil in its economic
relations with the West. Thus the Soviet Union shares problems
common to many primary commodity exporting developing countries:

Table 5.9: Soviet Energy Exports to the Hard Currency Area. 1970–84. Volumes of Oil in Million Tonnes. Volumes of Natural Gas in Million Cubic Metres. Values in Million Dollars.

| | PlanEcon Estimates (Volume) | | | | | OECD/IEA Estimates (Volume) | | | |
| | Crude | | Products | | Gas | Crude | | Products | |
	MDCs	LDCs	MDCs	LDCs	MDCs only	OECD	OECD less Finland	OECD	OECD less Finland
1970	23.15	2.35	18.37	1.39	956	22.90	16.20	16.00	13.25
1971	25.10	2.58	20.44	1.53	1,428	23.90	18.02	16.50	13.92
1972	21.95	2.30	21.00	1.53	1,163	22.10	16.11	17.70	14.89
1973	24.32	1.76	23.36	1.17	1,975	23.30	16.71	18.80	16.08
1974	15.77	1.76	25.76	1.17	5,484	15.10	8.96	20.90	17.73
1975	21.11	3.00	26.66	1.72	8,042	19.20	13.38	23.40	20.50
1976	34.02	2.94	25.92	1.68	12,345	32.30	25.30	23.50	20.64
1977	40.00	4.20	25.20	1.80	16,300	35.00	27.38	22.00	18.96
1978	40.30	3.30	26.80	1.80	20,000	36.30	29.38	24.30	21.30
1979	35.40	5.10	21.10	1.70	24,600	36.50	29.13	22.00	19.25
1980	31.40	5.10	22.10	1.60	25,100	33.40	26.44	23.60	20.85
1981	30.60	5.30	24.40	1.70	28,500	29.00	22.08	23.90	21.58
1982	38.30	5.70	32.70	1.80	27,400	36.80	28.91	32.20	29.69
1983	48.30	6.90	34.30	2.20	26,600	44.60	35.77	33.30	30.54
1984	52.50	6.50	32.70	2.10	28,450	49.60	42.09	31.80	29.04

OECD Estimates (Value)

Year	Oil (Crude and Products)			Gas			% Share of Energy in Total Exports to OECD less Finland[b]
	OECD	OECD less Finland[a]	% Share of Oil in Total Exports to OECD less Finland	OECD	OECD less Finland	% Share of Gas in Total Exports to OECD less Finland[a]	
1970	659	485	21.8	14.9	14.8	0.7	29.2
1971	846	640	25.7	23.1	23.0	0.9	33.2
1972	880	664	23.9	26.2	25.7	0.9	30.5
1973	1,421	1,141	26.2	27.3	27.1	0.6	30.9
1974	3,105	2,248	33.7	127.6	99.3	1.5	39.9
1975	3,782	3,025	41.9	266.4	220.2	3.0	45.0
1976	5,173	4,285	45.6	412.3	358.3	3.8	54.1
1977	5,777	4,736	44.6	593.5	540.0	5.1	53.1
1978	6,380	5,387	46.4	1,086.6	1,021.4	8.8	57.8
1979	10,110	8,436	51.6	1,316.7	1,246.7	7.6	61.5
1980	13,450	11,009	53.7	2,777.5	2,644.5	12.9	68.6
1981	13,903	11,323	55.4	4,072.0	3,930.1	19.2	75.6
1982	15,549	13,054	60.0	3,912.1	3,806.7	17.5	78.3
1983	15,891	13,343	62.2	3,326.8	3,234.3	15.1	78.8
1984	16,140	13,952	60.6	3,943.1	3,846.4	16.7	79.3

Notes: (a) The movements in these series broadly agree with those reported in various issues of the CIA *Handbook*.
(b) Including oil, natural gas, coal, coke and electric power.

Sources: PlanEcon, 1986
OECD/IEA, *Oil and Gas Statistics*, various issues
OECD, *Foreign Trade by Commodities*, *Series C*, various issues

it suffers from the undesirable consequences of heavy dependence on one commodity for its foreign exchange earnings; and the balance of the external account, and hence that of the entire economy, have become precariously dependent on the state of the market in a single commodity – oil. In this respect, the role of oil has grown to the extent that it is now a major factor in balancing the Soviet economy.

The Soviet Union's ability to import Western technology and feed grain in large quantities is in this sense contingent upon its ability to maintain and expand oil export revenues. Though Soviet dependence on imported goods may not be large at the aggregate level, its dependence on imports for the relief of critical production bottlenecks at the micro level can be very high. For example, more than 60 per cent of the specialized machinery in the chemical industry is reported to be of foreign origin (Treml, 1983). The agricultural sector would also suffer heavily from any withdrawal of imported grain. It is well known that hard currency imports play an important role in the Soviet economy in sustaining technological advances, in raising the production of key industries, and in easing bottlenecks in the agricultural sector. Oil exports have provided the economy with a core source of finance for these long-term import needs.

However, as discussed above, Soviet planners also need a *flexible* export commodity in order to deal effectively with short-run adjustments of the external balance. For a commodity to be capable of playing this role, it must possess several distinct features. On the domestic side, it should have flexibility of supply, or at least flexibility of delivery and distribution, so that it can be easily diverted from the other users as needs arise. To find a commodity with such a property is not easy in an economy governed by excess demand. As for the export market structure, the commodity should be well traded, probably in highly developed spot markets where any quantity supplied can be absorbed quickly and efficiently, and the market share occupied by Soviet exports should be small enough to ensure that variations in the level of supply do not affect the world price level unduly.

Obviously, for Soviet planners oil is a good candidate for this task. It is a highly tradable commodity in export markets with active spot deals. Yet, the Soviet market share in the total oil imports of the OECD countries is only about 6–7 per cent, and is not large enough to alarm planners about its effect on prices. Soviet planners are known to perceive that they can export any quantity they need at, or slightly below, the ruling price. In fact, for most export commodities (notable exceptions are gold, platinum and diamonds), Soviet planners take it for granted that they can vary the quantities supplied without influencing the price, since the Soviet Union is a marginal supplier to the world market. Thus they act typically as price takers on the world market (Portes, 1980; Jensen et al, 1983, p. 685; Hewett, 1983a; Wolf, 1982).

However, as argued by Roberts, 1984, in an application to the oil market of a concept developed by Arrow, 1959, every oil exporter faces a downward-sloping demand curve when the market is in disequilibrium, and thus has some discretion over price. Since markets are usually out of equilibrium, every small supplier is potentially a price setter and, on occasions, can exert a disproportionately large effect on price at the margin. Soviet planners' behaviour suggests either that they are unaware of their potential ability to affect the oil price or that they choose to ignore it.

On the domestic side, oil is the swing fuel with flexibility of delivery, though Soviet planners have no flexibility of supply through further expansion of oil *production*, which is subject to severe physical and economic constraints. The flexibility of supply of Soviet oil exports thus reflects flexibility in the allocation of delivery; and the surge of oil exports to the hard currency area in the early 1980s, while production remained stagnant, is largely explained by the diversion of oil deliveries to the West at the expense of the CMEA countries and domestic consumers. This was facilitated in part by a successful gas-for-oil substitution programme. However, as an unforeseen cut in production in 1985 amply demonstrated, Soviet planners operate with very little freedom in allocation, since they face constraints of different kinds in each of the three markets. Once production falls below a critical point, the volume of oil available for export to the West drops sharply. The oil allocation policy and its flexibility are analysed in Chapters 7 and 8.

Nevertheless, in terms of both the flexibility of its allocation and the structure of the Western market to which it is exported, oil appears to be the only commodity available that has all the properties required to facilitate short-run balance-of-payments adjustments. Indeed, Goldman claims that 'foreign trade planners have really only *petroleum* to manipulate when they want to adjust exports in any meaningful way.' (Goldman, 1980, p. 92, *our italics*.)

To substantiate this claim, we examine briefly the other export commodities at planners' disposal for similar purposes. The commodities examined are: natural gas, military goods, metals, lumber and cotton, which are among the top ten Soviet export commodities. Gold and capital borrowing from the West are then discussed separately, because they are handled separately from trade in other commodities (see Section 5.5).

(*a*) *Natural Gas*. Natural gas is a star performer in Soviet exports. The volume exported increased from 0.96 bcm in 1970 to 35.5 bcm in 1985 (see Table 5.9). Accordingly, its share in Soviet hard currency earnings grew from a mere 0.7 per cent in 1970 to 16–19 per cent in the early 1980s. Natural gas has become a leading export commodity, second only to oil.

The Soviet Union has a greater share of the world's reserves of gas than of oil. Its proved gas reserves were 42.5 tcm at end 1985, representing 43.2 per cent of the world total (BP, 1986). Moreover, the true extent of Soviet natural gas reserves is still far from certain. For example, estimates of ultimately recoverable gas reserves in East Siberia range widely between 2.5 and 9.8 tcm. The geological structures of the Soviet gas fields are also less problematic for development and extraction than those of the new oilfields of West Siberia. Exploration and production is said to be between 33 and 50 per cent cheaper for gas than it is for oil (Bethkenhagen, 1985, p. 181).

Gas production has grown faster than that of all other fuels and has over-fulfilled the planned level for some years. However, the export supply flexibility of gas, and hence the possibility of using it as a short-run balancing tool, are severely limited by technical constraints and also by the marketing method. On both accounts, natural gas requires long-term commitments and arrangements. Soviet natural gas is transported to domestic and foreign users by pipeline (although there are plans for future LNG deliveries to Japan), which of itself tends to reduce the flexibility of supply and segment the potential market. There is hence no world gas market as such (Hannigan and McMillan, 1984).

Furthermore, Soviet natural gas is usually sold under long-term supply arrangements based on the compensation format. Under this format, the Western partners are committed to deliver large-diameter steel pipes and equipment for high-capacity compressor stations under government-guaranteed credits in exchange for Soviet natural gas over the long period. Because of this compensation format, gas exports can not provide a hard currency surplus over and above the debt obligations incurred in the purchase of pipes and equipment for the first five or six years (Stern, 1984).

This type of arrangement is naturally well suited to long-term planning of hard currency earnings.[7] Over the longer term, Soviet planners have succeeded, and will probably succeed in the future, in complementing hard currency revenues from oil exports with revenues

---

[7] However, the contracts usually allow some flexibility in the quantities of actual gas deliveries. It is said that in 1982 and 1983 the Soviet Union suffered from the negative consequences of this, i.e. the purchase clauses that allowed Western buyers to reduce the quantity of gas purchased because of a decrease in demand (Bethkenhagen, 1985, p. 181).

from gas exports.[8] However, gas is unlikely to replace oil in the short term as the flexible export commodity. On the contrary, when energy demand is weak and the oil market in excess supply, gas demand and gas prices are also depressed. It is known that the formulae for calculating gas prices in export agreements link gas prices to oil prices, either to the f.o.b. price of crude oil or to the price of residual fuel oil.[9] The average ratio of gas prices to crude oil prices in Soviet export contracts is said to be around 75 per cent (Hewett, 1983b). It seems, therefore, that there is little room for *short-run* substitution of gas for oil in the Western market for revenue-raising purposes.

(*b*) *Military Goods*. It is reported that exports of military goods to developing countries have become an increasingly important source of Soviet hard currency earnings. According to CIA estimates (there are no useful Soviet data), arms sales to LDCs have recently accounted for about 17 per cent of Soviet hard currency merchandise export earnings (see Table 6.1). The increase in arms sales is usually explained by political considerations, namely the Soviet Union's desire to expand its political and strategic influence in the Third World and provide active support for national liberation movements.

Some argue, however, that economic forces are also at work. Until the early 1970s, vitually all Soviet arms transfers to Third World countries took the form of non-commercial deals, usually involving medium- and long-term credits. These deals carried low interest rates and were to be repaid in kind with the traditional exports of the recipient country. Further, the sales of Soviet weapons were heavily subsidized. Approximately 40 per cent of the value of Soviet military hardware was effectively written off as grants. In recent years, however, hard currency exports of military goods have accounted for more than 80 per cent of all military exports (Zoeter, 1983; Kanet, 1983).

Some argue (e.g. Deger, 1985) that arms production is uniquely characterized by excess supply owing to the high priority given to the defence industry in the Soviet Union's allocation of resources. Planners have economic incentives and pressure to sell these abundant weapons to the oil-rich developing countries in order to supplement their hard currency earnings.

However strong this pressure may be, the technical characteristics of most modern hardware, often built to customer's specification, prevent

[8] The further expansion of demand for Soviet gas in the West European countries is, however, limited by political and security considerations in East–West relations.

[9] There have been reports that in 1982–3, there were sporadic Soviet spot sales of gas, for which the spare capacity of the pipeline network was used to deliver extra volumes to West European customers at very attractive prices (Stern, 1984, p. 56).

the mass production needed to generate abundant supplies of weapons. More importantly, given the severe supply constraints governing the whole economic system, Soviet planners would not be able to indulge in a programme to expand the production of arms earmarked for the export market, because of the general scarcity of resources. The burden and opportunity cost to the civilian sector of producing a surplus of weapons are known to be very high, given the overfull employment of resources. Our view is that, while the military sector may have happened, *ex post*, to have a surplus of weapons and to have generated hard currency earnings, planners did not plan *ex ante* to have a large exportable surplus for this purpose.

For all these reasons, military goods possess neither the supply flexibility nor the market structure required for them to be used directly for short-run balance-of-payments adjustments. The one aspect of the sales of Soviet arms to OPEC countries that is directly relevant to our study is the barter trade of military goods for Middle East oil. This has increased the volume of oil available to planners for re-export to earn additional hard currency. This issue will be addressed in Chapter 7.

(*c*) *Other Export Commodities*. An examination of the other main Soviet export commodities – aluminium, copper, manganese, cotton and timber products (coniferous sawlogs and lumber) – in terms of their supply flexibility and market structure reveals that none of them has the production and delivery flexibility required to generate sufficient hard currency to serve for purposes of balance-of-payments adjustments in the short run. Nor are they marketed in a flexible manner, since they are all sold mainly through bilateral sales arrangements, requiring lengthy negotiations before their conclusion. Furthermore, irrespective of their market shares in these individual markets, Soviet traders tend to consider themselves as 'residual suppliers' to the world market and act as price followers instead of using their potential market power.

The analysis presented above leads us to support Goldman's statement that Soviet planners possess no flexible export commodity other than oil with which to balance the hard currency trade deficit (Goldman, 1980).

5.5 Gold Sales and Capital Borrowing

Apart from the above-mentioned export commodities – chiefly oil – that are at the planners' disposal, the Soviet Union has two other means by which to combat its trade deficit: gold sales and capital borrowing on the international financial market. These transactions are based on highly liquid assets, and are managed by *Gosbank* and the Ministry of Finance, which hold ultimate responsibility for balancing the monetary flows of all foreign transactions. Possessed of three means of adjusting its external trade imbalances, the Soviet Union attempts to use all three in the most efficient combination.

We shall now look at some characteristics of Soviet behaviour with respect to gold sales and capital borrowing, before turning to the issue of how oil exports have been used in conjunction with these two other instruments in the management of trade adjustments.

(*a*) *Gold Sales*. The Soviet Union is the world's second-largest gold producer after South Africa. Its share in world gold production is approximately 20–25 per cent, with South Africa accounting for nearly half of world production (see Table 5.10). Furthermore, while South African output has been on a declining trend since 1970, Soviet gold production has been steadily increasing. The same ranking holds for exports. However, while South Africa regularly sells about 80 per cent of its production, Soviet sales fluctuate considerably from year to year. As quoted elsewhere, '[South Africa] provides "the hard core" of the supply while the Soviet Union "plays it at the top".' (Kaser, 1983a, p. 162.) In comparison with the sales of other Soviet export commodities, gold sales are the least constrained by production capacity. Soviet gold reserves are large, and several experts forecast a substantial expansion of gold production.[10] It appears, therefore, that Soviet gold sales are constrained only by market behaviour.

Gold is traded twice daily on the international exchanges (in Zurich and London) where prices are transparent and can change violently from day to day. The gold price is influenced by speculative demand and as such is highly correlated with the state of the currency markets.

Since the Soviet Union is the world's second-largest producer and exporter of gold, and not a marginal supplier as for other commodities, Soviet dealers are well aware of the potential impact of their own supply on world prices. They know that sudden and large increases in the volume of gold supplies may not achieve their purpose of increasing hard currency earnings because of the adverse effect on gold prices, and they are known to study and follow the market very closely, involving themselves actively and skilfully in daily transactions.

However, the large variations in volumes of Soviet gold sales, as shown in Figure 5.4, are not easily explained in terms of cautious and

[10] For example, Kaser, 1983a, projects a production level of nearly 500 tonnes per annum for the 1990s.

Table 5.10: Various Estimates of Reserves, Production and Trade in Gold. 1970–84. Volumes in Tonnes. Gold Price in Dollars per Troy Ounce. Sales in Million Dollars.

	1970	1971	1972	1973	1974	1975	1976	1977	1978	1979	1980	1981	1982	1983	1984
Soviet Reserves															
CIA	1,631	1,797	1,842	1,747	1,836	1,900	1,797	1,702	1,526	1,581	1,811	1,888	2,118	2,391	n.a.
Production															
(i) Soviet Union															
(a) Kaser	264	271	285	298	301	309	322	325	331	336	345	348	n.a.	n.a.	n.a.
(b) CIA	218	224	243	250	262	258	276	285	296	307	317	327	329	332	n.a.
(ii) Non-Communist World (*Gold*)	1,273	1,233	1,177	1,111	996	946	964	962	972	959	954	976	1,025	1,112	1,149
of which South Africa	1,000	976	910	855	759	713	713	700	706	705	675	658	664	680	683
Soviet Sales to West															
(i) Kaser	n.a.	n.a.	150	280	227	141	326	400	407	229	50	280	n.a.	n.a.	n.a.
(ii) *Gold*	−3	54	213	275	220	149	412	401	410	199	90	283	203	93	205
(iii) BIS	50	90	220	330	150	150	350	450	450	290	90	300	200	80	100
(iv) CIA	3	19	158	304	131	147	328	332	401	220	80	200	n.a.	n.a.	n.a.
Annual Average Gold Price (*Gold*)	35.94	40.80	58.13	97.17	159.13	161.05	124.83	147.71	193.29	304.98	612.38	459.85	374.96	423.68	360.68
Gold Sales (CIA)	n.a.	24	289	962	683	725	1,369	1,618	2,522	1,490	1,580	2,700	1,100	750	1,000
Ratio of Gold Sales to Export Earnings (%)	n.a.	0.9	9.8	19.3	8.6	8.7	13.4	13.6	18.9	7.7	6.7	11.4	4.1	n.a.	n.a.
Ratio of Gold Sales to Production (%) calculated from:															
(i) CIA Estimates	1.4	8.5	65.0	127.6	50.0	56.0	118.2	116.6	135.5	71.7	25.2	61.2	n.a.	n.a.	n.a.
(ii) Kaser Estimates	n.a.	n.a.	52.6	94.0	75.4	45.6	101.2	123.1	123.0	68.2	14.5	80.5	n.a.	n.a.	n.a.

Sources: Kaser, 1983b and 1984
CIA, *Handbook*, various issues
Gold, various issues
BIS, *Annual Report*, various issues

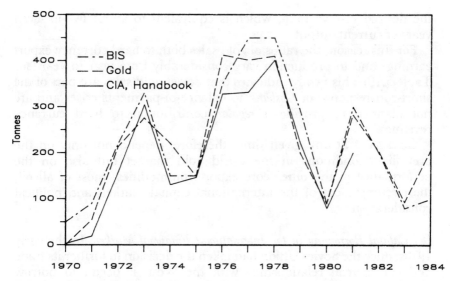

Figure 5.4 Western Estimates of Soviet Gold Sales to the West. 1970–84.

calculated market behaviour.[11] When volumes of Soviet gold sales are examined in relation to price changes in the market, their possible destabilizing effect on the world market is very clear.

Therefore, we must turn to other factors underlying Soviet behaviour in the world gold market, namely the role of gold as an indispensable tool in the management of the short-run balance-of-payments adjustments of the Soviet economy. Naturally, as Soviet dealers are well aware of their market position, we must assume that only *force majeure* will lead them to increase their sales in adverse market circumstances.

It is only when the Soviet Union has no readily available and better alternative that it increases gold sales on the open market above the desired normal level. These sales are often related to the need to import grain in larger quantities (e.g. in 1973, 1976, 1978 and 1981). Whenever sales are dictated by domestic needs, we find that annual sales are not positively related to world price movements.

The years of high gold sales are usually followed by years in which sales are below the normal level. The planners' aim is to rebuild reserves, and this explains why in 1974, 1979, 1980 and 1983, when gold prices were on the increase, Soviet sales were reduced sharply to restore

[11] Official Soviet data on gold sales are not available. The various published Western sources differ substantially in their estimates of the *levels* of gold sales to the West (see Table 5.10). Their reports of the *variations* in the level of sales over the period show, however, a similar pattern (see Figure 5.4).

the desired reserve ratio, which is equivalent to about five-to-seven years of current output.

For this reason, the ratios of gold sales both to hard currency export earnings and to production vary considerably from year to year (see Table 5.10) This firmly indicates that Soviet gold sales are part of the short-run response of *Gosbank* to balance-of-payments crises and are not planned to provide a *regular* contribution to hard currency revenues.

Gold sales at any given time, therefore, depend not only on the prevailing conditions in the world gold market but also on the performance of the other core export commodities, most of all oil, the circumstances of the international capital market, and political considerations.

(*b*) *Capital Borrowing in the International Financial Market*. In the early 1970s, once the Soviet Union had taken the decision to further its trade and commercial relationships with the West, it began to borrow actively on the Western capital market (see Tables 5.11 and 5.12 and Figure 5.5).[12] The figures for government and government-backed debt in Table 5.11 are for Soviet debt associated with long-term trade contracts, which was mainly used for financing purchases of Western technology and capital equipment, often as part of a compensation agreement. This debt increased steadily throughout the 1970s, from $1.4 billion in 1971 to $7.6 billion in 1979, with big jumps in three consecutive years (1974, 1975 and 1976). Thereafter, according to the CIA estimates, it levelled off except in 1982, when the Soviet Union used official credits to purchase pipe and equipment for the Yamburg gas pipeline. According to the OECD estimates, the government debt then decreased sharply in 1983 and 1984.

However, commercial debt, which represents Soviet borrowing from Western banks and other commercial sources, was subject to greater and more frequent changes and fluctuations. It climbed from $400 million in 1971 to $10.5 billion in 1979. Soviet borrowing increased vigorously in the period 1971–6, especially in 1975 when large syndicated general purpose loans were taken out (see Table 5.12). However, in 1977, the growth of the commercial debt was abruptly arrested, and since then borrowing has been kept very much under control. The next sharp rise in commercial debt, in 1981, was mostly in

---

[12] As official data on Soviet borrowing and debt are not available, the data used for our analysis are CIA and OECD estimates. Though both estimates are based on information given by Western commercial banks and government agencies, they are not comparable because of differences in their coverage of information and methods of calculation. The UN Economic Commission for Europe publishes its own estimates from time to time. However, UN estimates are reviewed substantially from one issue to another and consequently UN data are not consistent over time.

Table 5.11: Estimates of Soviet Hard Currency Debt. 1971–85. Million Dollars.

	Gross Debt		Commercial Debt		Government Debt		Assets in Western Banks		Net Assets in Western Banks		Net Debt	
	US	OECD	US	OECD	US	OECD	US	OECD	US	OECD	US	OECD
1971	1,808		407		1,401		1,225		818		582	
1972	2,408		858		1,550		1,854		996		555	
1973	3,748		2,041		1,707		2,583		542		1,165	
1974	5,175		2,787	3,600	2,388		3,522	3,300	735	−300	1,654	
1975	10,577		6,947	7,900	3,630		3,127	3,100	−3,820	−4,800	7,450	
1976	14,707		9,662	10,400	5,045		4,738	3,700	−4,924	−6,700	9,969	
1977	15,609		9,858	11,620	5,751		4,428	4,360	−5,430	−7,260	11,181	
1978	16,373		9,513	12,760	6,860		5,980	5,850	−3,533	−6,910	10,393	
1979	18,047		10,479	12,900	7,568		8,806	8,620	−1,673	−4,280	9,241	
1980	17,861		10,013	13,390	7,848		8,572	8,570	−1,141	−4,820	9,289	
1981	20,900	26,548	13,000	15,880	7,900	10,668	8,430	8,450	−4,040	−7,430	12,470	18,098
1982	20,100	26,361	11,300	14,210	8,700	12,151	10,000	10,030	−1,300	−4,180	10,100	16,331
1983	20,500	24,031	11,500	16,150	9,000	7,881	9,600	11,040	−1,900	−5,110	10,900	12,991
1984	20,200	23,185	11,300	16,640	8,900	6,545	10,000	11,340	−1,300	−5,300	10,200	11,845
1985		30,000		21,140		8,860		11,130		−10,010		19,000

Sources: CIA, *Handbook*, various issues

Zoeter, 1983

OECD, *Financial Market Trends*, March issues, 1984, 1985, 1986

Table 5.12: Indicators of Soviet Hard Currency Debt and Estimates of Medium- and Long-term Borrowing, 1971–84.

	1971	1972	1973	1974	1975	1976	1977	1978	1979	1980	1981	1982	1983	1984
(a) Ratio of Net Debt to Merchandise Exports (%)														
(i) CIA	24.0	18.8	23.3	20.9	90.0	97.5	94.2	77.9	47.6	39.4	52.4	38.1	n.a.	n.a.
(ii) OECD	n.a.	n.a.	n.a.	n.a.	n.a.	n.a.	n.a.	n.a.	n.a.	n.a.	55.4	44.6	34.9	32.2
(b) Ratio of Net Debt to Hard Currency Earnings including Gold Sales (CIA)	16.6	13.5	14.1	14.6	69.7	73.1	66.2	52.0	36.8	31.4	41.0	30.9	33.1	n.a.
(c) Share of Commercial Debt in Gross Debt (%)														
(i) CIA	22.5	35.6	54.4	53.9	65.7	65.7	63.2	58.1	58.0	56.1	62.2	56.2	56.1	55.9
(ii) OECD	n.a.	n.a.	n.a.	n.a.	n.a.	n.a.	n.a.	n.a.	n.a.	n.a.	59.8	53.9	67.2	71.8
(d) Soviet Assets/Liability Ratio vis-à-vis Western Banks														
(i) CIA	3.01	2.16	1.27	1.26	0.45	0.49	0.45	0.63	0.84	0.86	0.65	0.88	0.83	n.a.
(ii) OECD	n.a.	n.a.	n.a.	0.92	0.39	0.36	0.38	0.46	0.67	0.64	0.53	0.71	0.68	0.68
Borrowing (Million Dollars) OECD	–	–	–	–	750	282	–	400	320	50	50	153	68	867
Average Margin (Basis Points above Libor for East European Countries)	–	–	–	74	134	128	111	83	70	88	62	103	112	88

Note: The OECD series are not fully comparable throughout since the area reported expanded at the end of 1980 and the end of 1982.
Sources: Zoeter, 1983
    CIA, *Handbook*, various issues
    OECD, *Financial Market Trends*, March issues, 1984, 1985, 1986

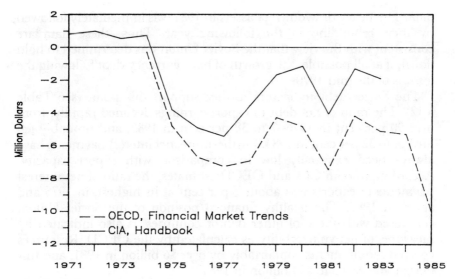

Figure 5.5 Net Assets in Western Banks at End of Year. 1971–85.

the form of increased short-term credits, and was followed by a reduction in 1982. The debt stayed at this reduced level until rising sharply again in 1985.[13]

The initial increase in borrowing from Western banks was so marked that the share of this component in gross debt increased from 22 per cent in 1971 to 66 per cent in 1975 and 1976, but it then stabilized below 60 per cent for some years. The share of commercial debt increased again in 1983 and 1984 (according to OECD estimates) but this reflects a reduced level of government-backed debt rather than a disproportionate growth of Soviet borrowing in the private sector capital market.

The same pattern emerges from an examination of Soviet asset management with Western banks. The Soviet Union became a net debtor in 1974 and 1975 in the international capital market, having borrowed massively in the earlier years. In 1975, it drew down so heavily on its assets that its assets/liquidity ratio worsened in one year from 1.26 to 0.45 according to the CIA estimates quoted in Table 5.12 (or from 0.92 to 0.39 according to the OECD estimates). The Soviet Union then attempted to restore the ratio to its previous level and improve its net assets position, as can be seen clearly from both sets of

---

[13] According to calculations based on estimates by the Vienna Institute for Comparative Economic Studies, short-term credits with a maturity of less than one year constituted 41 per cent of Soviet liabilities with Western banks in 1979. This share increased to 50 per cent in 1981 but declined to 45 per cent in 1982 (WIIW (ed), 1985).

data. The heavy drawdown of assets in 1981 was immediately followed
by their rebuilding in the following year. Thus, these data are
consistent with the view that the Soviet Union was determined to hold
down, if at all possible, the growth of hard currency debt following the
lessons of the mid-1970s.

The Soviet debt indicators further support this point (see Table
5.12). The ratio of net debt to export earnings declined rapidly, from
over 90 per cent in 1976–7 to 38 per cent in 1982, and probably fell
further to 32 per cent in 1984. Furthermore, net interest payments have
always been extremely low in comparison with export capacity.
According to both CIA and OECD estimates, the ratio of net interest
payments to exports was about 7 per cent at its highest, in 1975 and
again in 1981. The healthy financial position of the Soviet Union,
compared with those of other debtor countries, is also indicated by
measures of net vulnerability as calculated by the OECD. Resources
covered requirements comfortably by over $6 billion in 1981, and this
margin increased to $14 billion in 1984.[14]

This leads to the conclusion that Soviet borrowing and the level of
Soviet indebtedness have not been limited on the supply side, by the
availability of Western credits or the willingness of bankers to lend, but
rather on the Soviet side, by its self-imposed discipline and its
preference for self-reliance as against financial dependence on the
West.

This Soviet preference was reinforced by the deterioration in political
relations with the West in the late 1970s and by new economic factors.
The latter included the rise in interest rates internationally and the
related world debt crisis, which seriously affected the Soviet Union's
East European allies, notably Poland and Romania.

To conclude, when faced with sharp deteriorations in its hard
currency trade balance, the Soviet Union has resorted from time to
time to borrowing on the Western capital market in order to overcome
its liquidity crisis. However, it has raised very little money by means of
medium- and long-term commercial loans since 1975 (see Table 5.12).
Borrowing has predominantly been in the form of short-term credits
with a maturity of less than one year.[15] This reflects a desire on the part
of the Soviet Union to pay off its debt as quickly as possible with the
proceeds of increased exports. Because of the present political and
economic climate, the Soviet Union limits its recourse to Western

[14] The resources consist of Soviet deposits in BIS-area banks and unused credits, while the
requirement includes the current account deficit and Soviet liabilities with Western banks. The
vulnerability is calculated as the difference between the resources and the requirement (OECD,
Financial Market Trends, March 1986).
[15] See footnote 13 above.

capital for balance-of-payments purposes except in the very short run. While it endeavours to obtain government-backed credit on preferential terms for big development projects, it uses commercial credit mainly for bridging unexpected liquidity crises on the external account. The Soviet Union does not consider commercial credit to be a substitute for the necessary adjustments of real trade flows except in the very short run. This policy creates enormous pressure on export commodities, mainly on oil, for meeting debt repayments in the short term.

6 OIL EXPORTS AND BALANCE-OF-PAYMENTS ADJUSTMENTS: A HISTORICAL EXAMINATION

6.1 Introduction

In Chapter 5, the possible role of oil exports as a decision variable used by Soviet planners for purposes of balance-of-payments adjustments was discussed in the context of the overall balance-of-payments problem. We now turn to the question of how oil exports to the hard currency area have actually been used, in conjunction with gold sales and capital borrowing on the international financial markets, to adjust the trade balance during the period 1970–84. This analysis will provide us with some partial but nevertheless useful explanations of the considerable annual fluctuations in Soviet oil exports to the West. The levels and growth rates of Soviet exports of crude and products to the West are presented in Figures 6.1 and 6.2.

We begin with a brief look at balance-of-payments statistics. The only available comprehensive source on the Soviet hard currency

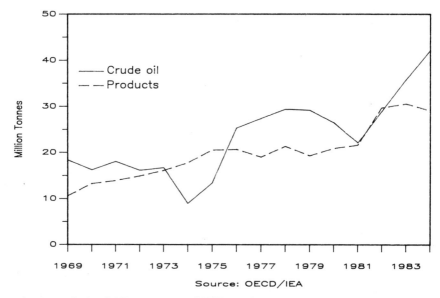

Figure 6.1 Soviet Oil Exports to the OECD (excluding Finland). 1969–84.

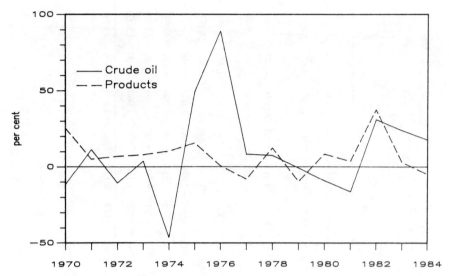

Figure 6.2 Annual Growth Rates of Soviet Oil Exports to the OECD (excluding Finland). 1970–84.

balance of payments is that provided by the CIA (see Table 6.1). Soviet official data are, however, available for the trade balance. The data presented in Table 6.2 are the figures from the Soviet source, which we have converted from foreign trade roubles into US dollars using the official rates published by *Gosbank*. In order to make the Soviet data comparable with the US estimates, which refer to trade with the hard currency area, we have excluded Finland from the Soviet data on trade with MDCs, since no direct hard currency payments are involved in the long-standing bilateral clearing arrangement that regulates trade between the Soviet Union and Finland.[1] The trade balances as derived from Soviet and US sources are shown in Figures 6.3 and 6.4 respectively.

According to the US estimates, Soviet merchandise trade with the hard currency area has been consistently in deficit. However, exports of military goods to LDCs reduced this deficit increasingly over the years, keeping total trade in near balance during most of the period (see Figure 6.4).

A comparison of the data from the Soviet source with the CIA estimates of the trade balance, assuming that this is a meaningful

[1] Some argue that Soviet trade with the hard currency area should include trade with Finland, on the grounds that Soviet imports from Finland are 'hard' goods, as opposed to the 'soft' goods it obtains from the CMEA partners. We exclude Finland, however, because of the two countries' bilateral trade agreement.

Table 6.1: Hard Currency Balance of Payments. 1970–84. Million Dollars.

	1970	1971	1972	1973	1974	1975	1976	1977	1978	1979	1980	1981	1982	1983	1984
(a) Current Account Balance															
(i) Exports (f.o.b.)	2,424	2,776	2,954	5,009	7,896	8,280	10,225	11,863	13,336	19,417	23,584	23,778	26,513	n.a.	n.a.
(ii) Additional Military Deliveries to LDCs (f.o.b.)[a]	400	400	600	1,600	1,500	1,500	1,850	3,220	3,965	3,855	4,200	4,200	5,464	n.a.	n.a.
(iii) = (i) + (ii)	2,824	3,176	3,554	6,609	9,369	9,780	12,075	15,083	17,301	23,272	27,784	27,978	31,977	32,392	31,726
(iv) Imports (f.o.b.)	2,984	3,093	4,342	6,744	8,695	14,577	15,478	14,805	17,026	21,435	26,070	27,778	27,501	27,697	27,292
Trade Balance A (i) − (iv)	−560	−317	−1,388	−1,735	−826	−6,297	−5,223	−2,942	−3,690	−2,018	−2,486	−4,000	−988	n.a.	n.a.
Trade Balance B (iii) − (iv)	−160	83	−788	−135	674	−4,797	−3,373	278	275	1,837	1,714	200	4,476	4,695	4,713
Net Interest	−80	−48	−60	−80	−103	−570	−724	−848	−881	−799	−710	−1,300	−1,500	−1,300	−1,050
Other Invisible Transfers	500	355	327	743	917	760	911	1,032	1,028	1,140	900	1,060	1,100	1,100	1,100
Current Account Balance	260	390	521	528	1,488	−4,607	−3,216	462	422	2,178	1,904	−1,000	4,076	4,495	4,484

(b) Capital Account Balance

(i) Borrowing from Abroad[b]	290	n.a.	600	1,340	1,427	5,400	4,130	902	764	1,675	-185	3,000	-865	560	-100
(ii) Change in Assets[c]	n.a.	n.a.	-629	-729	-939	395	-1,611	310	-1,552	-2,826	234	140	-1,575	400	-400
(i) + (ii)	n.a.	n.a.	-29	611	488	5,795	2,519	1,212	-788	-1,151	49	3,140	-2,440	960	-500
(iii) Gold Sales	n.a.	24	289	962	1,178	725	1,369	1,618	2,522	1,490	1,580	2,700	1,100	750	1,000
Capital Account Balance (i) + (ii) + (iii)	n.a.	260	1,573	1,666	6,520	3,888	2,830	1,734	339	1,629	5,840	-1,340	1,710	500	
Errors and Omissions[d]	n.a.	-753	-2,101	-3,154	-1,915	-672	-3,292	-2,156	-2,516	-3,532	-5,840	-2,736	-6,205	-4,984	

Notes: (a) This item excludes the values of arms-related commercial exports included in Soviet reporting on exports to individual LDCs.
(b) Borrowing = Gross drawings – Repayments, (both government-backed and commercial loans).
(c) Net change in Soviet assets held with Western commercial banks: a negative sign signifies an addition to assets.
(d) Including Soviet hard currency aid to and trade with other CMEA countries and trade credits extended to finance Soviet exports – including arms – to non-Socialist hard currency trade partners.

Sources: CIA, *Handbook*, various issues
   Zoeter, 1983

Table 6.2: Hard Currency Balance of Trade. 1970–84. Million Dollars.

	Imports			Exports			Trade Balance			Normalized Trade Balance (%)			
	Total	MDCs	LDCs	Total	MDCs	LDCs	Total	MDCs	LDCs	Total	MDCs	LDCs	US Estimates
1970	3,793	2,520	1,273	4,147	2,107	2,040	354	−413	767	8.5	−19.6	37.6	−23.1
1971	4,024	2,613	1,411	4,424	2,396	2,028	399	−218	617	9.0	−9.1	30.4	−11.4
1972	5,425	3,798	1,627	5,025	2,594	2,431	−399	−1,203	804	−7.9	−46.4	33.1	−47.0
1973	8,050	5,703	2,347	8,463	4,499	3,964	413	−1,203	1,617	4.9	−26.7	40.8	−34.6
1974	10,460	7,315	3,145	11,488	7,017	4,471	1,028	−298	1,326	8.9	−4.2	29.7	−10.5
1975	16,458	12,298	4,160	11,832	7,241	4,591	−4,626	−5,055	431	−39.1	−69.8	9.4	−76.1
1976	16,797	13,048	3,749	14,037	9,077	4,960	−2,760	−3,971	1,240	−19.7	−43.7	25.0	−51.1
1977	16,030	11,958	4,072	17,804	10,009	7,795	1,774	−1,405	3,179	10.0	−14.0	40.8	−24.8
1978	18,482	14,337	4,145	19,637	11,270	8,367	1,156	−3,067	4,223	5.9	−27.2	50.5	−27.7
1979	23,357	18,488	4,869	26,537	16,932	9,605	3,180	−1,638	4,736	12.0	−9.7	49.3	−10.4
1980	29,196	21,320	7,876	31,908	21,322	10,586	2,711	−27	2,738	8.5	−0.1	25.9	−10.5
1981	32,041	21,284	10,757	32,678	20,688	11,990	636	−598	1,234	1.9	−2.9	10.3	−16.8
1982	31,358	22,138	9,220	36,634	22,631	14,003	5,277	494	4,783	14.4	2.2	34.2	−3.7
1983	31,230	21,573	9,657	37,273	23,109	14,164	6,043	895	4,507	16.2	3.9	31.8	n.a.
1984	30,542	21,265	9,277	36,768	23,310	13,458	6,227	2,046	4,181	16.9	8.8	31.1	n.a.

Note: The series for MDCs exclude trade with Finland.
Sources: *VTSS* yearbook, various issues
US figures calculated from data in Table 6.1 (Trade Balance A ÷ Exports (i))

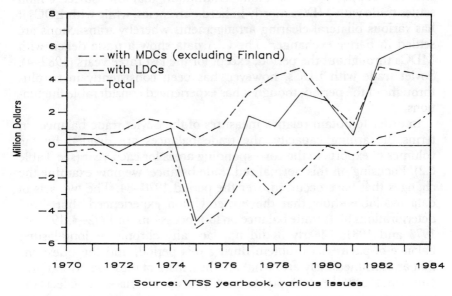

Figure 6.3 Soviet Official Data on Balance of Trade with non-Socialist Countries. 1970–84.

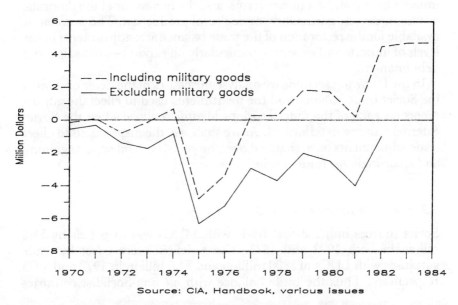

Figure 6.4 CIA Estimates of Soviet Hard Currency Balance of Trade. 1970–84.

exercise, supports the common assumption that the Soviet Union settles trade with MDCs mostly in hard currencies, while with LDCs it has various bilateral clearing arrangements whereby transactions are settled in barter exchange.[2] The CIA data show a trade deficit with MDCs throughout the period, except for the last three years (1982–4). Soviet trade with LDCs, however, has been consistently in surplus throughout the period, though it has experienced considerable fluctuations.

In order to obtain relative measures of the Soviet trade balances in terms of earning capacity, the trade balances are divided by the volumes of exports to the corresponding areas for each year (see Table 6.2). Focusing on this normalized trade balance, we now examine the changes that have occurred over the period 1970–84. The two sets of data available show that the Soviet Union experienced short-lived deteriorations of its trade balance on four occasions: in 1972–3, 1975–6, 1978 and 1981. Clearly it did not face any chronic or long-lasting balance-of-payments problem during this period, and the questions that arise immediately are: what are the causes of these deteriorations, and what are the techniques and procedures used to effect the necessary adjustments?

The possible *causes* of deteriorations are: the changes in the terms of trade, the factors accounting for the changes in the levels of exports and imports in real and monetary terms, and the behaviour of the domestic economic sector, particularly agricultural production. The *instruments* available for the restoration of the trade balance are: adjustments in the levels of imports and exports – particularly oil exports – gold sales, and debt financing.

In the following sections we analyse the causes of the deterioration of the Soviet trade balance and the instruments used to effect the adjustments on each of the four occasions identified above when the Soviet external balance deteriorated. As we shall see, the means used to effect trade adjustments have changed over the years, with oil exports gaining an increasingly prominent role.

6.2 The First Episode: 1972–3

Soviet sources indicate that trade with MDCs was in deficit by $1.2 billion in both 1972 and 1973. These deficits were offset by trade surpluses with LDCs of $800 million and $1.6 billion in 1972 and 1973 respectively. Thus the trade balance with *all* non-Socialist countries

---

[2] It is claimed, however, by some Western analysts that transactions between the Soviet Union and LDCs are settled in hard currency to a greater extent than officially acknowledged.

moved from a $400 million deficit in 1972 to a $400 million surplus in 1973.[3]

This was the time when Soviet planners, encouraged by the success of the new policy of *détente* and keen to alleviate bottlenecks in the domestic economy, promoted an expansion of commercial relations with the West. This started with a rapid increase in imports, with the growth of exports lagging one year behind. The Soviet source shows that imports from MDCs expanded by 45 per cent in 1972 and by 50 per cent in 1973, while the export drive began one year later. The export growth rates in 1972 and 1973 were 8 and 73 per cent respectively.[4] Furthermore, the increase in the value of trade was due to volume growth rather than price changes. The effects of significant rises in the prices of traded goods were not felt until a year later.

The Soviet Union responded to the trade deficit at that time mainly by increasing its borrowing on Western capital markets (see Tables 5.11 and 5.12). Commercial debt climbed from $400 million in 1971 to $2.0 billion by the end of 1973, increasing by 110 and 138 per cent in 1972 and 1973 respectively. This resulted in a deterioration of the net assets position with Western banks by 46 per cent and an increase in the Soviet net debt by 110 per cent in 1973 alone.

Sales of gold also had to be increased in 1972 and 1973, from 20–90 tonnes in 1971 to 275–330 tonnes in 1973. The share of gold in export earnings increased from 1 per cent in 1971 to 10 per cent in 1972 and further to 19 per cent in 1973 (see Table 5.10). The need for gold sales in 1972–3 was accentuated by the Soviet decision to increase grain imports (mainly of feed grain) massively from 4 million tonnes in 1971 to 16.2 million in 1972 and further to 24.4 million in 1973 (see Table 5.2 and Figure 5.3). This increase occurred despite a record good harvest in 1973, which followed the bad performance of agricultural production in 1972. Oil exports did not play much of a role in these years prior to the world oil price hike of October–December 1973. The share of oil sales in total exports to OECD countries (excluding Finland) was 24–26 per cent on average. In fact, oil exports, notably those of crude oil, dropped in both volume and value before picking up again in 1973 (see Table 5.9, Figures 6.1 and 6.2).

---

[3] According to CIA estimates the Soviet trade balance excluding deliveries of military goods to LDCs registered a deficit of $1.4 billion in 1972 and $1.7 billion in 1973. These deficits correspond to 47 and 35 per cent of export earnings respectively.

[4] The CIA estimates tell a similar story: imports increased in value by 40 and 55 per cent in 1972 and 1973 respectively, whereas exports increased by only 6 per cent in 1972, but increased massively by 70 per cent in 1973.

6.3 Trade Adjustments in 1974

In 1974, the Soviet trade balance improved notably according to both US and Soviet sources.[5] The Soviet source indicates that the 1974 deficit was a mere $300 million and that a large trade surplus with the LDCs turned the trade balance with the non-Socialist countries as a whole into a surplus of more than $1.0 billion (see Table 6.2 and Figure 6.3). The CIA estimates and the Soviet source both show that exports increased in value terms by twice as much as imports.

The increase in the value of exports in 1974 was principally due to increases in price rather than volume. This was particularly true for oil, the most important export commodity. According to OECD/IEA estimates (see Table 5.9), the volume of oil exports to the West dropped by 15 per cent, but there was an important difference in the export patterns of crude oil and products.[6] Exports of crude oil fell by 35 per cent from 23.3 million tonnes in 1973 to 15.1 million in 1974, while exports of products continued to increase in 1973 and 1974. If we exclude exports to Finland, the pattern of trade flows to the hard currency area becomes clearer. Exports of crude oil to the OECD countries excluding Finland fell by almost 50 per cent, from 16.71 million tonnes in 1973 to 8.96 million in 1974, while those of products increased steadily (see Table 5.9, Figures 6.1 and 6.2). Proceeds from oil sales rose by 97 per cent in 1974, following a 72 per cent increase in 1973. The share of oil in total Soviet earnings from exports to the OECD area went up from 26 per cent in 1973 to 34 per cent in 1974. The reduction in the volume of sales when prices were increasing demonstrates plainly that Soviet foreign trade policy is anti-mercantilist as mentioned earlier. The Soviet Union exports goods only in order to finance the planned required level of imports. If this objective is met as a result of price increases in the world market, export volumes are reduced.

In 1974, gold sales were reduced to restore the normal level of reserves (see Table 5.10). Borrowing from commercial banks levelled off and the assets position recovered. At the same time, the Soviet Union increased its borrowing from Western governments for long-term trade contracts in order to finance imports of Western technology on a large scale.

[5] According to the CIA estimates, the Soviet trade balance with the hard currency area improved from a deficit of $1.7 billion in 1973 to one of $800 million in 1974. Alternatively, this deficit fell as a proportion of export earnings from 35 per cent to 10 per cent.

[6] PlanEcon estimates, which also include shipments to LDCs, show Soviet oil exports following a similar historical pattern. For the purposes of the following analysis, the data quoted are mainly from the OECD/IEA *Quarterly Oil and Gas Statistics*.

This action reveals the optimistic view taken by the Soviet planners about the future purchasing power of oil exports, which they expected to remain high because of the rise in oil prices. Like their Western counterparts, they clearly failed to anticipate the impact of the oil price increases on the world economy – the world-wide stagflation in the years ahead. The effects of this stagflation in the West on the Soviet economy were a sharp reduction in the demand for other export commodities and increases in Soviet import prices.

6.4 The Second Episode: 1975–6

There was a major push to the import drive, which led to huge trade deficits in 1975 and 1976. Imports grew at the very high rate of 68 per cent in 1975, while exports stagnated, growing by a mere 3 per cent in that year. The Soviet source shows that the trade deficit with MDCs was in excess of $5 billion, or 70 per cent of export proceeds from the area in 1975.[7] As the surplus with LDCs was unusually small in that year, the trade deficit with the total non-Socialist area was $4.6 billion, or 40 per cent of export earnings. This dismal trade balance was partly explained by the very poor harvest of 1975. Grain production dropped from 222 million tonnes in 1973 to 140 million in 1975. As a result, the Soviet Union had to turn to the West for grain, and spent $2.8 billion on grain imports in 1975 and $3.1 billion in 1976.

Faced with this huge deficit in 1975, the Soviet Union first sought to borrow on the international capital market. Its commercial debt reached $6.9–7.9 billion in 1975 – an increase of 120–150 per cent over the previous year's level. Assets were drawn down, so that the net assets position worsened at a phenomenal rate (see Tables 5.11 and 5.12) and the ratio of net debt to export earnings reached 90 per cent. It is worth noting that the Soviet Union did not engage in large-scale sales of gold in that year.

In 1976, the Soviet trade balance began to improve, but was still in the red. The deficit was 40–50 per cent of export earnings. Faced with this problem, the Soviet Union continued to borrow but at a reduced rate. The growth rate of commercial debt fell to 32–39 per cent in 1976 and to 2–12 per cent in 1977. Having brought borrowing under control, the planners now turned to gold sales, which were increased from 150 tonnes in 1975 to 330–350 tonnes in 1976, which obviously depressed gold prices. Proceeds, however, almost doubled and gold sales were kept at that level until 1979 (see Table 5.10).

However, a real trade flow adjustment was clearly overdue. Import

[7] According to CIA estimates, the Soviet trade deficit reached over $6.3 billion, 76 per cent of its hard currency earnings in 1975.

growth slowed down significantly: the rate of growth of imports from MDCs was only 6 per cent in 1976 and became negative in 1977. Exports were increased by 25 per cent in 1976 and by a further 10 per cent in 1977. A large part of this increase in exports to the hard currency area was accounted for by oil. Since oil prices did not rise in these years (in fact they fell in real terms) an increment in oil export revenue could by obtained only through significant increases of deliveries to the export market. The volume of crude oil and products exported to the OECD countries increased by 18 per cent in 1975 and by 31 per cent in 1976. Furthermore, the burden of adjustment was borne largely by crude oil exports while products exports played only a minor role. The OECD/IEA estimates report increases in the volume of crude sales of 27 and 68 per cent in 1975 and 1976 respectively, with the volume of exports doubling from 15 million to 32 million tonnes. Data excluding Finland show a more dramatic increase of crude oil exports, which almost tripled, rising from 9 million tonnes in 1974 to 25.3 million in 1976. By 1976, oil exports provided 45 per cent of total earnings from exports to the OECD countries.

By means of this swift real trade flow adjustment, the Soviet Union managed to reduce its trade deficit with MDCs to $1.4 billion in 1976, i.e. 14 per cent of the normalized trade balance. Because of the substantial surplus with LDCs ($3.2 billion), the overall trade balance with non-Socialist countries registered a surplus of $1.8 billion according to Soviet data. Real trade flow adjustments continued in 1977, and according to the Soviet source exports to MDCs increased by 10 per cent and imports decreased by 8 per cent in that year.[8] The reduction in the volume of imports was particularly significant since it reduced the need for capital borrowing and, therefore, the growth of the commercial debt. Also, the growth in the volume of oil exports began to decelerate.

6.5 The Third Episode: 1978

In 1978, the Soviet trade balance showed a temporary deterioration, partly caused by a $1 billion increase in grain imports. Sales of gold remained at the level of 400–450 tonnes, generating much higher revenue because of the rise in world gold prices (see Figure 6.5). However, the deterioration was not critical and the difficulties encountered were not comparable with those of 1975–6. Import growth was kept firmly under control, and borrowing was not

[8] According to CIA estimates the hard currency trade balance halved: in 1977 imports decreased by 4 per cent while exports continued to grow, increasing by 16 per cent in the same year.

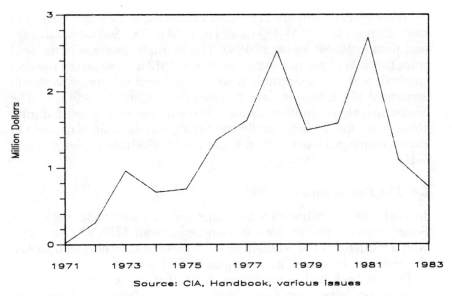

Figure 6.5 Estimated Soviet Hard Currency Earnings from Gold Sales. 1971–83.

increased. On the contrary, in 1978 the Soviet Union managed to rebuild its assets in Western commercial banks at a fast rate. Its net assets position improved and its net debt was reduced. Apparently, the balance-of-payments pressure was not sufficiently great to necessitate an oil export drive. In fact the combined volume of crude oil and products exports grew at a much lower rate in 1978. Crude oil exports to the OECD countries increased by only a small amount, and exports to LDCs declined.

The second oil price 'shock' of 1979 helped the Soviet trade balance during the following two years. The oil price increase was associated with a decline in the volume of Soviet oil exports. According to PlanEcon estimates, exports of crude oil and products fell by 12 per cent in 1979 and by 5 per cent in 1980 – from 72 million tonnes in 1978 to 63 million in 1979 and further to 60.2 million in 1980. Crude oil exports fell by 7 and 10 per cent in 1979 and 1980 respectively, while products exports registered a 20 per cent reduction in 1979 (PlanEcon, 1986). The OECD/IEA estimates show a less dramatic decrease of oil exports to the OECD countries as a whole, but when Finland is excluded the reduction appears to be of similar magnitude. Despite the lower volumes of exports, the Soviet Union still managed to raise its export revenues from the OECD countries by 57 and 31 per cent in 1979 and 1980 respectively. The share of oil in total export earnings from the OECD countries exceeded 50 per cent in 1979 (see Table 5.9).

Although grain imports continued to increase in 1979 and 1980, gold sales dropped from 400–450 tonnes in 1978 to 200–300 tonnes in 1979 and then to 50–90 tonnes in 1980. The dramatic increase in the gold price (from $193 per troy ounce in 1978 to $612 in 1980 on the London market), was of considerable help: the reduced volume of sales still generated $1.6 billion in hard currency (see Figures 5.4 and 6.5). The Soviet net assets position *vis-à-vis* Western banks improved during these years, the net debt hardly grew at all, and the ratio of net debt to export earnings fell to less than 40 per cent in 1980 (see Tables 5.11 and 5.12).

6.6 The Fourth Episode: 1981

In 1981, the Soviet trade balance experienced a further set-back. The Soviet source reports a $600 million deficit with MDCs.[9] Combined with a reduction of $1.5 billion in the Soviet trade surplus with LDCs, this reduced the overall trade surplus by $2.1 billion.

This set-back had many causes. First, there were poor harvests in three consecutive years (see Table 5.2). Grain production was 160 million tonnes in 1981 compared with 237 million in 1978. In 1981 grain imports had to be increased in value terms to $8.3 billion, requiring a rise of $2.6 billion over the previous year's level. Secondly, the world-wide economic recession and successful energy conservation measures in the OECD countries led to a fall in energy demand and a weakening of oil prices (and energy prices in general) in the Western market. In 1981, the volume of Soviet oil exported to the OECD countries dropped by 6.7 per cent, and crude oil sales were reduced by twice as much. Exports of crude oil to the OECD countries excluding Finland decreased from 26.4 million tonnes in 1980 to 22.1 million in 1981. Soviet hard currency earnings increased very little in that year because world oil prices had stopped rising. Energy export prices were, however, becoming a crucial factor in the state of the Soviet external balance, since oil and gas accounted for 67 per cent of total Soviet earnings from exports to the OECD countries in 1980 (oil, 54 per cent; gas, 13 per cent). Thirdly, in 1981 the Soviet Union had to provide Poland with $1.0 billion in hard currency in order to ease the serious financial crisis then faced by this ally.

However, the deterioration of the trade balance in 1981, when measured in relation to export capacity, was not very critical, and by no means comparable in its effects with the deficits of the early and mid-1970s. Nevertheless, the Soviet response to this set-back was swift and efficient. Gold sales were increased from the very low level of 1980 to

[9] The CIA estimates give a deficit of $4 billion.

200–300 tonnes in 1981, kept at a level of 200 tonnes in 1982, and then reduced in 1983 back to the 1980 level of 80–90 tonnes. The Soviet authorities did not hesitate to increase sales of gold in 1981–2, apparently disregarding the fall in its price on the world market in those years.

At the same time, borrowing from Western banks increased by 20–30 per cent, worsening the net assets and net debt positions sharply, but most of this borrowing took the form of short-term credits.

The Soviet Union, however, was determined not to become a chronic debtor, probably as a result of the deterioration in East–West relations and the increasing volatility of the international financial market which was increasingly affected by the global debt crisis. Within a year, the Soviet Union had begun both to reduce its commercial debt and to rebuild its assets, and it quickly improved its net assets position. The debt indicators improved impressively as shown in Table 5.12.

These efforts to improve the debt position continued for another two years. In 1982, long-term credits for the Yamburg gas pipeline were obtained, but in 1983 and 1984 the Soviet Union was able to ensure that the increase in its debt to Western governments was only marginal. This reflected a renewed determination to remain independent from the control of the international banking system. All the debt indicators point to the success of these efforts.

Naturally, the costs of this decision had to be borne by adjustments of the real trade flows. Import growth was checked promptly, and exports were increased in 1982. These trends continued in subsequent years, and the trade balance with MDCs registered a surplus for the first time in 1982, which was sustained through 1983 and 1984.

The burden of adjustment fell heavily on oil exports because demand for the other export commodities was stagnant or falling. The decline in world oil prices added to the burden, and forced a larger compensatory increase in the volume of oil exports to the OECD countries, which increased from 53 million tonnes in 1981 to 69 million in 1982, 78 million in 1983 and 81 million in 1984. The annual rates of increase were 30, 13 and 4.5 per cent in 1982, 1983 and 1984 respectively. Again, the adjustment was made largely through increases in the volume of crude oil sales, except in 1982, when the volume of products exports rose by 35 per cent. Crude oil exports to the OECD countries excluding Finland rose by 31, 24 and 18 per cent in 1982, 1983 and 1984 respectively. Oil revenues rose by 15 per cent in 1982, thanks to a volume increase of 30 per cent, and accounted for 60 per cent of total Soviet hard currency earnings from exports to the OECD countries.

This growth of oil exports was achieved at a time when oil production was stagnating. Between 1980 and 1983, oil production remained virtually constant, and it finally began to decline in 1984. Thus, the increase in oil exports to the West during this period was brought about almost entirely by a shift in the allocation of oil among the three markets: domestic consumption, the CMEA countries and the West. A small contribution was also made by the re-export of oil imported from OPEC countries.

Successful measures of gas-for-oil substitution in domestic Soviet consumption and in the composition of energy exports to the CMEA countries contributed to this change in oil allocation. However, the significant reduction in the level of *subsidized* oil deliveries to the CMEA partners also made an important contribution, although it entailed hardship for the CMEA–6. These countries did not suffer to any great extent from the oil price 'shocks' of the 1970s, since their supplies of subsidized oil imports from the Soviet Union continued. They faced their own 'energy crisis', however, in the early 1980s, when the Soviet Union reduced the protection afforded to them by this shield. These issues will be addressed in Chapter 7.

Our discussion so far has tended to support the hypothesis that the pattern of Soviet oil supplies to the West may be explained to some extent in terms of planners' decisions relating to the short-run adjustment of the external balance. Moreover, the role of oil exports as a vital instrument in the management of real trade flow adjustments has increased over time, while the time allowed for such adjustments has shortened in the 1980s, because of the deliberate policy shift away from financial dependence on the West. In recent years Soviet oil exports have been increased, even when the trade balance was in a healthy state. This can only reflect a desire on the part of the Soviet Union to improve its international debt position.

7 SOVIET OIL ALLOCATION POLICY

7.1 Introduction

This chapter examines Soviet oil allocation policy, which determines the amount of oil available for export to the West. Faced by severe physical and economic constraints on increases in oil production, Soviet planners have to reallocate the available supplies among the three main destinations, the domestic, CMEA, and Western markets, to enable them to use oil for short-run balance-of-payments adjustments. However, the degree of freedom enjoyed by the planners in deciding on these allocations is rather small, since their discretion is limited by the severity of the problems of oil production. In order to ease this bottleneck, planners sometimes supplement domestic Soviet production with oil imported from the Middle East for re-export, but they encounter other constraints in their three main markets, which reduce their ability to respond to changing market conditions by reallocating supplies.

In this chapter we first assess the constraints on oil production that determine initial oil availabilities (Section 7.2). We then turn to the means that enable planners to increase the volume of oil allocated to exports to the West. These are: first, oil imports for re-export (Section 7.3); secondly, domestic energy policies, such as conservation and inter-fuel substitution, aimed at reducing the level of oil consumption (Section 7.4); and thirdly, changes in the allocation of Soviet oil to the CMEA countries (Section 7.5).

7.2 Technical and Economic Constraints on Oil Production

The technical and physical difficulties facing the Soviet oil industry are well documented elsewhere (Goldman, 1980 and 1983; Hewett, 1984a; Gustafson, 1983 and 1985b; Estrada, 1984; Dienes and Shabad, 1979), and were discussed briefly in Chapter 2 above. The industry's current problems are partly due to the shortcomings of depletion policy in the past, which allowed excessive rates of extraction in the older oilfields.

Technological factors, such as drilling techniques and the water-flooding method used for enhanced oil recovery, are said to have worsened the situation, and the poor support provided to the oil sector by the machinery sector (the machine-building and metalworking industries) is also a chronic problem (Gustafson, 1985b). Furthermore, the incentive system for drilling crews encourages development drilling at the expense of exploratory drilling. In fact, the effort of all those concerned has been geared to maximizing output in the short run at the cost of shortening the useful lives of the oilfields. The planning system is often cited by Western economists as the underlying cause of the problems facing the Soviet oil industry.

The rapid depletion of the older fields has inevitably pushed the frontier of the major oil-producing areas further east, into the more hostile climatic zones and the less accessible regions of West Siberia. This shift in geographical location has raised the total capital cost per unit of oil output both directly and also indirectly, because of the need for investment in basic infrastructure for entire regions (e.g. the building of roads, housing, electric power stations etc.).

Table 7.1 shows the levels of Soviet capital investment in the energy sector, and in the industrial sector as a whole. As can be seen, the share of total industrial investment occupied by the (upstream) oil sector doubled in the fifteen years from 1970 to 1984. Furthermore, capital expenditure on oil pipeline transportation is estimated to account for around 15–20 per cent of upstream investment (Hewett, 1984a, Table 2–3, p. 41). Taking into account the capital outlay of the economic sectors that supply the oil industry with goods and services, either directly or indirectly, suggests that the economic burden of increasing oil production is unbearably heavy for the overstretched Soviet economy.[1]

[1] Gustafson presents the following estimates as an illustration of the real dimensions of the energy burden on the Soviet economy (Gustafson, 1985b, Table 1, p. 152).

Share of Total Output of Key Materials and Services Consumed by the Energy Sector, 1980

Type of Material or Service	Direct Share (%)	Indirect Share (%)
Industry		
Ferrous metals	10–12	21–27
Non-ferrous metals	3–5	18–21
Construction materials	11–13	16–20
Chemicals	3–5	7–11
Machinery and Equipment	6–8	12–16
Construction	12–14	15–18
Transportation (turnover)		
Rail	31–32	35–40
Shipping	47–49	48–50

Originally from: Yu. D. Kononov in L. A. Melentev and A. A. Makarov, *Energeticheskii kompleks SSSR* (Ekonomika, Moscow, 1983) and V. V. Kuleshov, 'Ne sekonomil? Ochen plokho!' *Ekonomika i organizatsiya promyshlennogo proizvodstva*, No. 11, Moscow, 1983.

Table 7.1: Soviet Investment in the Energy Sector. 1970–84. Billion 1984 Roubles. Percentage Shares of Oil Industry and Energy Sector in Soviet Capital Investment in Industry.

	1970	1975	1980	1981	1982	1983	1984
Coal Mining	1.8	2.0	2.4	2.4	2.6	2.8	2.8
Oil Extraction	2.8	4.2	7.5	8.9	9.6	10.0	9.9
Gas Extraction	1.2	2.0	2.3	2.3	2.7	3.1	3.7
Electric Power	3.7	4.3	5.2	5.3	5.3	5.4	5.8
Energy Total	9.5	12.5	17.4	18.9	20.2	21.3	22.2
Industry Total	32.5	44.9	53.3	55.4	57.0	60.1	61.9
National Economy Total	92.2	128.5	150.9	156.3	161.9	171.2	174.3
Oil/Industry	8.6	9.4	14.1	16.1	16.8	16.6	16.0
Energy/Industry	28.9	27.8	32.6	34.1	35.4	35.4	35.9

Source: *Narodnoe khozyaistvo SSSR*, various issues

The substantial increases in capital expenditure on oil over the period 1970–84 were associated with a reduction in capital efficiency. As shown in Chapter 2 above, oil production began to stagnate in the second half of the 1970s: the average annual growth rate of oil production dropped from 6.7 per cent in 1971–5 to 3.9 per cent in 1976–80, and further to 0.4 per cent in 1981–4, while capital investment in oil extraction more than doubled, rising from 4.2 billion roubles in 1975 to 10.0 billion in 1984.[2] The rapid rise in the incremental capital/output ratio implied by these figures indicates that the return on investment in the oil industry has been declining at a fast rate (Hewett, 1984a; Tretyakova and Heinemeier, 1986).

It is evident from the pattern of investment allocation shown in Table 7.1 that the rapid increase in capital investment in the oil industry was carried out at the expense of other sectors that are equally desperate for massive injections of capital for modernization (see Leggett, 1983, for an account of Soviet investment policy in recent years). Thus, the priority given to the energy sector, and in particular to the oil industry, in the determination of policy on the allocation of investments, imposed enormous strains on the rest of the economy. Hence, the economic constraints on the further expansion of output in the oil industry are now severely binding, and will continue to limit development in the short-to-medium term.

[2] *Narodnoe khozyaistvo SSSR*, 1984, reports that capital investment in the oil industry was 17.9 billion roubles for 1971–5, 29.3 billion for 1976–80 and 38.4 billion for 1981–4 (at 1984 prices). Hewett reports a similar rising trend of unit investment costs in the oil industry (Hewett, 1984a, p. 62, note 60). For a detailed and more recent study of the costs of producing oil to the Soviet economy, see Tretyakova and Heinemeier, 1986.

The existence of these formidable technical and economic constraints, which are responsible for the soaring marginal cost of oil
production (considering both extraction and investment costs), raises
the interesting question of whether it is still an economically justifiable
proposition for the Soviet Union to generate an export surplus of oil as
a means of earning hard currency. The opportunity cost to the rest of
the economy of its present trade strategy of exchanging oil for Western
technology and grain appears at first sight to be very high. Indeed, from
time to time an internal debate has taken place among Soviet
economists and politicians on this subject. Further, Goldman, 1983,
reports deep-rooted Russian popular sentiments 'that the Soviet Union
may be overexploiting its natural resources and that foreigners may be
benefiting at the expense of future Russians', and that 'Even those who
accept the need to exploit Soviet raw materials because they want
Western technology warn that such a policy is not always as simple as it
seems and that it necessitates ever increasing expenses because of the
need to go off farther into the North and the East' (Goldman, 1983, p.
635).

There is widespread and growing disillusionment with the performance of imported Western technology in the Soviet Union. Soviet
absorptive capacity, and in particular the Soviet economy's efficiency in
the adaptation of imported technology, have also been questioned
(Hanson, 1981). However, though imported technology does not
represent a large share of total investment, its contribution to the relief
of critical bottlenecks is said to be of considerable importance. For
example, in the chemical industry, Western technology is imported
only where local substitutes for imported machinery and equipment
are not readily available.

This restrictive import policy is also applied to imports of technology
for the energy sector. Gustafson, 1985b, in a detailed study of the role of
imported technology in the Soviet oil and gas industries, shows that,
although imports of foreign equipment have increased sharply in
recent years, their share of total investment in the Soviet oil and gas
industries remains modest, and does not exceed 20 per cent (see Table
7.2). While this estimated share is clearly only a crude indicator, since
the figures for imports and investment use different prices, the Soviet
campaign to boost oil production has not relied to any great extent on
foreign technology, and most of the rise in the share of imports during
the oil and gas campaign can be attributed to the imports of large-
diameter pipe and compressors for the gas industry (see Table 7.3), for
which no domestic substitutes were available at the time. In fact,
wherever possible, as in the case of the oil refining sector, the Soviet
Union has imported equipment from CMEA suppliers (especially East

Table 7.2: Oil- and Gas-related Imports as a Share of Total Soviet Oil and Gas Investment (including Transmission) (Categories 128 and 266). 1970–83. Million Roubles.

	Total Imports	Total Investment	Share of Imports (%)
1971–5	3.21	27.8	11.5
1976–80	6.60	48.5	13.6
1981	1.77	14.2	12.5
1982	2.83	~15.6	18.1
1983	3.23	~16.6	19.4

Note: Category 128 includes machinery etc. for drilling, well development, and geological exploration for the oil and gas industries. Category 266 is 'pipe'.
Source: Gustafson, 1985b, p. 167, Table 9, originally compiled from various Soviet sources

Table 7.3: Soviet Imports of Gas and Oil Equipment (Category 128). 1981–4. Million Roubles.

	Gas	Oil	Share of Gas (%)
1981	4.8	194.6	2.4
1982	381.7	278.1	57.9
1983	942.4	356.2	72.6
1984	789.6	241.6	76.6

Source: Gustafson, 1985b, p. 166, Table 8, based on *VTSS* yearbook, various issues

Germany and Czechoslovakia) in order to avoid spending hard currency.

Further, as has been noted elsewhere, 'since most of the gas-related equipment comes from the West, then much of the oil-related must come from CMEA.' (Gustafson, 1985b, p. 165.) Hence it can be seen that imports of Western technology have been kept to an absolute minimum even in such a high-priority sector as energy. Gustafson notes that the share of the energy sector in total imports of equipment has been surprisingly small, in view of its much publicized high priority and its importance as an earner of hard currency. According to his study, the average share of energy imports in total imports in 1980–84 was 6 per cent, while that of oil- and gas-related imports was 4.5 per cent.

Therefore, it appears that the import policy followed in the past was rather restrictive, and that the imputed relative shadow prices used to determine the allocation of resources must have justified the decision that was taken to import Western technology in preference to using the equipment and technology available either domestically or from CMEA suppliers. The level of grain imports, another major Soviet import from the West, must have been justified on similar grounds, since the reforms that would be needed to bring about any substantial improvement in the performance of the agricultural sector have not been forthcoming. In other words, the price that oil commanded on the world market (up to 1985), relative to the prices of technology and grain, must have provided planners with the economic rationale not to retreat into a strategy of autarky, despite the escalating costs of domestic oil production.[3] Since domestic prices and foreign trade prices are not comparable, the opportunity cost calculated using either set of prices as a base gives a somewhat misleading picture.

Another important consideration that planners must take into account in embarking on the expansion of energy production in West and East Siberia is undoubtedly the region's development over the longer term. Since not only energy-related resources but also other natural resources and raw materials in the European USSR have been progressively exhausted, sooner or later the frontier of development will have to be moved into Siberia, where the reserves of most resources are very promising and, in some cases, available in almost unlimited quantities. Infrastructural investments made now for oil and gas production can be regarded as a great asset, since they constitute a basic foundation for the future development of the whole of Siberia. Here we can see that the plans for energy production and Siberian regional development are closely interwoven.

Faced with little flexibility in domestic oil production, planners are left with two means of using oil to effect short-run balance-of-payments adjustments: first, they can adjust the level of total oil supply using imported oil for re-export; secondly, they can increase their flexibility in supplying exports to the West by adjusting the allocation of oil to the other markets.

Although the absolute volume of Soviet oil exports to the West in 1984, the peak year, exceeded 84 million tonnes (exports of crude to MDCs were 52 million and exports of refined products 32 million tonnes), oil exports to the West in that year were no more than 14 per cent of domestic production. In the case of crude oil alone, the share remained less than 10 per cent (the average share in 1980–84 was 6–7 per cent). The two options listed above, whose significance in the

---

[3] The immediate impact and possible long-run consequences of the drastic decline in world market oil prices in 1986 on the Soviet economy and foreign trade strategy are discussed in Chapter 8 below.

determination of total supply seems to be only marginal in relation to the level of domestic Soviet production, provided planners with a measure of flexibility in supplying oil to the West.

7.3 Soviet Oil Imports

The volume of Soviet oil imports has increased considerably, with large fluctuations from year to year (see Tables 7.4A and 7.5A). While the ratios of oil imports to domestic production and consumption are very small (in the case of crude oil, the ratio of imports to production was 2.4 per cent in 1984), their crucial role in supplementing Soviet exports to the West cannot be ignored, since it is known that all imports of crude oil are allocated to re-export.

In recent years, refined products have been imported both from the CMEA countries and from the MDCs, and the ratio of imports to exports of products has fluctuated around 2–3 per cent. Thus the contribution of imports to the total supply of products is very marginal (see Table 7.5B). Imports of crude oil, however, do play a significant role, and crude oil has been imported from a number of OPEC

Table 7.4A: Soviet Trade in Crude Oil. 1960–84. Million Tonnes.

		Exports				Imports
	Total	*CMEA–6*	*OCPEs*	*MDCs*	*LDCs*[a]	*Total*[b]
1960	17.8	6.2	2.6	8.2	0.8	1.2
1965	43.4	18.3	4.1	16.4	4.6	0.0
1970	66.8	34.7	6.6	23.1	2.4	3.5
1971	74.8	39.9	7.2	25.1	2.6	5.1
1972	76.2	44.4	7.5	21.9	2.3	7.8
1973	85.3	50.8	8.4	24.3	1.8	13.2
1974	80.6	54.2	8.9	15.8	1.8	4.4
1975	93.1	59.3	9.7	21.1	3.0	6.5
1976	110.8	63.6	10.2	34.0	2.9	6.4
1977	122.1	67.6	10.3	40.0	4.2	6.2
1978	123.4	68.8	11.0	40.3	3.3	9.0
1979	124.7	71.0	13.2	35.4	5.1	6.5
1980	121.1	72.6	12.0	31.4	5.1	3.6
1981	119.9	72.4	11.6	30.6	5.3	4.2
1982	121.8	66.2	11.6	38.3	5.7	7.6
1983	132.8	64.3	13.3	48.3	6.9	12.5
1984	138.3	64.8	14.5	52.5	6.5	14.1

Notes: (a) LDCs importing oil from the Soviet Union include India, Nicaragua, Morocco, Ethiopia, Brazil and Afghanistan.
    (b) For 1960, all imports are from LDCs.
Source: PlanEcon, 1986

Table 7.4B: Soviet Trade in Crude Oil. 1960–84. Percentage Shares.

	Exports/ Production	Exports to MDCs/ Production	Imports/ Exports	Imports/ Exports to MDCs	Shares of Destinations in Total Exports			
					CMEA–6	All CPEs	MDCs	MDCs + LDCs
1960–64 (Average)	14.0	7.0	2.81	6.26	34.2	47.8	45.6	52.2
1965–9 (Average)	19.0	7.6	0.52	1.31	44.6	53.8	39.8	46.2
1970	19.0	7.0	5.24	15.00	52.0	62.0	35.0	38.0
1971	20.0	7.0	6.82	20.10	53.0	63.0	34.0	37.0
1972	19.0	6.0	10.28	35.40	58.0	68.0	29.0	32.0
1973	20.0	6.0	15.45	53.30	60.0	69.0	29.0	31.0
1974	18.0	3.0	5.45	27.80	67.0	78.0	20.0	22.0
1975	19.0	4.0	6.98	30.80	64.0	74.0	23.0	26.0
1976	22.0	7.0	5.80	18.80	57.0	67.0	31.0	33.0
1977	23.0	7.0	5.11	15.50	55.0	64.0	33.0	36.0
1978	22.0	7.0	7.29	22.30	56.0	65.0	33.0	35.0
1979	22.0	6.0	5.22	18.40	57.0	68.0	28.0	32.0
1980	21.0	5.0	2.94	11.50	60.0	70.0	26.0	30.0
1981	20.0	5.0	3.50	13.70	60.0	70.0	26.0	30.0
1982	21.0	6.0	6.26	19.80	54.0	64.0	31.0	36.0
1983	22.0	8.0	9.39	25.90	48.0	58.0	36.0	42.0
1984	23.0	9.0	10.20	26.90	47.0	57.0	38.0	43.0

Source: Figures calculated from Table 7.4A

Table 7.5A: Soviet Trade in Refined Oil Products. 1960–84. Million Tonnes.

	Exports					Imports					Net Exports
	Total	CMEA–6	OCPEs	MDCs	LDCs	Total	CMEA–6	OCPEs	MDCs	LDCs	Total
1960	15.4	2.96	3.41	7.67	1.36	3.23	3.08	0.15	0.0	0.0	12.16
1965	21.0	4.14	2.34	11.32	3.18	1.90	1.86	0.00	0.0	0.04	19.08
1970	29.0	5.58	3.61	18.37	1.39	1.05	0.97	0.00	0.04	0.02	27.90
1971	30.3	4.86	3.42	20.44	1.53	1.50	1.45	0.00	0.03	0.04	28.75
1972	30.8	4.50	3.79	21.00	1.53	1.30	1.23	0.12	0.02	0.0	29.52
1973	33.0	4.41	4.01	23.36	1.17	1.50	1.34	0.02	0.04	0.0	31.46
1974	35.6	4.54	4.14	25.76	1.17	1.00	0.94	0.03	0.03	0.0	34.62
1975	37.3	4.18	4.72	26.66	1.72	1.06	0.92	0.02	0.11	0.0	36.22
1976	37.7	4.74	5.38	25.92	1.68	0.80	0.58	0.04	0.20	0.0	36.93
1977	38.9	5.77	6.10	25.20	1.80	0.73	0.53	0.03	0.17	0.0	38.13
1978	41.4	6.51	6.30	26.80	1.80	0.55	0.32	0.02	0.20	0.0	40.86
1979	36.7	7.09	6.80	21.10	1.70	1.03	0.32	0.02	0.69	0.0	35.66
1980	37.5	7.73	6.10	22.10	1.60	0.86	0.43	0.02	0.41	0.0	36.67
1981	40.3	7.28	6.90	24.40	1.70	1.50	0.68	0.02	0.80	0.0	38.79
1982	48.7	6.25	7.90	32.70	1.80	1.18	0.46	0.01	0.71	0.0	47.47
1983	50.6	6.29	7.80	34.30	2.20	1.16	0.49	0.01	0.66	0.0	49.43
1984	49.0	6.35	7.80	32.70	2.10	1.10	0.50	0.01	0.59	0.0	47.85

Source: PlanEcon, 1986

Table 7.5B: Soviet Trade in Refined Oil Products. 1960–84. Percentage Shares.

	Shares in Total Exports				Shares in Total Imports		Imports/Exports
	CMEA-6	All CPEs	MDCs	LDCs	CMEA-6	MDCs	
1960–64 (Average)	22.50	41.23	51.29	7.48	95.6	0.7	14.00
1965–9 (Average)	19.79	31.46	60.08	8.46	90.7	1.5	5.12
1970	19.28	31.74	63.45	4.81	91.9	4.1	3.64
1971	16.06	27.37	67.58	5.05	96.5	0.2	4.96
1972	14.60	26.89	68.13	4.97	94.5	1.8	4.22
1973	13.40	25.55	70.89	3.56	89.5	2.5	4.55
1974	12.75	24.38	72.32	3.30	94.2	3.4	2.80
1975	11.22	23.89	71.51	4.60	87.2	10.3	2.84
1976	12.57	26.84	68.70	4.46	72.8	24.6	2.11
1977	14.84	30.54	64.83	4.46	71.6	23.1	1.89
1978	15.72	30.94	64.72	4.35	59.0	36.4	1.32
1979	19.32	37.86	57.51	4.63	31.2	66.9	2.81
1980	20.60	36.85	58.88	4.26	50.5	47.7	2.29
1981	18.08	35.21	60.57	4.22	45.6	53.4	3.72
1982	12.85	29.09	67.21	3.70	39.0	60.0	2.43
1983	12.44	27.85	67.80	4.35	42.0	57.0	2.29
1984	12.98	28.91	66.80	4.29	45.4	53.5	2.25

Source: Figures calculated from Table 7.5A

countries (e.g. Libya, Iran and Iraq), for re-export to the West European market in exchange for hard currency. The importation of oil from the Middle East under a system of barter trade indirectly enables the Soviet Union to use military and other goods, which might not be easily exported to the hard currency area, into a source of foreign exchange earnings (see Chapter 5 above and Stern, 1983).

These deals clearly have strategic and political implications, but they also make a contribution to the external balance which cannot be ignored, given the constraints on the further expansion of domestic oil production. Although crude oil imports fluctuated from year to year throughout the 1970s and 1980s, as would be expected of deals tied to sales of military hardware, expressed as a proportion of total Soviet oil exports to the West they never dropped below 10 per cent, and indeed they reached levels of over 30 per cent in the early 1970s (see Table 7.4B).

It is interesting to note that, despite the stagnation of domestic oil production, a big push in oil exports to MDCs was apparently achieved during 1981–4, thanks to an equally big surge in oil imports. Crude oil imports rose from 3.6 million tonnes in 1980 to 7.6 million in 1982, and further to 14.1 million in 1984. Thus, increments in oil exports in 1982–4 were made possible in large part by the increased volume of oil imports, which in 1983 and 1984 represented 25 per cent of the total volume of Soviet oil exports to the West.

7.4 Soviet Domestic Consumption

The rapid rise of oil prices in the world market in the early 1970s and the declining rate of growth of domestic production induced planners to seek a reduction in the level of domestic oil consumption. Two policies were considered: the first was a programme of overall measures of energy conservation and the second was a programme of inter-fuel substitution – especially gas-for-oil substitution – in domestic consumption, and in exports to both the CMEA countries and the MDCs.

(*a*) *Energy Savings*. The results of the first measure are shown in Table 7.6, which shows the annual growth rates of total energy consumption and those of individual fuels. The average annual growth rate of total energy consumption has gradually declined from 5.9 per cent in 1961–5 and 4.8 per cent in 1966–70, to 2.7 per cent in 1981–4, but much of this decline can be explained by the general slow-down of growth in the economy as a whole. The average annual growth rates of NMP utilized in the three periods were 6.0, 7.1 and 3.2 per cent respectively. Nevertheless, the rate of growth of energy consumption

Table 7.6: Percentage Annual Growth Rates of Apparent Soviet Domestic Consumption of Various Fuels, and NMP Utilized. 1961–84.

	Total	Coal	Oil	Gas	Primary Electricity	Other	NMP Utilized	Ratio of Growth of Energy Consumption to Growth of NMP Utilized
1961–5 (Average)	5.9	1.6	8.7	26.2	7.5	1.7	6.0	0.98
1966–70 (Average)	4.8	1.6	7.8	9.4	6.2	-0.7	7.1	0.68
1971–5 (Average)	4.7	1.9	7.1	7.5	0.5	1.4	5.1	1.02
1976–80 (Average)	3.3	0.1	4.2	6.2	11.2	-2.1	3.9	0.96
1981–4 (Average)	2.7	0.4	-0.5	8.2	8.0	0.6	3.2	0.84
1970	5.3	1.6	9.0	8.9	4.5	-0.2	11.2	0.47
1971	4.6	2.3	6.4	9.1	-1.7	-1.0	5.9	0.78
1972	5.1	2.1	8.7	6.7	-1.5	3.0	3.5	1.46
1973	4.4	1.3	7.6	5.9	1.3	0.8	7.7	0.56
1974	4.6	1.6	7.0	7.3	8.9	-3.7	4.1	1.12
1975	4.9	2.0	5.7	8.3	-4.3	7.7	4.2	1.17
1976	3.3	1.4	2.9	8.6	10.4	-8.2	5.3	0.62
1977	3.8	1.2	3.6	6.4	12.1	3.8	3.5	1.09
1978	4.4	1.1	6.3	6.0	17.8	-4.7	4.5	0.98
1979	3.2	-0.2	3.8	5.8	3.9	5.4	2.0	1.60
1980	1.9	-2.8	4.1	4.2	11.9	-6.8	3.9	0.49
1981	2.6	-0.9	1.2	6.7	6.1	6.4	3.2	0.82
1982	2.6	3.1	-0.8	8.4	0.0	-4.0	3.6	0.72
1983	2.3	0.2	-1.0	7.8	6.1	0.3	3.6	0.64
1984	3.1	-1.0	-1.3	10.0	19.7	-3.0	2.6	1.19

Source: Figures calculated from PlanEcon, 1986

tended to be slower than the overall rate of economic growth, as is indicated by the declining ratio of the two growth rates – from 1.02 in 1971–5 to 0.84 in 1981–4. This points to a slowly decreasing trend in the energy intensity of the Soviet economy over the period 1970–84.

However, according to a UN study comparing trends in energy consumption in the ECE region, the Soviet Union has lagged far behind North America and Northern Europe in reducing its energy elasticity since 1973. Table 7.7 shows that, while North America and Northern Europe managed to halve their energy elasticities following the 1973 oil price increase, the countries of Eastern and Southern Europe increased their energy elasticities over the period 1973–80.[4] In the Soviet Union, the elasticity has shown little change.

Table 7.7: Energy Elasticities for Various Regions (Ratios of Growth Rates of Primary Energy Consumption to Growth Rates of GDP or NMP).

Region	1960–72	1973–80
North America	1.19	0.59
Northern Europe	1.05	0.48
Southern Europe	1.41	1.63
Eastern Europe	0.49	0.70
Soviet Union	0.84	0.85

Note: The energy elasticities were computed by regressing the log of primary energy consumption on the log of GDP or NMP.
Source: UNECE, *Economic Bulletin for Europe*, 1984, Vol. 36, No. 2, p. 158, Table 1

The same UN study also reports the results of a decomposition analysis of the decline in primary energy consumption into slow-down effects and conservation effects (UNECE, *Economic Bulletin for Europe*, Vol. 36, No. 2, July 1984, p. 159, Table 2). The results show that, while the slow-down and the conservation measures contributed almost equally to the reductions in energy consumption in both North America and the North European countries, for the Soviet Union and the three South European countries the decline in energy consumption is explained entirely by the slow-down, and was marginally offset by the increase in energy intensity. In the case of Eastern Europe, the increase in energy intensity outweighed the slow-down effect by a wide margin, and the growth of actual energy consumption in 1973–80 was above the historical trend rate observed in the previous period.

[4] In this context, 'Eastern Europe' refers to the European CMEA–6, 'Southern Europe' includes Spain, Portugal and Greece, and 'Northern Europe' refers to the remaining EEC countries, together with Austria, Finland, Iceland, Norway, Sweden and Switzerland.

The poor record of energy conservation in the Soviet Union and Eastern Europe is in part a reflection of the factor-extensive and energy-intensive growth path that their economies continued to follow, well after the big surge in world market energy prices in 1973. As stated in Chapter 5 above, the domestic energy prices in these centrally planned economies are not directly linked to world energy prices. The real progress that has been made in energy conservation in some East European countries (e.g. East Germany and Hungary) did not begin until after the second oil price increase, in 1979–80, when the Soviet Union adopted a less generous position with respect to its subsidized oil deliveries to these countries, and the gap between intra-CMEA energy prices and world market prices narrowed considerably.

As for the Soviet Union, the potential for future energy conservation appears to be sizeable. An earlier UN study, comparing energy intensities internationally, amply demonstrates this potential (UNECE, *Economic Survey of Europe: The European Economy in 1979*). The energy intensity of an economy (i.e. the level of energy consumption per unit of gross output produced) naturally depends first of all on the country's level of economic development and its socio-economic structure, but it also depends on efficiency in energy utilization.

Table 7.8 shows that the energy intensities of the Soviet Union and the East European countries are considerably higher than those of Western industrialized countries at comparable or higher levels of economic development (with the reservation that GDP per capita measured in US dollars is admittedly not the 'best' indicator of the level of development). This is partly explained by differences in economic structure, since energy-intensive industries account for a higher share of economic activity in the CMEA countries, which is another legacy of the factor-intensive heavy industrialization programmes pursued in the recent past. More importantly, however, as an earlier analysis of these data has shown, the high energy intensity in the CMEA region (including the Soviet Union) can be attributed to inefficient use of energy, i.e. it is 'due to the comparative obsolescence of fuel consumption and goods production patterns, technology, machinery and equipment.' (Balkay, 1984, p. 128.)

In the case of some East European countries (e.g. East Germany and Bulgaria) another contributing factor is the inefficient energy mix resulting from their heavy reliance on brown coal, which has a low calorific content. The inefficiency of energy use in these countries appears to be particularly problematic in the industrial sector, where the share of energy consumption is conspicuously high by international standards. The sectoral distributions of energy consumption in the ECE region and North America are shown in Table 7.9.

Table 7.8: Indicators of Energy Intensities of Various Countries. 1973 and 1978.

Country	Index of GDP per capita, 1973[1]	Index of Energy Intensity of GDP, 1973[1]	GDP per capita 1978, US $[2]	Energy Consumption per capita, 1978 (Kilograms Coal Equivalent)	Energy Consumption per Unit of GDP, 1978[2]
Bulgaria	38.8	97.2	3,200	5,020	1.6
Czechoslovakia	55.8	90.0	4,720	7,531	1.6
East Germany	58.4	93.2	5,660	7,121	1.3
Poland	42.3	81.1	3,660	5,596	1.5
Hungary	42.5	64.9	3,450	3,451	1.0
Romania	33.1	90.0	1,750	4,042	2.3
Soviet Union	45.3	92.1	3,700	5,582	1.5
Yugoslavia	30.3	50.6	2,390	2,035	0.9
USA	100.0	100.0	8,700	11,374	1.2
Canada	92.6	109.4	9,170	9,930	1.1
UK	70.9	68.1	5,030	5,212	1.0
Italy	51.7	56.4	3,840	3,230	0.8
Netherlands	73.9	74.9	8,390	5,327	0.6
Japan	64.5	58.3	7,330	3,825	0.5
Sweden	82.8	84.3	10,210	5,954	0.6
West Germany	72.7	71.2	9,600	6,015	0.6
France	64.6	65.8	8,270	4,368	0.5

Sources: 1. UNECE, *Economic Survey of Europe: The European Economy in 1979*, p. 173 (USA = 100)
2. Balkay, 1984, p. 124, Table 6

Table 7.9: Final Energy Consumption by Sector for Various Regions. 1973–80. Percentage Shares.

Region	Industry	Transport	Other
North America			
1973	33.7	31.4	34.9
1978	30.4	35.8	33.8
1980	31.4	35.0	33.6
Northern Europe			
1973	40.8	19.8	39.0
1978	38.9	21.7	40.0
1980	38.4	22.2	39.9
Southern Europe			
1973	47.3	31.3	21.0
1978	46.2	30.8	23.0
1980	45.1	31.3	24.6
Eastern Europe			
1973	52.7	8.8	38.5
1978	54.7	7.4	37.9
1980	54.0	7.3	38.7
Soviet Union			
1973	65.7	11.5	22.9
1978	63.6	13.4	23.0
1980	64.3	12.9	22.8

Note: 'Other' includes agricultural, commercial, public and residential use.
Source: UNECE, *Economic Bulletin for Europe*, 1984, Vol. 36, No. 2, Table 4, p. 161

Hewett, in a detailed analysis of Soviet energy consumption, demonstrates the potential for future energy conservation by comparing industrial energy consumption in the Soviet Union and the United States. According to his calculations, in 1980 the Soviet Union required 58 per cent more energy per dollar value added in the industrial sector than the United States (Hewett, 1984a, p. 108).

Now that the potential for energy conservation has been recognized, the Soviet campaign on this front has been intensified in recent years. It is hard for Soviet planners to ignore the fact that 'the capital costs of energy-conservation measures are one-third to one-half the new investment that would be involved in extracting and transporting to consumers energy equivalent to that saved through conservation.'[5]

[5] Quoted by Hewett, 1984a, p. 113. Originally it is from the paper by A. Lalayants: 'Problemy ekonomii toplivno-energeticheskikh resursov v narodnom khozyaistve' (Problems economizing fuel-energy resources in the economy), *Planovoe khozyaistvo*, No. 1, Moscow, January 1981.

Despite an intensive campaign in the media and a series of decrees, however, the results have not been very encouraging. It is generally agreed that the obstacles to substantial progress in energy conservation are the inappropriate incentives given to energy savings, obsolete technology, the shortage of capital and the slow adoption of energy-saving innovations. For example, Hewett, 1984a, argues that the fundamental impediment to rapid progress in energy conservation is the planning and incentive system governing the whole economy, which places far more emphasis on the requirement that enterprises meet their output targets than on the achievement of the cost efficiencies embodied in the input plan, including energy savings.[6]

(*b*) *Inter-fuel Substitution*. The need to promote a gas-for-oil substitution programme was already apparent in the early 1970s, given the relative sizes of the reserves of the two fuels. At that time Soviet decision-makers and planners started to debate issues of long-term energy policy within a twenty-year framework (up to 1990) in the broader context of regional development planning for Siberia. The implementation of the gas-for-oil substitution policy gained momentum in the early 1980s when the need to reduce domestic oil consumption became paramount. In contrast to the discouraging results obtained from energy conservation measures to date, the policy of inter-fuel substitution, namely gas-for-oil substitution, has been very successful in recent years. The conspicuous decline in the rate of growth of oil consumption, compared with that of total energy consumption (and gas consumption in particular), can be seen immediately from Table 7.6. The average annual growth rate of oil consumption fell from 7.1 per cent in 1971–5 to 4.2 per cent in 1976–80 and further to −0.5 per cent in 1981–4, whereas that of gas consumption was sustained at 6–8 per cent throughout. Hence, by 1984, oil and gas each held a share of approximately one-third of total Soviet domestic energy consumption (see Table 7.10).

Over the five years 1980–84, the share of oil dropped from 37.5 to 33.2 per cent, while that of gas increased from 26.4 to 32.6 per cent, compensating also for the reduced shares of coal and other energy sources. The share of primary electricity also increased marginally but steadily over time, from 3.5 per cent in 1960 to 5.5 per cent in 1984. This shift in the energy balance of consumption, and in particular the substitution of gas for oil, were supported by the rapid increase in gas production as shown in Soviet energy balances of production (see

---

[6] This issue has often been addressed by Soviet leaders and economists as for example in the case of the abortive Kosygin reforms of the late 1960s. The possible effects of the more resolute reforms under the new Gorbachev leadership on energy savings remain to be seen.

Table 7.10: Soviet Energy Balance: Percentage Shares of Various Fuels in Apparent Consumption. 1960–84.

	Coal	Oil	Gas	Primary Electricity	Other
1960	51.3	24.7	7.9	3.5	12.6
1965	41.7	28.1	16.3	3.7	10.2
1970	35.8	32.4	20.2	3.9	7.7
1971	35.0	33.0	21.1	3.7	7.3
1972	34.0	34.1	21.4	3.4	7.2
1973	33.0	35.1	21.7	3.3	6.9
1974	32.0	35.9	22.3	3.5	6.4
1975	31.1	36.2	23.0	3.2	6.5
1976	30.6	36.0	24.2	3.4	5.8
1977	29.8	35.9	24.8	3.6	5.8
1978	28.9	36.6	25.2	4.1	5.3
1979	27.9	36.7	25.8	4.1	5.4
1980	26.6	37.5	26.4	4.5	4.9
1981	25.7	37.0	27.4	4.7	5.1
1982	25.9	35.8	29.0	4.6	4.8
1983	25.3	34.7	30.5	4.8	4.7
1984	24.3	33.2	32.6	5.5	4.4

Source: Figures calculated from data in PlanEcon, 1986

Tables 7.11 and 7.12). The average annual growth rate of gas production was sustained at a high level throughout the period 1970–84: it was 8.1 per cent in 1971–5, 9.9 per cent in 1976–80 and 7.8 per cent in 1981–4. By contrast, the growth rate of oil production fell from 6.8 per cent in 1971–5 to 0.4 per cent in 1981–4.

As a result, gas production doubled from 270 bcm in 1975 to 548 bcm in 1984, as shown in Table 7.13. Most of these increases were due to the expansion of gas production in West Siberia (especially in Tyumen province), which now accounts for more than half of all Soviet gas production.

As mentioned in Chapter 5 above, the Soviet Union enjoys a far higher reserves/production ratio for gas than for oil, and can count on sufficient reserves to permit substantial increases in gas production in future. The rapid growth of gas production has offset the poor performance of the coal and oil industries in recent years, and increased the share of gas in total Soviet energy production from 20 per cent in 1975 to 31 per cent in 1984. As long as the present trend continues, therefore, the supply side is unlikely to present any immediate limitation on further substitution of gas for oil.

The future success of the gas-for-oil substitution programme within

Table 7.11: Percentage Annual Growth Rates of Soviet Energy Production. 1971–84.

	Total	Coal	Oil	Gas	Primary Electricity	Other
1971–5 (Average)	4.92	1.74	6.82	8.05	1.25	1.35
1976–80 (Average)	4.03	0.22	4.24	9.89	11.19	−2.10
1981–4 (Average)	2.63	−0.02	0.41	7.80	7.78	−0.42
1971	4.53	2.05	6.83	7.33	−0.48	−1.08
1972	4.16	1.63	6.22	5.58	−1.32	3.05
1973	4.68	1.30	7.15	6.72	2.95	0.74
1974	5.48	1.93	6.97	10.28	9.13	−3.66
1975	5.74	1.81	6.94	10.12	−4.01	7.70
1976	5.01	1.53	5.90	10.90	9.90	−8.16
1977	4.79	1.45	5.04	7.80	11.18	3.73
1978	4.13	0.28	4.73	7.59	16.90	−4.67
1979	3.58	−0.22	2.48	9.22	5.06	5.41
1980	2.64	−1.92	3.04	6.73	12.91	−6.84
1981	2.36	−1.34	0.96	6.94	5.73	6.42
1982	2.57	1.92	0.62	7.64	0.38	−4.00
1983	2.48	−0.03	0.62	6.99	6.47	0.39
1984	3.12	−0.62	−0.58	9.64	18.50	−3.05

Source: PlanEcon, 1986

the Soviet Union depends rather on the speed with which problems on the demand side can be resolved. As for domestic consumption, it is argued that the shortage of gas storage facilities and deficiencies in upgrading refining capacity will impose serious constraints on the future substitution of gas for oil in boiler uses (Sagers and Tretyakova, 1986). The planned substitution of gas for oil as a major export commodity has also run into several problems, although total exports of gas increased rapidly from a mere 3.3 bcm in 1970 to 19.5 bcm in 1975 and further to 65.7 bcm in 1984 (see Table 7.13). In 1984, the Soviet Union exported 37.2 bcm of natural gas (56 per cent of total gas exports) to the Socialist countries, and 28.5 bcm to the West European countries.

Further increases of Soviet gas deliveries to the East European countries are planned, partly in order to compensate for reductions in oil exports to these countries. Soviet natural gas exports to Eastern Europe could reach 60 bcm by the early 1990s, provided that both pipeline construction and the substitution of gas for oil and coal in these countries proceed smoothly as planned. At present, natural gas

Table 7.12: Soviet Energy Balance: Percentage Shares of Fuels in Production. 1960–84.

	Coal	Oil	Gas	Primary Electricity	Other
1960	49.0	28.7	7.4	3.2	11.7
1965	39.0	33.9	14.6	3.4	9.1
1970	33.1	38.6	17.9	3.6	6.8
1971	32.3	39.5	18.3	3.4	6.5
1972	31.5	40.3	18.6	3.2	6.4
1973	30.5	41.2	18.9	3.2	6.1
1974	29.5	41.8	19.8	3.3	5.6
1975	28.4	42.3	20.6	3.0	5.7
1976	27.4	42.6	21.8	3.1	5.0
1977	26.6	42.7	22.4	3.3	4.9
1978	25.6	43.0	23.2	3.7	4.5
1979	24.6	42.5	24.4	3.8	4.6
1980	23.6	42.7	25.4	4.2	4.2
1981	22.7	42.1	26.5	4.3	4.4
1982	22.6	41.3	27.8	4.2	4.1
1983	22.0	40.6	29.1	4.4	4.0
1984	21.2	39.1	30.9	5.0	3.8

Source: PlanEcon, 1986

accounts for about 18 per cent of energy consumption in the CMEA–6 as a whole.[7]

In contrast, Soviet efforts to increase sales of gas to Western Europe have encountered serious obstacles in recent years. Obviously the stagnation and slight decline in energy consumption, and hence gas consumption, in the region, together with the presence of competing supply sources (e.g. the Netherlands, Algeria and Norway), are contributory factors. More importantly, however, the prospects for the Soviet Union to increase its gas sales are hindered first by the express policy of the West European countries to diversify their supply sources for security reasons, partly in response to pressure from the Reagan Administration, and secondly by the recent agreement between Norway and certain West European countries for future sales of gas from the Troll field.

Nevertheless, there is no doubt that the successful implementation of the gas-for-oil substitution programme has made an important contribution to generating the flexibility required in Soviet oil allocation policy, and hence to the freeing of oil for the Western market. This

[7] The 1984 figures for the individual countries were: Bulgaria 14 per cent, Czechoslovakia 12 per cent, East Germany 9 per cent, Hungary 30 per cent, Poland 8 per cent and Romania 49 per cent (PlanEcon, 1986).

Table 7.13: Soviet Natural Gas Balance. 1960–84. Billion Cubic Metres.

	Production	Exports				Total Imports[b]	Apparent Consumption	Exports/ Production (%)	Export Structure (%)	
		Total	CMEA–6	OCPEs	MDCs[a]				Socialist/ Total	MDCs/ Total
1960	42.2	0.2	0.2	0	0	0	42.0	0.5	100.0	0
1965	119.0	0.4	0.4	0	0	0	118.6	0.3	100.0	0
1970	184.4	3.3	2.3	0	1.0	3.6	184.7	1.7	68.2	31.7
1971	197.9	4.6	3.1	0	1.4	8.1	201.5	2.2	66.1	33.8
1972	206.3	5.1	3.4	0	1.6	11.1	212.3	2.4	65.2	34.9
1973	220.2	6.8	4.9	0	2.0	11.4	224.8	3.0	68.4	31.6
1974	242.8	14.0	8.6	0	5.5	11.9	240.7	5.4	60.0	40.0
1975	269.6	19.5	11.4	0	8.0	12.4	262.5	6.8	58.0	42.1
1976	299.1	26.1	13.8	0	12.3	11.8	284.8	8.1	57.3	47.4
1977	322.5	31.7	15.4	0	16.3	11.8	302.6	9.1	48.2	51.8
1978	346.9	36.3	16.2	0.1	20.0	9.6	320.2	9.7	44.7	55.3
1979	378.9	47.5	22.0	0.9	24.6	6.4	337.9	11.6	48.1	51.9
1980	405.6	56.2	29.4	1.7	25.1	3.2	352.6	12.9	55.2	44.8
1981	433.6	59.7	29.2	2.0	28.5	2.2	376.1	12.8	52.2	47.8
1982	466.7	61.1	31.1	2.6	27.4	2.4	408.0	12.1	55.0	45.0
1983	499.3	61.6	32.3	2.7	26.6	2.4	440.1	11.4	56.7	43.3
1984	547.5	65.7	33.9	3.3	28.5	2.5	484.3	11.1	56.6	43.4

Notes: (a) There are no exports to LDCs.
(b) Most imports are from LDCs.
Source: PlanEcon, 1986

can be clearly seen from the difference between the shares of oil in
domestic Soviet energy consumption and production. While the share
of oil in consumption had fallen to 32 per cent in 1984, its share in
production was still 39 per cent. This gap shows up as a proportion of
net exports in the energy balance. Oil still commands a predominant
share in Soviet energy exports – over 70 per cent – despite the increase
in the share of gas (see Table 7.14).

Table 7.14: Soviet Energy Balance: Percentage Shares of Fuels in Exports. 1960–84.

	Coal	Oil	Gas	Electricity
1960	22.5	77.1	0.5	0.0
1965	20.6	78.5	0.4	0.5
1970	15.6	80.8	2.4	1.2
1971	14.7	81.0	3.0	1.4
1972	14.2	81.1	3.3	1.4
1973	13.0	81.3	4.0	1.6
1974	13.3	77.2	7.8	1.7
1975	11.7	77.2	9.6	1.6
1976	10.4	77.0	11.2	1.4
1977	9.8	76.5	12.4	1.3
1978	8.6	76.3	13.8	1.3
1979	8.1	72.8	17.5	1.6
1980	8.0	69.7	20.3	2.0
1981	6.7	70.0	21.3	2.0
1982	6.2	70.9	20.8	2.1
1983	6.2	71.9	19.8	2.1
1984	6.3	71.1	20.4	2.1

Source: Figures calculated from PlanEcon, 1986

7.5 Soviet Oil Exports to the CMEA Countries

The lowering of the growth rate of domestic oil consumption was the
result of a long-term planned policy, carried out over a period of years,
to free oil for the hard currency export market. By contrast, the
reallocation of oil deliveries away from the CMEA–6, although it
served the same purpose, was put into effect suddenly in late 1981.[8] The

[8] Although the statistics presented below treat the CMEA–6 in the aggregate, Romania is
significantly different from the other five countries (Bulgaria, Czechoslovakia, East Germany,
Hungary and Poland), since until 1975 it was a net exporter of oil, and specialized in the refining of
domestically produced crude oil, supplemented by imported crude oil. It continued, after 1975, to
engage in transit refining, depending heavily on imported crude oil from the Middle East, thus
apparently incurring substantial losses. Romania began to import from the Soviet Union in the
mid-1970s, but unlike the other CMEA countries it has always paid world market prices in hard
currency or hard goods.

significance of this event is better understood when placed in its historical context. After the first world oil price increase in 1973, the Soviet Union continued to subsidize the oil import bills of the East European countries for almost a decade, retaining the existing pricing formula for intra-CMEA trade (the five-year moving average of the world market prices for the guideline prices).[9] Marrese and Vanous, 1983, estimate that the East European countries benefited from the application of this formula to the tune of $33 billion between 1970 and 1978 as compared with only $3.3 billion between 1960 and 1969.[10]

Soviet exports of crude oil to the CMEA–6 countries increased from 44.4 million tonnes in 1972 to 72.6 million in the peak year 1980, and those of refined products from 4.5 million tonnes to 7.7 million in the corresponding years. During this period the share of the CMEA–6 in Soviet crude oil exports fluctuated between 55 and 60 per cent, recording a temporary drop in the years 1976–8, when exports to the West were stepped up in order to restore the hard currency balance on the external account.

In addition, since the Soviet Union either allowed the CMEA–6 to run substantial deficits or agreed to provide supplier credits in transferable roubles so as to soften the potential burden of the terms-of-trade changes, the impact of world oil price changes on Eastern Europe was considerably delayed.

The reasons for the long-standing willingness of the Soviet Union to mitigate the adverse effects of sudden changes in world energy prices on the CMEA countries are known to be primarily of a political nature. The Soviet Union obviously has a significant stake in the political stability of Eastern Europe, and was for a long time unwilling to risk the political repercussions of a possible 'energy crisis' in the form of either an increase in the domestic energy prices of these countries or a sudden deterioration of their hard currency trade balances. It has been said

[9] The sliding price formula (the 'Moscow Principle') was introduced in 1975, in response to rapid changes in the world market prices of many commodities. Previously, the intra-CMEA pricing formula had been based on the 'Bucharest Principle', which set guideline prices for each year based on world market prices in five previous years, the choice of which was itself a subject of annual negotiations between the Soviet Union and the CMEA partners.

[10] Others (e.g. Dietz, 1985; Balkay, 1985) obtain much more modest sums for the size of the Soviet subsidy than Marrese and Vanous. They assert that 'the small CMEA member countries' relative price advantages have in fact been considerably reduced by adverse changes in the price levels of their offsetting goods: these have made up for a substantial part of the income forgone by the CMEA's prime-commodity exporters.' Importantly, it is argued that '"subsidies" to the prime-commodity importers are *no inherent feature of the* [intra-CMEA] *pricing system*; rather, they are triggered by price hikes, if any, in the non-CMEA (world) market. In fact . . . intra-CMEA prices used to be *higher* till about 1973; also at times of declining commodity prices, the current pricing formula reverses the opportunity cost/forgone gains picture, starting a "subsidy" flow *from* the *importers towards* the *exporters* of primary commodities.' (Balkay, 1985, pp. 65, 67, *original emphasis*.)

that the Soviet Union accepted considerable economic losses in intra-CMEA energy trade in return for an economically and politically stable Eastern Europe and that it was a 'way of paying through economic relations for political gains' (Hewett, 1984b, p. 242). Up to the early 1980s it appeared that Soviet oil allocation policy towards the CMEA countries was firmly attached to this position. Although there had been variations in the *growth* rates of exports to these countries, until 1981 the Soviet Union never *reduced* its oil shipments to them in absolute terms in response to its own domestic economic considerations.

Only factors of a critical nature could change this long-standing Soviet position on oil allocation policy, but such a change was brought about in the autumn of 1981, when the Soviet Union unilaterally announced a 10 per cent reduction in future 'concessionary oil deliveries', apparently in a desperate search for an additional source of oil exports to the West. This caught the CMEA–6 countries by surprise, as they had been led to expect that Soviet oil deliveries would be held constant at the 1980 level.

Soviet crude oil exports to the CMEA countries were reduced by 8.6 per cent in one year, from 72.4 million tonnes in 1981 to 66.2 million in 1982. Further, it is estimated that approximately 10 per cent of these CMEA imports were purchased for hard currency at world market prices. These reduced shipments continued in the following years: crude oil exports to the CMEA–6 were 64.3 million tonnes in 1983 and 64.8 million in 1984, while shipments to the West grew by 25 per cent in each of these consecutive years, from 30.6 million tonnes in 1981 to 52.5 million in 1984 (see Table 7.4A).[11]

Soviet exports of refined products to the CMEA–6 countries were also reduced, from 7.3 million tonnes in 1981 to 6.3 million in 1982. This reduction of some 14 per cent followed a reduction of 5 per cent in the previous year. At the same time, exports of refined products to MDCs expanded from 24.4 million tonnes in 1981 to 34.3 million in 1983 (see Table 7.5A). The share of the CMEA–6 in Soviet exports of refined products had never exceeded its 1980 level of 20.6 per cent, since many of these countries possess well-established refining industries, which not only meet their domestic demand for products but also export to the West.[12] In 1981–4, however, the share of the CMEA–6 in

[11] The share of the CMEA–6 countries in Soviet crude oil exports dropped from 60 per cent in 1981 to 47 per cent in 1984. In contrast, the share of MDCs increased from 26 to 38 per cent (see Table 7.4B).

[12] For example, in the peak year, 1980, Bulgaria exported 2 million tonnes of refined products to the West; Czechoslovakia increased its exports of refined products to 1.1 million tonnes from less than 500,000 tonnes in 1977 and 1978; Hungary and Poland exported 500,000 and 1.3 million tonnes of oil products respectively to earn extra hard currency; and East Germany increased its

Soviet oil products exports had shrunk to 12–13 per cent, while that of MDCs climbed to 68 per cent at the peak in 1983.

This shift in the allocation of Soviet oil exports between the two regions in recent years may be taken as a reflection of the increasing pressure and heavier burden placed on the single export commodity – oil – to balance the external hard currency account of the Soviet economy over a relatively short period. The ever-rising marginal capital costs of oil production, in particular the soaring investment costs discussed earlier, must have been an important determinant of the new Soviet allocation policy. The other crucial factor was probably the Soviet Union's increased preference for financial independence from the West (see Chapter 5 above).

To stave off the immediate impact of this sudden change in policy on the CMEA countries, the Soviet Union allowed them to continue running large deficits in transferable roubles on their bilateral trade accounts. In assessing the impact with the benefit of hindsight, however, it can be seen that the subsidy element of Soviet oil deliveries to CMEA countries would have been gradually reduced in any case, because of the general reduction in world oil market prices.[13]

Nevertheless, the abrupt change in policy in such a sensitive area as the volume of oil supplies has surely had enduring consequences, in both real and psychological terms, for the economic relationships between the Soviet Union and its East European neighbours. The latter have suddenly woken up to realize that the 'umbrella' of Soviet protection is not necessarily available in times of hardship.

The immediate effects of this reduction in Soviet oil shipments varied from country to country, first because the Soviet Union differentiated among its East European allies in the application of the policy, and secondly because the energy positions of these countries, particularly the degrees of their economic dependence on imported Soviet oil, were significantly different.

The five European members of the CMEA that import significant

exports of oil products by one-third to 2.8 million tonnes in 1980, as it enjoyed a stable and profitable market for oil products in West Berlin. These products exports provided substantial hard currency proceeds to these countries. For example, Bulgaria derived 32.3 per cent of its total export revenue *vis-à-vis* the OECD countries from oil exports in 1980: for Czechoslovakia, East Germany, Hungary, Poland and Romania, the corresponding shares were 10.5, 22.7, 5.7, 5.0 and 39 per cent respectively (OECD, *Foreign Trade by Commodities, Series C*).

[13] According to Bethkenhagen, 1985, furthermore, the price formula adopted for intra-CMEA trade changed again in 1980. Since then, prices seem to have been calculated on the basis of average world market prices for the previous three years rather than five. If this is the case, by 1983 intra-CMEA clearing prices must have been higher than world market prices by nearly 10 per cent (Bethkenhagen, 1985, p. 186). It should be noted, however, that such a straightforward comparison of intra-CMEA and world market prices is not the criterion applied in practice in planning these countries' trade, since intra-CMEA trade also involves transactions in 'soft' goods.

volumes of oil from the Soviet Union were, in order of relative importance (1980–84): East Germany, Czechoslovakia, Poland, Bulgaria and Hungary (see Table 7.15). Romania, which was itself a net exporter of oil until 1975, has been importing small and fluctuating amounts of crude oil from the Soviet Union ever since, but these have rarely been more than 1.0–1.5 mtpa, and Romania can therefore be ignored in the context of this analysis.[14] Turning to the five other countries we note that between 1980 and 1984 Czechoslovakia and Hungary suffered the largest percentage cuts in their oil imports from the Soviet Union (13.5 and 12 per cent respectively); Bulgaria and East Germany, a slightly smaller reduction (about 11 per cent); and Poland the smallest relative cut (only 7.5 per cent).

The percentage reductions in Soviet oil exports to *Czechoslovakia* and *Hungary* were the largest, although the energy profiles of these two countries are markedly different. Hungary is a small oil producer while the oil deposits of Czechoslovakia are of negligible importance. Both countries are heavily dependent on the Soviet Union for oil imports, and both re-export some Soviet oil in order to obtain hard currency.[15] The main difference, however, is that the share of oil in the energy consumption mix is much smaller in Czechoslovakia (25 per cent in 1980), where domestic coal production is very significant, than in Hungary (35 per cent in 1980). It is believed that the latter incurred high adjustment costs as a result of the reduction in deliveries of Soviet oil in the early 1980s. Hungary was then facing a debt crisis, and tried to ease its balance-of-payments difficulties by increasing its bilateral trade with Middle Eastern countries, and then re-exporting some of its oil to the West to obtain much needed hard currency.

The Soviet Union reduced its oil exports to *Bulgaria* and *East Germany* by almost the same amount (about 11 per cent between 1980 and 1984), despite considerable differences in both the energy profiles and the economic structures of these two countries.

Bulgaria is the country in the CMEA–6 with the highest dependence on the Soviet Union for its energy requirements. In 1980 it imported 95 per cent of its oil consumption from the Soviet Union, as well as natural gas and electric power, so that its overall energy dependence on imports from the Soviet Union was 75 per cent. The share of oil in the energy consumption mix was also high (46 per cent in 1980) thanks to a significant programme of oil-for-coal substitution undertaken successfully in the 1960s and 1970s. Because of this dependence on oil, and particularly on imports from the Soviet Union, the Bulgarian economy was very vulnerable to adverse changes in Soviet oil export policy.

[14] See footnote 8 above.
[15] See footnote 12 above.

Table 7.15: Soviet Oil Exports to Eastern Europe. 1980–84. Million Tonnes.

	Bulgaria			Czechoslovakia			East Germany	Hungary			Poland		
	Crude	Products	Total	Crude	Products	Total	Crude	Crude	Products	Total	Crude	Products	Total
1980	12.7	2.4	15.1	18.5	0.5	19.0	19.3	7.3	1.8	9.1	13.3	3.0	16.3
1981	12.3	2.3	14.6	17.9	0.5	18.4	19.3	7.1	1.5	8.6	13.2	2.9	16.1
1982	11.5	2.2	13.7	16.7	0.5	16.8	18.0	6.8	1.5	8.3	13.2	2.1	15.3
1983	11.2	2.1	13.3	16.1	0.4	16.5	17.3	6.0	1.4	7.4	12.5	2.3	14.8
1984	11.2	2.2	13.4	16.0	0.4	16.4	17.3	6.5	1.5	8.0	12.9	2.2	15.1
% Reduction 1980–84			−11.3			−13.5	−11.0			−12.0			−7.5

Source: PlanEcon, 1986

Furthermore, Bulgaria used to re-export some of the Soviet oil at its disposal in order to earn hard currency. By greatly reducing the oil allocation to Bulgaria in the 1980s, the Soviet Union caused both energy and balance-of-payments problems. Bulgaria at first found it hard to make the necessary adjustments to domestic oil consumption. It increased instead the volume of its oil imports from the Middle East and paid for them in kind under new barter agreements. The Soviet Union also helped by increasing the supply of natural gas by 30 per cent over the period 1981–4.

In East Germany, the share of oil in the energy consumption mix is small thanks to significant production of coal. Oil never accounted for more than 20 per cent of energy consumption; and the overall energy dependence on imports from the Soviet Union is relatively low (28 per cent). Soviet oil exports to East Germany are entirely in the form of crude oil because it has sufficient refining capacity to meet its own needs. East Germany does not re-export Soviet crude as such but generates a surplus of petroleum products which it exports to the West. The forced reduction in oil imports from the Soviet Union naturally caused some adjustment problems, but it seems that they were less severe for East Germany than for the other CMEA countries surveyed here.

The Soviet Union cut its oil exports to *Poland* by the smallest percentage amount because its ally was then in the midst of a serious economic and financial crisis. It seems that the supply reduction was tailored to match a decline in oil consumption caused by the economic recession of the early 1980s and brought about by small adjustments in energy policy, and that the Soviet Union was careful not to impose a large additional burden.

However, the share of oil in Poland's energy consumption has never been very high: it increased from a mere 5 per cent in 1960 to just over 16 per cent in the late 1970s. Poland is a large producer, and indeed a net exporter, of high-quality hard coal. (In this respect it compares very favourably with East Germany, Czechoslovakia and Bulgaria, which mainly produce brown coal of much lower quality.) Poland's overall energy dependence on the Soviet Union is thus relatively low, indeed the lowest of the five CMEA countries considered here. Because of the severity of its current economic problems, however, Poland is probably more vulnerable to cuts than countries that are more dependent for their energy requirements, in relative terms, on imports of Soviet oil.

Poland imports both crude and products from the Soviet Union and does not re-export Soviet crude. The reduction in Soviet oil exports to Poland between 1980 and 1984 was mainly in products. (These exports declined by almost one-third from 3.0 million to 2.2 million tonnes while crude oil exports were reduced only slightly, from 13.3 million to 12.9 million tonnes in the respective years.)

It seems, therefore, that the Soviet Union reduced its oil exports to four of its East European allies in 1980–84 in roughly the same proportion, with the sole exception of Poland from this across-the-board cut. Because of differences in the energy profiles, degrees of energy dependence and economic circumstances of the four countries most affected, however, the similar proportional cuts in Soviet exports caused greater adjustment problems for some countries (Bulgaria and Hungary) than for others (Czechoslovakia and East Germany).

The aggregate indicators of the dependence of the CMEA–6 on Soviet imports are shown in Table 7.16, in order to show the effects of these cuts on the region as a whole. According to these indicators, the dependence of total domestic energy consumption in the CMEA–6 on Soviet supplies gradually increased from 10 per cent in the early 1960s to 29 per cent at the peak in 1981, but then declined by 2–3 per cent. The overall energy dependence of the region is not alarmingly high because domestically produced coal still accounts for more than 55 per cent of energy consumption, although the share of coal has been

Table 7.16: Energy and Oil Dependence of CMEA–6 Consumption on Imports from the Soviet Union. 1960–84. Percentage Shares.

	Total Energy	Oil
1960–64 (Average)	10.2	66.6
1965–9 (Average)	15.5	77.4
1970	17.8	74.4
1971	19.0	71.9
1972	20.3	72.8
1973	21.6	71.3
1974	23.2	74.7
1975	24.3	76.9
1976	24.7	75.7
1977	25.8	76.4
1978	25.6	74.5
1979	27.0	77.3
1980	28.8	81.6
1981	29.3	85.9
1982	27.6	81.4
1983	27.5	82.9
1984	27.7	82.9

Source: PlanEcon, 1986

Table 7.17: CMEA–6 Energy Balance: Percentage Shares of Fuels in Consumption. 1960–84.

	Coal	Oil	Gas	Primary Electricity	Other
1960–64 (Average)	82.1	9.2	6.1	1.1	1.5
1965–9 (Average)	74.1	14.3	3.9	1.4	1.3
1970	68.7	17.8	10.6	1.7	1.2
1971	67.0	19.1	11.0	1.8	1.2
1972	64.7	20.7	11.4	2.0	1.2
1973	62.5	22.5	11.9	2.1	1.0
1974	61.1	22.6	12.8	2.6	0.9
1975	60.3	22.6	13.6	2.6	0.9
1976	58.3	23.2	14.8	2.8	0.8
1977	57.5	24.0	14.7	3.0	0.8
1978	56.6	24.9	14.7	3.1	0.7
1979	56.6	24.2	14.9	3.5	0.7
1980	56.0	23.3	16.0	4.0	0.7
1981	55.5	22.5	16.8	4.4	0.8
1982	56.7	21.4	16.8	4.2	0.8
1983	56.7	20.6	17.4	4.6	0.9
1984	56.1	20.4	17.9	4.7	0.8

Source: PlanEcon, 1986

steadily declining from a level of over 80 per cent in the early 1960s (see Table 7.17).

For oil, however, the dependence of the region on imports from the Soviet Union is indeed high. It reached a peak of over 85 per cent in 1981, after increasing from an average level of about 67 per cent in the early 1960s (see Table 7.16). Moreover, the favourable terms available from the Soviet Union enabled the CMEA–6 to increase their oil consumption by almost 50 per cent, from 67.3 million tonnes in 1972 to 99.2 million in 1980. As shown in Table 7.7 above, the energy elasticities of these economies increased rather significantly after the first oil price shock, in contrast to those of the market economies in the West. Furthermore, the contribution of the conservation effect towards energy savings in these countries was even negative in 1973–80. As discussed earlier, the energy intensities of these economies were extremely high by international standards, given their comparative levels of development, which indicates that the countries concerned were effectively shielded from the first world-wide energy crisis.

The Soviet Union's reductions of oil deliveries to the CMEA–6 countries in the 1980s led to their 'real' energy crisis, forcing the authorities for the first time to make cut-backs in private consumption and to take various measures of thrift and austerity. Moreover, the timing of this 'energy crisis' was very unfortunate for them, since they were severely hit by a debt crisis at the same time. The two crises contributed significantly to the further slow-down of economic growth in the region.

In view of these experiences, the flexibility at the disposal of the Soviet planners in reallocating oil supplies between the East and West European markets became rather limited. It seems that there was a critical limit beyond which they could not go on pushing the East European partners into further austerity in order to earn hard currency for the Soviet Union's own needs. In this sense, Soviet planners' decisions on oil allocation are made in an environment of constant tension between the competing priorities of oil shipments to the CMEA countries and those to the Western markets (Jensen et al, 1983, p. 683).

In order to use oil exports for the management of balance-of-payments adjustments, Soviet planners have frequently reallocated oil supply among the three markets, fully utilizing their authority and control over allocation decisions. However, there are a number of specific constraints that planners encounter in dealing with the three markets, which they cannot afford to ignore, and which considerably reduce their freedom in allocation decisions. In this sense, the capacity of the Soviet Union to export oil to the West still depends in the last resort on its ability to increase production.

8 SOVIET OIL EXPORTS IN 1985–6

8.1 Introduction

1985 and 1986 witnessed important and, in some cases, sudden developments, which call for a separate analysis. There was a marked decline in Soviet oil production in 1985, an oil price collapse in 1986, and the Chernobyl accident in April 1986. These developments affected Soviet oil exports dramatically, and may bring about drastic changes in many parameters, fundamentally affecting planners' decisions on oil production and allocation in the future. At the same time they have brought many interesting features of the Soviet system into sharper focus, including certain basic aspects of planners' behaviour with respect to oil exports and the precarious nature of Soviet trade relationships with the West.

8.2 The Decline of Oil Production in 1985

After a slight decline in 1984 (0.6 per cent), Soviet oil production dropped by a further 2.9 per cent in 1985 (see Table 8.1). The causes of previous declines in Soviet oil production were manifold, and related to the earlier Soviet depletion policies discussed in Section 7.2. In 1984 and 1985, however, it was the particular problems encountered in the West Siberian oilfields (especially the Nizhnevartovsk fields of Tyumen province) that were mainly responsible for the industry's dismal performance. The West Siberian oilfields account for over 63 per cent of total Soviet oil production. Nevertheless, chronic shortages of equipment and spare parts and the low reliability of electricity supply to these oilfields, which suffer from repeated power interruptions, are said to have caused frequent stoppages of production.[1]

[1] For example, according to Soviet Press reports in late 1985 (*Ekonomicheskaya gazeta, Izvestia*), 'official plans for manufacturing spare parts for drilling equipment are not being met. The Ministry for Chemical Machinery fell 14.3 per cent short of plan in delivering spare parts for drilling and oilfield equipment and the Ministry for Heavy Machinery had a 24.9 per cent under-fulfilment. Even worse, however, the plans themselves do not meet the oil workers' needs.' *Pravda* criticized poor supply of equipment reporting that '20 million tonnes of output were lost because the Ministry for Chemical Machinery failed to install equipment for secondary recovery in 10 out of 11 sites where it was to be put into operation.'

Table 8.1: Soviet Oil Production: Volume and Growth Rates. 1983–6. Million
Tonnes.

	Volume				Growth Rate (%)	
	1983	1984	1985	1986	1984–5	1985–6
1Q	153.3	153.0	147.0	148.7	−3.92	1.16
2Q	153.7	154.0	148.0	153.2	−3.90	3.5
3Q	156.1	154.0	150.0	156.0	−2.60	4.0
4Q	152.9	152.0	150.0	157.1	−1.30	4.7
Annual	616.3	613.0	595.0	615.0	−2.94	3.36

Note: The figures quoted include gas condensate.
Source: *Ekonomicheskaya gazeta*, various issues

As drilling crews in the West Siberian oilfields spent considerable
time repairing equipment, instead of drilling new wells, existing
deposits were over-exploited and depleted at faster than optimal rates.
Coupled with the long delays in the delivery of equipment and the
installation of gaslift, this caused approximately 4,000 wells to be shut
down in West Siberia alone while awaiting repair or conversion to
pumping (EIU, 1985, No. 3, p. 25). Furthermore, the lack of basic
infrastructure, such as housing for workers in the oilfields, resulted in a
chronic and acute labour shortage.

In addition to these technical and organizational problems, which
had been building up over many years, oil production in West Siberia
in the first quarter of 1985 was particularly badly hit by one of the
coldest winters on record. It is reported that the temperatures recorded
in oilfields were too low for the installed waterflooding systems, which
were designed to keep working at temperatures as low as −40 °C.
These systems froze and disintegrated when the temperature fell to less
than −55 °C (EIU, 1985, No. 2, p. 26).

8.3 The Soviet Response to the 1985 Decline in Oil Production

(*a*) *Oil Allocation*. It is interesting to see how Soviet planners, faced with
a decline in domestic oil production of 18 million tonnes in 1985 (2.9
per cent), allocated the available supplies among the three destinations
(the internal market, the West and the CMEA–6). Our analysis will be
based on OECD/IEA sources since Soviet data on actual deliveries to
CMEA countries and domestic consumption in 1985 are not available
at the time of writing. According to the figures presented in Table 8.2,

Table 8.2: Soviet Oil Exports to OECD Countries. 1983–6. Thousand Tonnes.

		Crude Oil				Refined Products			
		Total OECD		OECD excluding Finland		Total OECD		OECD excluding Finland	
1983	1Q	7,152	(−3.8)	5,480	(−7.7)	6,600	(−1.4)	6,319	(−1.8)
	2Q	11,803	(10.2)	9,827	(10.8)	9,063	(5.5)	8,457	(4.4)
	3Q	13,244	(45.7)	10,739	(55.5)	8,572	(2.4)	7,489	(−1.0)
	4Q	12,436	(30.3)	9,722	(35.2)	9,069	(6.4)	8,275	(9.2)
Annual		44,635	(21.3)	35,768	(23.8)	33,304	(3.5)	30,540	(2.9)
1984	1Q	10,394	(45.3)	9,148	(66.9)	6,450	(−2.3)	5,917	(−6.4)
	2Q	12,913	(9.4)	10,562	(7.5)	7,721	(−14.8)	7,003	(−17.2)
	3Q	13,744	(3.8)	11,400	(6.2)	9,045	(5.5)	8,149	(8.8)
	4Q	12,577	(1.1)	10,976	(12.9)	8,598	(−5.2)	7,963	(3.9)
Annual		49,628	(11.2)	42,086	(17.7)	31,814	(−4.5)	29,032	(−4.9)
1985	1Q	3,978	(−61.7)	2,761	(−69.8)	4,939	(−23.4)	4,703	(−20.5)
	2Q	9,783	(−24.2)	7,682	(−27.3)	8,847	(14.6)	8,160	(16.5)
	3Q	14,427	(5.0)	12,929	(13.4)	8,590	(−5.0)	7,621	(−6.5)
	4Q	9,547	(−24.1)	7,147	(−34.9)	7,371	(−14.3)	6,579	(−17.4)
Annual		37,735	(−24.0)	30,519	(−27.5)	29,747	(−6.5)	27,063	(−6.8)
1986	1Q	4,863	(22.2)	3,038	(10.0)	6,343	(28.4)	5,881	(25.0)
	2Q	12,084	(23.5)	9,874	(28.5)	8,271	(−6.5)	7,654	(−6.2)
	3Q	14,923	(3.4)	12,429	(−3.9)	9,919	(15.5)	8,271	(8.5)
	4Q	13,858	(45.2)	11,470	(60.5)	7,839	(6.3)	7,043	(7.1)
Annual		45,728	(21.2)	36,811	(20.6)	32,372	(8.8)	28,849	(6.7)

Note: Figures in brackets are growth rates over the same period in the preceding year.
Source: OECD/IEA, various issues

the volume of crude oil exported to the OECD countries declined by 11.9 million tonnes in 1985 (24 per cent), compared with the peak level reached in 1984. This represents almost two-thirds of the decrease of oil production that occurred in 1985. There was a huge drop in exports of crude (6.4 million tonnes, or 62 per cent compared with the previous year) in the first quarter of 1985, when production and transportation were severely disrupted by the very cold weather. The decline in products exports was not so drastic: there was a reduction of just over 2 million tonnes (6.5 per cent) in 1985 as a whole from the 1984 level.

Preliminary estimates of Soviet oil imports in 1985 show a reduction of about 6 per cent from the 14 million tonnes attained in 1984 (PlanEcon, 1986). Obviously, the decline in world oil prices reduced the potential for sales of Soviet military hardware to the oil-exporting countries of the Middle East.

It is therefore clear that the adjustments to oil allocation necessitated by the 1985 decline in production fell mainly on export sales to the OECD countries. This episode clearly demonstrates that the small operational flexibility that planners had previously enjoyed in making oil allocation decisions had been exhausted by 1985.

In 1984, the planners nearly reached the limit, at least in the short run, of their ability to reduce oil deliveries to the domestic market and the CMEA countries. The easy phase of gas-for-oil substitution, concentrated mainly in the power stations, was over. As discussed earlier, energy conservation measures have not produced any significant savings to date. Therefore, planners were unable to reduce domestic oil consumption any further in response to the decline in oil production, and were also hindered by the inadequate stock of upgrading facilities in refineries and by the shortage of gas storage capacity. In fact, the extremely cold winter forced them to allocate more oil to domestic consumption, at a time when they would have preferred to allocate less.

The planners were also constrained *vis-à-vis* the CMEA countries, since they could not reduce deliveries to these countries significantly for fear of straining the relationships between the Soviet Union and its allies even further.

In these circumstances, Soviet planners had no option but to reduce the volume of oil exports to the West for a while, and wait for a recovery of oil production. Unlike many Western observers, they regarded the decline in oil output in 1984–5 as a temporary phenomenon and were optimistic about their ability to solve the production problems within a year or two.

Their decision to reduce oil exports to the West is better understood if we recall that the Soviet balance of payments had shown considerable improvement since 1981. By 1984, the Soviet Union enjoyed a favourable balance on both trade and capital accounts (see Chapters 5 and 6).

None the less, the consequences of the planners' decision to adjust the oil allocation by reducing oil exports to the West, at a time of declining world oil prices, were significant. According to Soviet sources (see Table 8.3), the value of total Soviet exports to the MDCs declined from 21.3 billion roubles in 1984 (about $26.2 billion at the official rate) to 18.6 billion roubles in 1985 (about $21.9 billion), a reduction of nearly 13 per cent in nominal terms. Most of this drastic decline in export earnings, which was largely due to the reduction in oil revenues, occurred in the first quarter of the year.

(*b*) *Other Trade Adjustments*. The planners reacted to this immediate shock by cutting imports from the West as early as the third quarter of

Table 8.3: Soviet Foreign Trade. 1984–6. Billion Foreign Trade Roubles.

		Socialist Countries		MDCs		MDCs excluding Finland		LDCs	
(a) Exports									
1984	1Q	10.1	(10.8)	4.6	(10.3)	4.2	(12.5)	2.4	(−2.6)
	2Q	10.8	(12.5)	5.7	(16.6)	4.9	(14.0)	2.3	(−11.6)
	3Q	10.2	(14.6)	5.5	(8.3)	4.8	(9.1)	2.8	(0.7)
	4Q	10.9	(7.9)	5.6	(−0.7)	5.0	(4.2)	3.5	(27.5)
Annual		42.1	(11.6)	21.3	(8.6)	19.2	(10.2)	10.9	(3.8)
1985	1Q	10.1	(0.0)	3.3	(−28.3)	2.9	(−31.0)	2.2	(−8.3)
	2Q	11.4	(5.6)	4.9	(−12.5)	4.3	(−12.2)	2.2	(−4.3)
	3Q	11.0	(7.8)	5.1	(−7.3)	4.6	(−4.2)	2.1	(−25.0)
	4Q	11.7	(7.3)	5.2	(−7.1)	4.6	(−8.0)	3.1	(−11.4)
Annual		44.3	(5.2)	18.6	(−12.7)	16.3	(−15.1)	9.6	(−11.9)
1986	1Q	10.9	(7.9)	3.2	(−3.0)	2.8	(−3.4)	2.1	(−4.5)
	2Q	11.6	(1.8)	3.4	(−30.6)	3.0	(−30.2)	2.0	(−9.1)
	3Q	11.1	(0.9)	3.1	(−40.4)	2.7	(−41.3)	1.9	(−38.7)
	4Q	12.1	(3.4)	3.4	(−34.6)	3.0	(−34.8)	3.6	(16.1)
Annual		45.7	(3.2)	13.1	(−29.6)	11.5	(−29.4)	9.6	(−0.7)
(b) Imports									
1984	1Q	9.6	(10.3)	4.6	(−14.8)	3.9	(−15.2)	1.8	(5.9)
	2Q	10.2	(15.9)	5.1	(0.4)	4.5	(2.3)	1.9	(−5.1)
	3Q	8.7	(10.1)	4.4	(10.9)	3.9	(14.7)	2.0	(4.8)
	4Q	9.7	(15.5)	5.5	(29.5)	5.0	(38.9)	1.8	(20.8)
Annual		38.2	(13.4)	19.6	(4.8)	17.3	(8.1)	7.5	(5.6)
1985	1Q	10.0	(4.2)	5.0	(8.7)	4.5	(15.4)	1.8	(0.0)
	2Q	11.6	(13.7)	5.7	(11.8)	4.9	(8.9)	2.1	(10.5)
	3Q	10.0	(14.9)	3.7	(−15.9)	3.1	(−20.5)	2.0	(0.0)
	4Q	10.6	(9.3)	4.8	(−12.7)	4.1	(−19.0)	1.7	(−5.6)
Annual		42.2	(10.5)	19.3	(−1.5)	16.6	(−4.0)	7.6	(1.3)
1986	1Q	10.3	(3.0)	4.4	(−12.0)	4.0	(−11.1)	1.4	(−22.2)
	2Q	11.4	(−1.7)	4.4	(−22.8)	3.8	(−22.4)	1.3	(−38.1)
	3Q	9.5	(−5.0)	3.4	(−9.5)	2.7	(−13.9)	1.1	(−45.0)
	4Q	10.6	(0.0)	3.7	(−22.9)	3.0	(−26.8)	1.1	(−35.3)
Annual		41.8	(−0.9)	15.9	(−17.8)	13.5	(−18.7)	4.9	(−36.0)

Note: Figures in brackets are growth rates over the same quarter in the preceding year.
Source: *VTSS*, monthly, various issues

1985,[2] and their efforts to reduce imports have continued ever since (see Table 8.3). A higher volume of grain production in 1985 (191.6 million tonnes compared with 170 million in 1984) helped to reduce the need for imports in the short run. However, as shown in Table 8.4, these reductions in imports could not offset the trade deficit completely, which amounted to almost 2.2 billion roubles in the first two quarters of 1985 (MDCs excluding Finland), and the external balance recorded an overall annual deficit of about 300 million roubles for the year as a whole. Some Western observers believe, however, that the Soviet trade deficit with the West in 1985 was much higher than the figure suggested by the Soviet source.

Table 8.4: Soviet Trade Balance with non-Socialist Countries. 1984–6. Million Foreign Trade Roubles.

		MDCs	*MDCs excluding Finland*	*LDCs*
1984	1Q	65	−179	587
	2Q	549	644	370
	3Q	1,128	1,191	813
	4Q	33	5	1,625
Annual		1,775	1,661	3,395
1985	1Q	−1,709	−1,577	354
	2Q	−731	−601	119
	3Q	1,381	1,445	143
	4Q	370	432	1,362
Annual		−689	−301	1,978
1986	1Q	−1,246	−1,181	674
	2Q	−1,058	−815	706
	3Q	−198	−17	806
	4Q	−215	78	2,470
Annual		−2,717	−1,935	4,656

Source: *VTSS*, monthly, various issues

To finance this deficit, the Soviet Union stepped up its capital borrowing. OECD studies estimate that the Soviet net debt increased to $19 billion in 1985 from $11.8 billion in 1984 (OECD, *Financial Market Trends*, March 1986), and the Soviet Union is also held to have increased its gold sales in 1985, despite the decline in world gold prices

[2] Imports from the OECD (excluding Finland) fell by more than 20 per cent on an annual basis.

in that year (the average price of gold fell from $360 per troy ounce in 1984 to $317 in 1985).

(*c*) *Attempts to Reverse the Oil Production Decline*. Soviet planners' attempts to reverse the declining trend of oil production started in 1985. The problems of the West Siberian oilfields were reported widely in the Press, poor management and organizational bottlenecks were severely and openly criticized, and this led the authorities to make new appointments of several middle- and high-ranking managers in the Ministry of the Oil Industry, in the supply industries, and in the regional production units. Visits by several senior politicians from Moscow, including Gorbachev's widely publicized visit to West Siberia, emphasized further to all concerned the strategic importance of oil production for the Soviet economy.

Investment in oil extraction was stepped up by 31 per cent in 1986 from the 1985 level. Most of the increase in investment was directed to the West Siberian oilfields (where investment had in fact been *reduced* in 1984), despite the very tight constraints on the availability of resources for investment in other sectors of the economy.

To alleviate the labour shortage, highly qualified and experienced oil workers from all over the Soviet Union (from the Volga–Urals region, the Bashkir and Tatar republics, and from Belorussia, Tadzhikistan, the Ukraine and Uzbekistan) were rushed into West Siberia as touring duty crews for drilling and repairs. Arriving with their own equipment, they helped to commission new deposits and repair existing wells in addition to building roads and laying pipelines. The provision of electricity to the oilfields was also improved with the commissioning of the Surgut No. 2 power station.

This new injection of money and labour on a large scale demonstrated the Soviet planners' determination to arrest the decline in oil production. These efforts, which began in 1985, produced some encouraging results in 1986. As shown in Table 8.1, after a small increase in oil production in the first quarter (1.2 per cent), there was a 3.5 per cent increase (on an annual basis) in the second quarter. Production rose further in the second half of 1986, yielding a total output of 615 million tonnes for the full year (see Table 8.1), which was almost as high as the level attained in 1983, and very close indeed to the plan target (99.7 per cent).

This recovery in oil production was reflected in the volume of oil shipments to the West in the first half of 1986. The level in the first quarter already showed some improvement over the disastrous first quarter of 1985 (see Table 8.2): crude oil exports to the OECD countries increased by 22 per cent (although this figure falls to 10 per cent if Finland is excluded). Nevertheless, the export volume of 4.9 million tonnes in the first quarter of 1986 was still below the levels attained in any first quarter in 1976–84, and less than half the export volume in the comparable period in 1984. This was not good enough, and the effort to induce a recovery of oil shipments in the West continued: the export volume in the second quarter of 1986 rose to the level of the corresponding quarter in 1983. Furthermore, exports of refined products made a remarkable recovery as early as the first quarter of 1986, when they regained their 1984 level after the difficulties experienced in 1985.

The performance of Soviet oil exports to the West in the first two quarters of 1986 reveals the planners' determination to respond to the slide in world oil prices and the deterioration in the hard currency trade balance by reallocating oil availabilities as they had done in the past. In 1985–6, however, they also mobilized resources to increase availabilities through higher oil production.

8.4 The Oil Price Collapse of 1986

The development that dominated the world oil market throughout 1986, i.e. the sharp decline in and high volatility of world market oil prices, had an enormous immediate impact and also a deep and lasting influence on Soviet oil trade policy in particular and foreign trade policy in general.

The sharp and sudden drop in world market oil prices resulted in a huge reduction in Soviet export earnings in 1986 to the tune of $6–7 billion. The position worsened with the depreciation of the dollar in 1985, which caused a further reduction in Soviet purchasing power in Europe. This contrasted unfavourably with the experience of the previous few years, during which the dollar had appreciated against the other major Western currencies. During the period 1981–5, the Soviet Union had not suffered any substantial loss from the gradual decline of oil prices (which are denominated in dollars), because it purchases most of its capital goods from Europe and Japan.

Furthermore, the oil price collapse brought about dramatic and permanent changes in the Soviet terms of trade *vis-à-vis* the Western countries, thus forcing Soviet planners to review the whole range of their trade and economic strategies. It painfully revealed to Soviet planners the precarious nature of the trade strategy they had pursued since the early 1970s of expanding the exchange of oil for Western technology and grain, and the heavy dependence of the Soviet economy on a single export commodity – oil.

Having realized belatedly the weakness of their trade structure, which involves such a heavy dependence on oil exports, Soviet planners are reported to have reorganized their foreign trade operations in the hope of expanding exports of manufactured goods in the future. In recognition of the importance of the Soviet Union's continued participation in the international division of labour with developing countries and countries in the West, a new organization, the State Foreign Economic Commission, has recently been set up, under the Council of Ministers. This new body is charged with the functions of directing the activity of the foreign economic ministries and departments.

It is reported that 'the measures designed to upgrade foreign economic activity are among the measures being undertaken in the USSR for the significant expansion of the rights and responsibilities of combines and enterprises and for their conversion to full self-financing and cost-accounting operations. These measures aim to increase the incentives for product manufacturers to expand the output of highly export-orientated goods and to use imported resources effectively. As from 1 January 1987, over twenty ministries and departments of the USSR, and seventy of the largest combines and enterprises, will have the right to carry out direct export–import operations.' (*Ekonomicheskaya gazeta*, October 1986.) This will affect only 6–7 per cent of Soviet trade, and the export of raw materials and the import of turnkey plants will continue to be handled directly by the Ministry of Foreign Trade, but it represents a significant departure from the principle of the state monopoly of foreign trade, which had always been applied very strictly in the past.

However, the effects of these changes on the structure of Soviet foreign trade will be slow to materialize. As Soviet planners have no other export commodities with which to replace oil in the near future, their most likely response in the short term is to try to increase the volume of oil exports to the West to compensate for the heavy loss of revenues resulting from the lower prices. Western experts predicted a huge increase in Soviet oil exports in 1986.

The high volatility of oil prices, manifested by large day-to-day fluctuations, has caused Soviet traders to adopt new pricing strategies in order to minimize their losses. It is reported that they quickly adopted netback pricing to protect the volume of their oil sales to the West against the competition of other exporters.

Further, the Soviet Union for the first time openly showed interest in supporting OPEC's attempts to stabilize oil prices, and responded positively in mid-1986 to an Iranian request for curbs on exports to back up OPEC's cuts in production. Western observers remained sceptical, however, regarding Soviet promises that exports to the

OECD would be cut by 100,000 b/d, from an unspecified level and for an unspecified period, as a symbolic political gesture. In fact, however, the Soviet Union's gesture was motivated by its own real interests, as it has much to lose from lower prices. Table 8.2 shows that the growth of exports to the West abated temporarily in the summer of 1986, when spot market prices fell below $10 per barrel. It is understood that Soviet planners feared the further impact on oil prices of aggressive supply policies. It was only in the fourth quarter that they resumed their export drive, when prices began to firm up on the world market. Exports of crude oil to the OECD in the fourth quarter rose to an all-time high, leading to a recovery for the year as a whole to above the level attained in 1983.

8.5 Chernobyl

A domestic event that shocked the Soviet leaders and people and indeed the whole world was the Chernobyl disaster in April 1986. In a sense, the accident is a reminder of the very tight circumstances of energy supply faced by the Soviet Union and the systematic pressures on its planned economy. It has been widely reported in the Soviet Press that regular maintenance service was often neglected in nuclear power stations because of overloading. The Chernobyl station had been operating at a capacity of 8,000 hours per year, compared with the norm of 6,500. Whatever the sequence of events that led directly to the disaster, the common Soviet practice of maintaining heavy workloads was certainly an indirect contributory cause.

Apart from concern about the real causes of the accident and the extent of casualties, there was much speculation about the immediate impact and long-term consequences of the accident for Soviet energy policy on production, consumption and trade, including the level of oil exports to the West. Initially, the discussion was dominated by the view that the Soviet Union would be forced to use more oil domestically and hence reduce (or be unable to increase) its oil exports to the West. However, as time passed by, it became clear that the impact of the Chernobyl accident on Soviet oil exports would be minimal.

Immediately after the accident, a shut-down of all fourteen reactors of the Chernobyl type (RBMK-1,000) was ordered, and this action temporarily reduced the supply of electricity by 7 per cent. This shortage, which fortunately occurred in the summer, was soon compensated by the increased use of gas and coal in thermal power stations, but it is significant that the use of oil for the generation of electricity was *not* increased. These fourteen reactors were soon brought back on stream at full capacity, except for Chernobyl itself, which had previously accounted for only 1.3 per cent of the total Soviet electricity generating capacity.

It is now generally agreed that the Chernobyl accident did not alter the Soviet Union's long-term plans for its energy supply mix. Within the Soviet Union, the accident was attributed mainly to human error, and the Soviet authorities are said to be satisfied with the fact that nearly all the 41,500 MW of new reactor capacity planned for the 1986–90 period is of the PWR type. These reactors are thought to be technically superior to RBMK reactors of the Chernobyl type, and safer to operate, incorporating containment domes as an integral part of their design.

Thus, the Soviet nuclear power programme is set to continue unabated, and it seems, for the moment at least, that Chernobyl will have little if any long-term effect on Soviet oil export policy. However, the accident may have indirect repercussions on the future pattern of Soviet oil allocation, if the other CMEA countries significantly alter their energy programmes by reducing their own dependence on nuclear power.

8.6 Soviet Oil Exports to the West in the Longer Term

When we turn to the longer-term prospects for Soviet oil exports to the West, forecasting becomes increasingly speculative. As mentioned earlier, Soviet oil exports to the West reflect planners' behaviour in three interrelated fields: foreign trade, national energy policy and allocation policy. These are areas of strategic importance, in which political factors play a decisive role. Predicting changes in any of these is hazardous, and it is therefore very difficult to make reliable forecasts of the future level of Soviet oil exports.

To complicate matters further, the entire Soviet economic system will shortly undergo a number of fundamental changes if the thorough and far-reaching economic reforms now being debated by the new leadership are implemented. This series of reforms may significantly alter the rules and factors that govern Soviet decisions on oil exports.

We expect, for example, that the future criteria for determining the level of oil production will differ considerably from the present ones. The Soviet Union is likely to become more concerned about its oil reserves. Proved reserves were estimated to be 8.3 billion tonnes at end 1985, equivalent to 14.0 years of output at the 1985 level. This ratio compares unfavourably not only with those of the major oil-producing countries of the Middle East but also with the estimated reserves/production ratios for gas and coal in the Soviet Union. The comparable proved reserves/output ratio for natural gas is 66.1 years (BP, 1986).

Soviet oil depletion policy the past was far from optimal. Since exploratory drilling was neglected in favour of development drilling, the rate of accretions to reserves was often outpaced by the rate of production. There is therefore now a real danger that the Soviet oil reserves position will worsen in the near future. More importantly, as discussed in Chapter 7 above, the main problem of the Soviet oil industry at present arises from the economic and technical difficulties encountered in the exploitation of existing reserves.

The oil price collapse of 1986 may also bring about significant changes in Soviet foreign trade policy and hence in the future development of oil trade. It will inevitably influence depletion policy, and the recent decline of oil prices in relation to the cost of imported goods undoubtedly raises serious questions about the economics of attempting to increase oil production in the face of soaring extraction and investment costs. The opportunity costs to the rest of the Soviet economy may be very high.

However, there is no strong evidence yet to show that oil production in the Soviet Union is a function of world market prices. We believe, therefore, that the efforts to maintain the current level of oil production are likely to continue, irrespective of world market prices, so long as the marginal extraction and investment costs of yielding an export surplus do not exceed the costs of providing for domestic needs by a wide margin.

The Soviet Union is probably determined to remain a net oil exporter for the foreseeable future. Judging from the 1986 experience, and assuming other things remain equal, the Soviet Union will not allow oil production to drop far below 600 mtpa. This is less than the planned target for 1990 of 625–640 million tonnes but would still be higher than the levels forecast by many Western experts. Soviet planners are more optimistic: the new head of *Gosplan*, Nikolai Talyzin, has announced a plan target of 617 million tonnes of oil production for 1987.[3] Western experts think that this level of production is not sustainable over the longer term. Even if production does not meet the planned target levels, oil exports may be sustained as a result of successful measures of energy saving. The 1986–90 five year plan incorporates an ambitious energy savings plan: annual savings of 200–230 mtoe are to be achieved, with 64 per cent of the increase in domestic energy demand being met through savings. The plan aims to reduce the energy intensity of NMP by 7–9 per cent by 1990.

The Soviet Union may remain an important exporter of oil to the

---

[3] *Financial Times*, 18 November 1986.

West for some years to come, provided that oil production, energy savings and investment in refinery upgrading capacity do not fall too far short of their plan targets. The expectation of continued growth in gas production and a healthy recovery in coal production reinforce this conclusion.

9 SOVIET OIL EXPORTS TO THE WEST: AN ECONOMETRIC ANALYSIS

9.1 Introduction

In Chapters 5 and 6, we examined the Soviet planners' *need* to use oil exports to the West for purposes of *short-run* balance-of-payments adjustments. In Chapter 7 we discussed the *constraints* that planners encounter in pursuing an oil export policy with a trade adjustment objective. We now attempt to examine the actual outcome of the interplay of the *need* and the *constraints* as it is manifested by the actual behaviour of Soviet oil exports. The method followed is to estimate oil export supply functions.

A number of studies in recent years have modelled the foreign trade flows of centrally planned economies (Burkett et al, 1981; Charemza and Gronicki, 1987 forthcoming). These focus on the interactions between the foreign trade sector and other macroeconomic variables at the aggregate level. They usually address the question of how foreign trade flows (import and export volumes) are adjusted to restore both internal and external balance in the CPEs. For this purpose, the export supply and import demand equations are construed as the planners' equilibriating mechanism, and modelled and estimated accordingly. For example, in Burkett et al, 1981, current volumes of exports and imports are related to four key determinants: domestic output, foreign trade prices, the balance-of-trade target and the requirements of the internal balance.

As discussed in Chapters 5 and 6, the role of oil exports in the equilibriating mechanism of the Soviet economy has increased markedly over the last fifteen years, as external and internal disturbances not foreseen in the medium-term planning stages (the five year plans) have become larger and more frequent, and have required sizeable *annual* adjustments of trade flows. We suggested in Chapter 6 that the fluctuations in Soviet oil shipments to the West revealed by the trade statistics may be partly explained by the planners' need to use oil exports as a critical instrument for the adjustment of real trade flows needed to restore the external balance.

9.2 The Model

In order to test this hypothesis, we shall model Soviet oil export supply as a planners' behavioural equation, adopting Burkett et al's specification of the export supply function.

Accordingly, the volume of oil exported to the West in period t, X_t^s, is a function of lagged hard currency trade balances TB_{t-i} and world market oil prices P_{t-i} (or rather the terms of trade TOT_{t-i}) and so on. At the same time, the amounts of oil available to planners for balance-of-payments adjustments are limited by the levels of oil production Y_{t-i}, and by other exogenous factors, including those affecting planners' decisions on oil allocations Z_{t-i}. Therefore, an oil export supply function can be expressed as:

$$X_t^s = X^s \, (TB_{t-i}, \, P_{t-i} \, (\text{or } TOT_{t-i}), \, Y_{t-i}, \, Z_{t-i}) \qquad (9.1)$$

$$i = 0, \ldots, k$$

$$(i > 0 \text{ for } TB_{t-i})$$

In this general form, the subscripts $t-i$ represent an unknown lag structure for the variables.[1] A simple way to convert this to a regression equation with a specified lag structure is to introduce a Koyck distributed-lag model.

The second and perhaps more realistic way is to construct a partial adjustment model. As we discussed in Chapter 7, Soviet planners, faced with severe difficulties in increasing oil production, have tried to generate some flexibility in the allocation of export supplies to the three destinations, but do not have much room for manoeuvre. Supplies to the three main markets are determined by a number of factors, many of which are subject to rigidities. Similarly, there may be some constraints on the demand for Soviet oil in these markets.

Though supply constraints are partially dealt with in equation 9.1, the effects of constraints arising on both supply and demand sides are more effectively captured in the partial adjustment model, in which the actual change in the export volume $X_t - X_{t-1}$ is expressed as a fraction

---

[1] Since oil is such a dominant export commodity in Soviet trade with the West, we might expect a high correlation between the two explanatory variables in our model, i.e. the trade balance TB_{t-i} and the price index (PI_{t-i} or TOT_{t-i}). An estimation of simple contemporaneous correlations using annual data yields correlation coefficients of 0.45 between TB_t and PI_t and 0.42 between TB_t and TOT_t. These values are somewhat lower than expected, which may imply that planners adjust trade flows relatively quickly in response to price changes. In fact, this point will be confirmed by our regression results presented below. In any event, the potential problem of multicollinearity among the independent variables is avoided in our estimations, since we use the *lagged* trade balance, not the *current* one.

of the change required by the planners to adjust the trade balance $X_t^s - X_{t-1}$. Thus:

$$X_t - X_{t-1} = \delta(X_t^s - X_{t-1}); \ 0 < \delta < 1 \tag{9.2}$$

where X_t^s is the level of oil exports desired by the planners in period t in the absence of constraints.

Combining the two equations, 9.1 and 9.2, we obtain a regression equation with a lagged dependent variable, whose functional form is similar to that of the Koyck distributed-lag model.

The oil export equation thus specified is estimated with both annual data (1970–84) and quarterly data (4Q76–4Q84) for crude oil and refined products separately.[2] As shown in Figure 6.1 above, Soviet oil exports of crude and products have followed different historical patterns. This is explained by the planners' use of different decision rules for crude and for products.

9.3 Estimation Results for Crude Oil Exports

After some experiments with different sets of variables and lag structures, the estimation results presented in Table 9.1 are taken to represent the export equations of crude oil to the West.

The dependent variable CO_t is Soviet crude oil exports to the OECD countries (excluding Finland) in million tonnes per annum. In equations (1)–(3) and (7), the lagged hard currency trade balance TB_{t-1} is the Soviet trade balance with MDCs (excluding Finland) lagged by one year. In equations (4)–(6), TB_{t-1} is the trade balance with *all* non-Socialist countries (MDCs and LDCs), also lagged by one year.

These trade balances are expressed in three different ways: in million roubles, in million dollars converted from roubles at the official exchange rate, and as a normalized trade balance, obtained by dividing the nominal trade balance by exports in the corresponding year as suggested by Hewett, 1983a. The model is then estimated with these different expressions of the trade balance in order to identify the indicators of the trade balance to which planners are most likely to respond. If our hypothesis is correct, the expected sign of the estimated coefficient of the variable representing this indicator is negative. Other relevant variables relating to the Soviet balance of payments such as debt indicators are not included, because no consistent time-series are available.

---

[2] The OECD/IEA statistics do not report reliable quarterly data on Soviet exports to the member countries until the fourth quarter of 1976, which limits the number of observations available for our regression analysis.

Table 9.1: Estimation Results of the Export Equation for Crude Oil (Annual Data). 1970–84 (15 Observations). Dependent Variable: CO_t

Trade Balance TB_{t-1}	Constant	CO_{t-1}	TB_{t-1}	PI_t	TOT_t	t^2	$\bar{R}^2$	DWS	$\zeta(1)$
(1) TBR_{t-1}	8.84 (3.28)	0.319 (2.08)	−0.0021 (−3.51)	−0.211 (−4.43)		0.17 (6.26)	0.94	1.94	0.17
(2) TBU_{t-1}	9.07 (3.40)	0.313 (2.05)	−0.0015 (−3.55)	−0.215 (−4.51)		0.17 (6.32)	0.94	1.95	0.16
(3) TBC_{t-1}	6.86 (1.93)	0.396 (2.16)	−0.105 (−2.35)	−0.169 (−3.04)		0.15 (4.80)	0.92	1.60	1.03
(4) $TTBR_{t-1}$	7.71 (2.58)	0.48 (2.91)	−0.0016 (−3.07)	−2.03 (−4.00)		0.17 (5.79)	0.93	2.21	0.34
(5) $TTBU_{t-1}$	7.42 (2.45)	0.501 (2.96)	−0.0012 (−3.06)	−0.194 (−3.86)		0.17 (5.72)	0.93	2.24	0.44
(6) $TTBC_{t-1}$	8.15 (2.68)	0.507 (2.91)	−0.161 (−2.90)	−0.173 (−3.39)		0.14 (4.87)	0.93	1.91	0.05
(7) TBR_{t-1}	14.11 (4.53)	0.196 (1.26)	−0.0027 (−4.30)		−0.270 (−4.67)	0.20 (6.32)	0.94	1.67	0.68

Notes: (a) Figures in brackets are t-statistics.
(b) $\zeta(1)$ is L–M test statistic for first-order autocorrelation. The critical value of $x^2_{1,\,0.95}$ is 3.84.
(c) Definitions of variables and data sources are given in Appendix 4.

PI$_t$ is the world market oil price index, i.e. the average oil price index (1980 = 100) of major fuel-exporting countries as reported in IMF statistics. Since the price vector is an exogenous variable in the model, we cannot use the price index of Soviet oil. The average world oil price index seems to be a more appropriate variable for our purposes than the price indices of specific non-Soviet crudes. *TOT$_t$* is the terms-of-trade index (1980 = 100), computed as a ratio of the oil price index to the import price index, calculated here as the weighted average of the US wheat price index and the unit value index of manufactured exports of the developed market economies. As mentioned above, the expected sign of the estimated coefficient of *PI$_t$* or *TOT$_t$* is negative if planners are thought to follow an anti-mercantilist policy.

The results shown in Table 9.1 reveal that the coefficients of all explanatory variables are of the expected sign, and support our hypothesis that Soviet oil exports to the West increase (decrease) with the deterioration (improvement) of the trade balance with the West. For instance, according to the result shown in equation (1) of Table 9.1, if all other variables are held constant, a deterioration of the trade balance by 1 billion roubles in year $t-1$ leads to an increase of crude oil exports by 2.1 million tonnes in year t.

Furthermore, a one-point increase in the world oil price index in year t results in a drop of shipments of crude oil to the West by 211,000 tonnes in the same year. A re-estimation of equation (1) of Table 9.1, using ln *CO$_t$* and ln *PI$_t$* instead of *CO$_t$* and *PI$_t$*, yields an estimate of the short-run price elasticity of crude exports of -0.645.[3] Our estimate of the price elasticity falls within the expected range of values suggested by the literature on the foreign trade of the CPEs. The negative sign is consistent with the hypothesis of a backward-bending export supply curve. Our estimate of the short-run elasticity has an absolute value of less than 1, and does not correspond exactly to the view of Holzman, 1968, that there is a one-to-one relationship between a rise in export prices and an associated decline in export volume. Our estimate probably reflects supply constraints, short-run oil market rigidities and the asymmetry of planners' responses to rises and falls in oil prices. When the oil price rises they do not compensate fully for the change by reducing export volumes in a proportionate manner. Thus they are able to finance an upward revision of their import plans when this occurs.

[3] The estimation result thus obtained is as follows:

$$\ln CO_t = 3.003 + 0.10 \ln CO_{t-1} - 0.00015 \; TBR_{t-1} - 0.645 \ln PI_t + 0.217 \; t$$
$$\quad\;\; (5.71) \quad (0.63) \qquad\quad (-4.11) \qquad\qquad (-4.83) \qquad\quad (5.87)$$

$$\bar{R}^2 = 0.91, \; DWS = 1.60, \; Z(1) = 1.39$$

The negative coefficient of PI_t, which implies a backward-bending supply curve of Soviet *exports* to the West, should not be taken as evidence supporting the 'backward-bending supply' hypothesis mentioned but refuted by Hewett, 1984a, p. 46. This hypothesis argues that planners cut both production *and* exports, when oil prices rise on world markets. Yet, as we have seen earlier, Soviet oil production is believed to be unresponsive to changes in world oil prices. Stagnant oil production is a sign of the difficulties encountered by the oil industry in the supply-constrained Soviet economy. It can therefore be argued instead that it is precisely *because* of the severity of production problems and the tight supply schedules that Soviet oil exports to the West display the features of a backward-bending supply curve.

In order to compare the size of the price and lagged trade balance effects on oil exports, we have computed the beta coefficients $\beta_{PI(t)}$ and $\beta_{TB(t-1)}$. The results of the estimation are $\beta_{PI(t)} = -0.91$ and $\beta_{TB(t-1)} = -0.30$. Thus, in terms of beta coefficients, that is in standard deviation units, the price effect is three times as large as the nominal trade balance effect.

The estimated coefficient of the lagged dependent variable in this specification, λ, can either be used to calculate an adjustment coefficient of the model, $\delta = 1 - \lambda$, or viewed as a geometric weight for the distributed-lag model. As an adjustment coefficent, the estimated value, $\delta = 1 - 0.32 = 0.68$, indicates that, despite the presence of various constraints, Soviet planners, by and large, manage to adjust the volume of oil exports to the West each year in accordance with their planned targets for the external balance. Alternatively, the relatively small value, $\lambda = 0.32$, interpreted as the distributed-lag coefficient, suggests relatively swift quantity adjustments of oil exports in response to planners' objectives. In both cases the estimated coefficient supports our view that the real trade flow adjustments the planners seek to achieve through changes in the level of oil exports are of a *short-term* nature, i.e. they are annual adjustments. This point is also supported by the results of other regressions in which we introduced longer lags for the explanatory variables: the coefficients on these longer lags were insignificant in all cases.

The long-run growth trend of crude oil exports is captured with a polynomial regression on time t (1969 = 1).[4] The coefficient on t

---

[4] In order to control the effects of trends common to the different time-series more effectively and have a cross-check of the underlying relationships between the variables, the export equations are also estimated in first-difference form. The results show that the functional relationships in the model are upheld well: the changes in two key variables – the export price, in both nominal and relative terms, and the lagged trade balance – explain well over 50 per cent of the variation in the changes in the export volume of crude oil.

turned out to be positive but insignificant in this specification, but the coefficient on t^2 is highly significant, indicating that growth rates have been increasing in recent years.

Our tests also included oil production as a regressor, using data published in *Ekonomicheskaya gazeta*, in order to test the significance of the level of domestic oil production in determining the flow of oil to the West. However, as might be expected from our earlier discussion, both current and lagged production proved to be insignificant statistically. This confirms our view that the level of oil production does not have a significant influence on the annual fluctuations of crude oil shipments to the West, so long as production is above the critical level that yields an export surplus sufficient to allow the necessary adjustments to be made by means of allocation policy.

As argued in Chapter 7, the increases in oil exports to the West, particularly after production began to stagnate in the late 1970s, were facilitated on the one hand by a greater flexibility in the allocation of oil to the three main markets and, on the other hand, by changes in the volume of oil imported into the Soviet Union from OPEC countries.

To test this explicitly, the volume of total Soviet oil imports and the volume of Soviet exports to the CMEA countries were alternately introduced into the model as additional explanatory variables. However, both variables were found to be statistically insignificant. This may be explained partly by the fact that the allocation policy has not been consistent throughout the estimation period 1970–84. The allocation policy has shifted over time from one of favouring subsidized deliveries to the CMEA countries to one of seeking higher hard currency earnings from oil exports to the West. The insignificance of the coefficients of these variables may also be explained statistically. Variations in these variables may reflect the same factors that cause changes in the dependent variable. Hewett, 1983a, for example, shows that Soviet primary product shipments to the CMEA area increase when the lagged hard currency trade balance improves.

The other important variable that exerts a significant influence on Soviet oil allocation, i.e. domestic consumption, is not tested in our analysis, since the only available data are those for *apparent* consumption, which is derived as a residual by subtracting net exports from production.

We conduct further tests with the model, using different concepts of the hard currency trade balance. We use measures of the trade balance in dollars TBU_{t-1} and the ratio of the trade balance to export capacity TBC_{t-1} instead of TBR_{t-1}. The estimates are shown as equations (2) and (3) of Table 9.1. These results show that the volume of crude oil exported to the West changes more in response to the lagged hard currency trade balance in nominal terms than to the balance measured relative to export capacity.

We then carry out further tests, using the trade balances with *all* non-Socialist countries ($TTBR_{t-1}$, $TTBU_{t-1}$, $TTBC_{t-1}$) instead of those with only the industrialized West. The results are reported in Table 9.1 as equations (4)–(6). These results are similar to the estimates obtained from the earlier regressions with TBR_{t-1}, TBU_{t-1} and TBC_{t-1} respectively. When the trade balances are expressed in nominal terms, the estimates of the coefficients of the trade balance and price variables are marginally smaller than those in the corresponding earlier equations. This suggests that planners are more sensitive to the trade balance with the industrialized West, with which transactions are settled in hard currency. However, a comparison of equations (3) and (6) indicates that planners take a more global stance towards the adjustment of oil export volumes to the lagged trade balance when this is measured in real terms.

The estimates of the coefficients λ on CO_{t-1} are, however, higher and more significant, in all cases, which shows that the export volume of crude to the West is adjusted more slowly in response to changes in the trade balance with *all* non-Socialist countries than in response to changes in the trade balance with the industrialized West *alone*.

As argued in Chapter 5 above, planners in charge of foreign trade flows, both imports and exports, are more likely to respond to the price of oil exports relative to imports than to the oil export price in nominal (dollar) terms. In order to test this proposition we construct an oil terms-of-trade index TOT_t, a ratio of the oil price and aggregate import price indices (for details see Appendix 4). We then estimate the model using TOT_t instead of PI_t, and the results are shown in Table 9.1 as equation (7). This confirms that the level of Soviet crude oil exports is negatively correlated with the Soviet terms of trade: improved purchasing power of oil (increased TOT_t) leads to a reduction in the volume of crude oil deliveries to the West, and deteriorating terms of trade induce attempts to stem the decline in revenue through an increase in the volume of oil exports. However, the estimated supply elasticity with respect to relative prices is not very different from the price elasticities obtained from the other equations, mainly because the terms-of-trade index is constructed with the oil price index for the estimated period as the numerator (see Figure 9.1).

Since the number of observations is limited, a more sophisticated specification of the dynamic structure is precluded. However, we attempt to construct a simple 'error correction (feedback)' model as suggested by Davidson et al, 1978, in which steady-state long-run equilibrium relationships between variables are modelled explicitly.

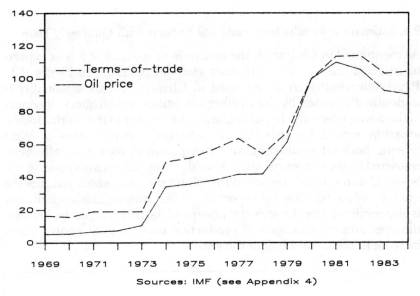

Figure 9.1 Oil Price and Terms-of-Trade Indices. 1969–84 (1980 = 100).

In order to avoid scaling problems, all variables are now expressed in natural logarithms, and the trade balance is expressed in ratio form. Thus $\ln TB_t = \ln EX_t - \ln IM_t$, where EX_t and IM_t represent Soviet exports to and imports from the MDCs respectively. An estimation of a simple version of the feedback model, which incorporates a long-run equilibrium relationship between crude exports and the lagged trade balance, $CO_t^* = kTB_{t-1}^*$, yields the following:

$$\Delta_1 \ln CO_t = 0.798 - 0.420\Delta_1 \ln TB_{t-1} - 0.186\,(\ln CO_{t-1} - \ln TB_{t-2})$$
$$ (2.03)(-1.93) \phantom{- 0.420\Delta_1 \ln TB_{t-1}} (-1.53)$$

$$-0.640\Delta_1 \ln PI_t \qquad\qquad (9.3)$$
$$(-4.90)$$

$\bar{R}^2 = 0.78,\ DWS = 1.48,\ \zeta(1) = 1.11$

The basic relationships between the variables presented in Table 9.1 are thus upheld by this specification. Furthermore, the finding that the estimated coefficient on the proportionate term ($\ln CO_{t-1} - \ln TB_{t-2}$) is statistically insignificant confirms our earlier interpretation of the oil export equation: that it reflects the planners' *short-run (annual) adjustment mechanism*, i.e. the process whereby planners try to equilibriate the external balance by adjusting the annual volume of crude oil exports to the West.

9.4 Estimation Results for Crude Oil Exports with Quarterly Data

As mentioned in Chapter 3, the quarterly time-series of Soviet exports of crude oil exhibit a very distinct seasonal pattern (see Figure 9.2). Regression results are as reported in Chapter 3. This seasonality is undoubtedly caused by the weather conditions, which affect all sectors of the Soviet economy. In particular, as the frontier of the oil-producing area has moved towards the more hostile climatic zones of West Siberia, both oil production and transportation have naturally been restricted in the winter months. Also, domestic oil consumption in the Soviet Union is much higher in the winter months, which reduces the quantity of oil available for export in the first quarter. This seasonality is also reinforced by the seasonal pattern of the planning cycle, because the pressures on managers of production units to fulfil annual plans increase in the second half of the year.

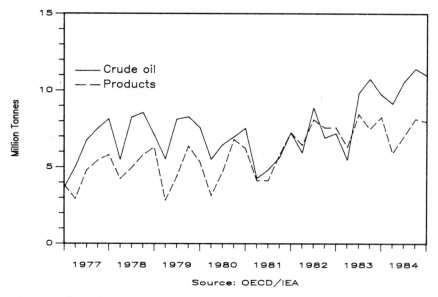

Figure 9.2 Soviet Exports of Crude Oil and Refined Products to the OECD (excluding Finland). 4Q76–4Q84.

The other key explanatory variables, i.e. Soviet trade balances, also exhibit a clear seasonal pattern (see Figure 9.3 and Table 9.2).

Following the data-based inference method suggested by Hendry (Davidson et al, 1978; Hendry, 1979), and after a number of experiments with different lags, we obtain a better specification for controlling these seasonalities by transforming the variables into four-quarter

Table 9.2: Seasonal Patterns of Soviet Trade Balance with the West (Quarterly Data). 4Q76–4Q84 (33 Observations). Dependent Variable: *TBR*

Constant	1Q	2Q	4Q	t (Trend)	$\bar{R}^2$	DWS	Mean of Dependent Variable
95.0 (0.50)	−1,554.7 (−7.83)	−890.2 (−4.49)	−298.5 (−1.55)	30.7 (4.23)	0.77	1.25	−57.2

Note: Figures in brackets are *t*-statistics.

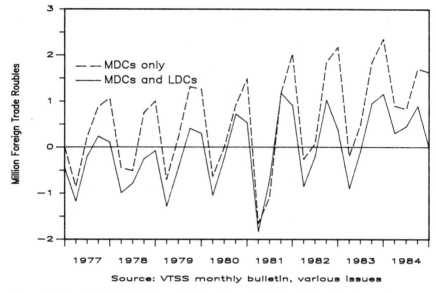

Source: VTSS monthly bulletin, various issues

Figure 9.3 Soviet Trade Balance with the West (excluding Finland). 4Q76–4Q84.

(annual) differences, $\Delta_4 \ X_t \ = \ X_t \ - \ X_{t-4}$, which capture an *annual* planning cycle effect.

Estimations of the error correction model discussed earlier (see equation 9.3), using quarterly data, yield the results shown in Table 9.3. In equation (1) the estimation is performed using the series of official prices for Arabian Light, and in equation (2) the terms-of-trade index discussed above is used. In both cases, once the seasonality of the variables is controlled, these estimations using quarterly data confirm the general Soviet export pattern of crude oil in relation to the two key explanatory variables as revealed by the annual data, and provide support for our hypothesis.[5] Thus the differences that emerge between the results obtained with annual and quarterly data, e.g. the implied larger stabilizing feedback effects between the volume of crude exports and the lagged trade balance, probably reflect the difference in the estimation periods. Unfortunately, the model as formulated above

---

[5] As before, oil production is shown to have little influence on the export volume, once the seasonality is controlled. Furthermore, in place of the series of official prices, a series of spot prices taken from the *OPEC Bulletin* was also tried, and this showed that Soviet foreign trade planners adjust the export volume marginally more in response to movements of official prices than in response to those of spot prices. In place of the variations in the quarterly trade balance, the accumulated trade balances over the preceding four quarters were also modelled. However, when we carried out tests with different lags, going as far back as we could without losing too many observations, this stock variable in any transformed form remained insignificant.

Table 9.3: Estimation Results of Export Equation for Crude Oil (Quarterly Data). 4Q78–4Q84 (25 Observations). Dependent Variable: $\Delta_4 \ln CO_t$

	Constant	$\Delta_4 \ln TB_{t-4}$	$\ln CO_{t-4} - \ln TB_{t-8}$	$\Delta_4 \ln PO_t$	$\Delta_4 \ln TOT_t$	$\bar{R}^2$	DWS	$\zeta(1)$
(1)	0.80 (2.49)	−0.52 (−2.16)	−0.31 (−2.01)	−0.36 (−2.40)		0.56	1.23	3.59
(2)	0.88 (2.97)	−0.45 (−1.88)	−0.37 (−2.53)		−0.42 (−2.41)	0.56	1.16	4.12

Note: Figures in brackets are t-statistics.

cannot reflect any ability planners might have to respond to changes in external factors on a quarterly basis. Nevertheless, we believe this formulation is valid on the grounds that the annual cycle is the shortest in the Soviet system in which major planning decisions are clearly manifested.

In summarizing our regression results for *crude oil* exports, we may conclude that the 'balance-of-payments adjustments' model can explain to a great extent the annual fluctuations in Soviet crude oil shipments to the West. The burden placed on crude oil exports to effect trade adjustments in the Soviet economy appears to be considerable, simply because there are no other flexible export commodities that can be used.

Faced with stagnation in oil production and falling oil prices in the 1980s, the planners needed oil for export quantity adjustments and had to seek supply flexibility somewhere in their severely supply-constrained economic system. The required flexibility was in the end created by a change in the allocation of oil supplies, i.e. by a reduction of crude oil shipments to the CMEA countries and a stabilization of the levels of refinery throughput for domestic consumption. This second measure was made possible largely by implementing the gas-for-oil substitution programme at a faster rate. Additional flexibility was also gained by the negotiation of arms-for-oil (or technology-for-oil) deals with Arab countries. Thus, despite several constraints restricting planners' allocation decisions, they appear in retrospect to have succeeded in the use of crude oil exports as a key instrument for the annual adjustment of the external trade balance with the hard currency area.

Furthermore, the pro-cyclical pattern of Soviet oil supply to the West, analysed in this chapter, points to its *potentially* destabilizing influence on the world oil market. On the one hand, when the oil price increases, i.e. excess demand prevails on the world market, the Soviet Union tends to reduce its supply, as its revenue requirement is fulfilled with a smaller volume of exports. This downward quantity adjustment is explained by the anti-mercantilist stance that has characterized planners' decision rules on foreign trade in the past. On the other hand, when excess supply pushes oil prices down, the Soviet Union tries to prevent its revenue from falling by increasing oil shipments to the world market. This appears to provide some justification for the common belief that the impact of Soviet exports on the market may be disproportionately large in relation to its actual market share. Historically, the Soviet Union, as one of larger non-OPEC oil exporters, was frequently blamed by the other suppliers for destabilizing the market (by the major oil companies in the 1960s and by OPEC more recently), when they were trying to arrest downward price movements.

However, it should be noted that the *potentially* destabilizing influence of Soviet oil supplies can only be translated into a real threat to the world market's stability if two further conditions are met: first, the adjustments to Soviet export prices required for the achievement of planned revenue targets must be substantial and unpredictable; secondly, the Western oil market must itself be volatile and incapable of absorbing extra supplies easily.

9.5 Estimation Results for Refined Oil Products Exports

As shown in Chapter 3, refined oil products have shown far less variation in their export volume than crude oil exports. The standard deviation of refined products exports to the West was 5.47 million tonnes, compared with a figure of 8.93 million for crude oil exports in the period 1970–84.

Furthermore, the export pattern of refined products is, as expected, not explained by our 'balance-of-payments adjustments' model. Our regression analysis shows that neither the lagged trade balances nor the time trend are significant in any of the various specifications of the model that we attempted to estimate.

The estimation results for Soviet products exports using annual data are reported in Table 9.4. The coefficients of the current oil price variable turn out to be negative, but insignificant, and are therefore omitted from the reported regressions.

The results in equation (1) of Table 9.4 show some evidence that, in contrast with that of crude oil exports, the export volume of products in year t responds positively to world petroleum prices with a one-year lag, though the price elasticity is small.[6] Price data used for this analysis are, however, crude oil prices, rather than aggregate product prices weighted with the volumes of the separate products traded. We are assuming, therefore, either that the two price series move closely together or that products prices adjust to crude prices within a year. The coefficient of the lagged dependent variable in the above equation is larger than in the case of crude exports, and suggests that products exports adjust to lagged price changes rather slowly. However, definite

---

[6] The estimation in log-linear form yields a short-run price elasticity with respect to one-year lagged prices of 0.11 in the following form:

$$\ln RP_t = 1.31 + 0.446 \ln RP_{t-1} + 0.111 \ln PI_{t-1}$$
$$(3.11) \quad (2.32) \qquad\qquad (2.29)$$

$\bar{R}^2 = 0.896$, $DWS = 1.77$, $\zeta(1) = 0.21$

Table 9.4: Estimation Results of the Export Equation for Refined Oil Products (Annual Data). 1970–84 (15 Observations). Dependent Variable: RP_t

	Constant	RP_{t-1}	PI_{t-1}	$RPCM_t$	$\bar{R}^2$	DWS	$\zeta(1)$
(1)	8.21	0.455	0.076		0.907	2.34	0.78
	(3.60)	(2.93)	(3.45)				
(2)	14.11	0.410	0.103	−1.09	0.936	2.96	4.42
	(4.30)	(3.01)	(4.56)	(−2.25)			

Note: Figures in brackets are t-statistics.

conclusions on supply responses to prices cannot be made without disaggregated estimations for individual products.

Equation (2) in Table 9.4 reports slightly improved estimates. In this equation we add products exports to the CMEA–6 countries in year t, $RPCM_t$. The result suggests a possible inverse relationship between products exports to the West and products exports to the CMEA countries, i.e. a potential trade-off in the planners' allocation between the two destinations.

Moving now to quarterly analysis, we note that Soviet exports of refined oil products exhibit a clear seasonal pattern, as do crude oil exports (see Chapter 3).

Regression analysis with quarterly data further confirmed the result that refined products exports are not used for trade adjustment purposes. Lagged trade balances were found to be statistically insignificant and they do not explain the volume of products exports. (They did contribute to an explanation of changes in crude oil exports.) Crude oil production does not seem to be an important determining factor.

This important difference between crude oil exports and refined products exports may be explained by the fact that products exports are constrained by the country's refinery configuration, which does not provide the planners with the flexibility to use products exports for short-run adjustments. As the above analysis of the refinery system illustrates (see Chapter 4), once the level of refinery throughput is set to meet planned domestic demand and products export demand, both the output levels and the product mix are determined by the available refinery technology and refinery capacity. Changes in the latter involve major investment decisions with long lead-times, except for marginal alterations to capacity utilization rates. However, as is the case in the rest of the economy, the refinery system in the Soviet Union is utilized to the limit of the 'effective' capacity extant at any point in time (in other words excess capacity arises from technical constraints and not from a demand shortfall). This leaves little, if any, flexibility for discretionary quantity adjustments of products exports in the short run. Allocation adjustments to the two export markets (the CMEA–6 and OECD countries) have provided some additional flexibility, as shown by our estimation of equation (2) in Table 9.4. However, the potential gains from reallocation are limited because the share of exports of refined products taken by the CMEA–6 is already much smaller than their share of crude exports.

PART III

SOVIET OIL IN THE WORLD PETROLEUM MARKET
David Long

10 SOVIET OIL EXPORT MARKETS AND MARKETING STRATEGIES

10.1 Introduction

As shown in earlier chapters, Soviet oil exports have increased substantially in recent years. Almost all the growth in Soviet oil exports has been directed to the West. Between 1980 and 1984, gross oil exports (crude oil plus refined products) to the industrialized and industrializing nations of the West (MDCs and LDCs) expanded from 60.2 million to 93.8 million tonnes, according to PlanEcon estimates. At the same time exports to other Socialist countries (CMEA–6 and OCPEs) were held approximately constant. And in 1985 it was exports to the West that took the brunt, falling back to 70.8 million tonnes, while exports to other Socialist countries were hardly affected.

It is important to recall that the expansion in Soviet oil exports to the West took place at a time when the demand for oil in the non-Communist world was falling as a result of economic recession, conservation and substitution away from oil following the oil price rises of 1979–80. As a result the rate of market penetration by the Soviet Union was much greater than might appear at first sight. In 1980 oil exports from the Soviet Union to the non-Communist world represented about 4 per cent of world trade in oil. By 1984 this had risen to 8 per cent, and even during the export difficulties of 1985 it was still as high as 6 per cent.

How did the Soviet Union achieve this impressive gain in its market share? It is not sufficient just to have the oil available for export; it still has to be sold. And by the 1980s the world market was already awash with oil from new producing areas outside the OPEC region. Yet there is no evidence that the Soviet Union has ever had any serious difficulty in selling all the oil it had available for export.

The key to the success of the Soviet Union in increasing the volume of its oil exports to the West and its share of world oil trade throughout 1980–86 lies in its behaviour as an oil marketer. Without an effective strategy for selling its oil the Soviet Union could not have achieved the export gains of the 1980s. And in order to understand how this was done we will need to examine the types of crude oil and products being exported, the terms under which they are sold, the possible reasons

why this particular strategy was chosen, and the prices achieved by the
Soviet Union for its oil on the world market.

10.2 Soviet Oil and its Competitors in International Trade

Soviet oil exports compete in a world petroleum market which trades a
wide range of different types of crude oil, feedstocks and refined
products. Each type of crude oil and product has its own set of
characteristics that distinguish it even from other very similar crudes or
products. As a result there are no perfect substitutes in the oil market
and each type of oil traded tends to create a market of its own.

This does not mean, however, that prices in each of the many sub-
markets can be set independently of the prices of other types of oil
being traded on the world market. Most types of oil can be blended,
refined or otherwise converted (at a cost) into each other and so prices
in the various sub-markets tend to be highly correlated.

In addition, each market has evolved its own rules and methods of
doing business over time and many of the players are specialists who
survive by exploiting a particular trading niche created by the
characteristics of the type of oil they trade. All these features of the
world petroleum market will influence the sales strategy adopted by
the Soviet Union in selling its oil exports on the world oil market.

Various factors influence the trading characteristics of a particular
type of oil. The most important is the physical and chemical composition of the oil, which affects the mix or type of final product that can be
made, and hence its ultimate sales value. In addition, the seasonal
pattern of supply and demand, the method of shipment and the size of
parcel, the frequency and reliability of supply, the variation in quality
and the existence of close substitutes can each play a significant role in
determining the operation of the market.

(*a*) *Export Channels*. The Soviet Union, like all other major oil-
exporting nations, exports oil to the West by sea. The major export
terminals are in the Baltic (primarily Ventspils and Klaipeda) and the
Black Sea (Novorossiisk, Feodosiya and Tuapse). In addition there is
regular small-scale river and coastal barge traffic from inland refineries
(such as Gorkii) and railway terminals to destinations in North West
Europe.

There are a large number of links in the chain from production well
or refinery to export terminal and it is impossible to associate a given
export terminal with a particular source of oil. In the case of crude oil,
exports are delivered by a network of pipelines connecting oilfields in
West Siberia and the Caucasus/Caspian regions to export terminals on

the Black Sea and the Baltic (see frontispiece). In the case of products, exports are still mainly delivered by railcars which could have come from almost any refinery in the Soviet Union.

However, there is a broad distinction to be drawn between the quality characteristics of products exported from terminals in the Baltic and those from the Black Sea. Baltic products are of a higher, and more reliable, quality than Black Sea products, which suggests that terminals in the Baltic are usually supplied by a different group of refineries from those in the Black Sea. This probably results from the use of different collection systems for crude oil and refined products.

Most of the oil is transported in Soviet flag vessels and sold c.i.f. to Western buyers. However, for a variety of reasons, some operational and some political, Soviet vessels tend to be constrained to short-haul voyages. And buyers who want to move Soviet oil to long-haul destinations must buy f.o.b., but these are still in the minority. This helps to explain why, as we have shown in Chapter 3 above, the vast majority of Soviet oil exports to the OECD countries are to destinations in Western Europe, with less than 5 per cent going to the USA and Japan.

Since the boundaries of the export market for Soviet oil are largely determined by the range of Soviet flag vessels, the main sources of competition are limited to the Atlantic basin market for crude oil and the Mediterranean and North West European markets for refined products. For good geographical reasons, oil exports from the Baltic usually compete in northern European markets and exports from the Black Sea in southern European markets. Arbitrage between the two is infrequent as the additional shipping costs charged by the Soviet export agency or its subsidiaries can be high, but it will always occur if the differentials are right.

(*b*) *Properties of the Soviet Export Crude and Export Oil Products*. The Soviet Union used to export two similar but not identical crude oil blends; now it exports one grade of crude oil known as Soviet Export Blend (SEB), although it is sometimes described as Urals or Romashkino. In the past, crude oil exported from Baltic ports tended to be heavier and of a higher sulphur content than the blend exported from the Black Sea, although both were called Soviet Export Blend, and were usually sold at very similar c.i.f. prices in the Mediterranean and North West Europe (see Table 10.1).

Today the export blend has the heavier gravity of the old blend exported from the Baltic but has the lower sulphur content of the old blend exported from the Black Sea, as can be seen from the summary of refining characteristics given in Table 10.2.

Table 10.1: Characteristics of the Two Old Soviet Export Blends.

	Gravity (°API)	Sulphur (% weight)
Baltic to North West Europe	32–33	1.7
Black Sea to Mediterranean	33–34	<1.4

Source: *PIW*, 26 March 1984

Table 10.2: Characteristics of the Soviet Export Blend and of some Competing Crudes.

Characteristic	Soviet Export Blend	Flotta	Arabian Light	Saharan Blend	Brent
Crude Oil					
Gravity (°API)	32.50	35.70	33.40	46.20	37.20
Sulphur (% weight)	1.38	1.14	1.79	0.11	0.35
Distillation (% volume)					
C_1–C_4	n.a.	4.3	1.8	5.4	4.2
C_5–165 °C	23.8	22.7	20.3	35.3	24.4
165–235 °C	11.2	10.8	13.6	16.0	12.1
235–350 °C	16.0	21.5	20.6	20.1	21.1
350+ °C	49.0	40.7	43.7	23.2	38.2
Cracker Feed (370–520 °C)					
Yield (% volume)	22.7	22.3	18.9	14.6	22.5
Sulphur (% weight)	1.94	1.66	2.19	0.29	0.40
K-factor	11.8	11.8	11.9	12.1	12.1

Source: Mabro et al, 1986, pp. 23, 25

It can be seen that SEB is fairly similar to Arabian Light in terms of its gravity and refinery yields, although the long residue from SEB is greater (49.0 per cent) and the sulphur content lower (1.38 per cent). SEB is also very close to Flotta, its main competitor in the North West European crude oil market, although the sulphur content of Flotta is lower again.

SEB, Arabian Light and Flotta can be classed as medium-gravity, medium-sulphur content crudes, and all three have favourable cracking characteristics. As such they are much heavier and higher in sulphur content than the major crudes produced in the North Sea (e.g. Brent) or the Mediterranean (particularly Libyan and Algerian crudes). The main competition for SEB in terms of quality therefore comes from long-haul Gulf crudes such as Arabian Light and Dubai.

As with all blends, the quality of SEB varies depending on the mix of production streams in the blend, but the range of variations is not very wide and seems acceptable to refiners. Furthermore, SEB is free of major impurities. Finally, let us note that Soviet crude is exported in small cargoes in parcels of about 40,000 tonnes (almost 300,000 barrels), compared with Brent which moves in standard cargoes of more than twice this size (600,000 barrels).

The Soviet Union also exports the full range of oil products: gasoline, naphtha, kerosine, gas oil and LPG. However, the bulk of its products exports are accounted for by gas oil and fuel oil.

Gas oil provides the largest component of products exports from the Soviet Union to the OECD. According to OECD/IEA estimates, between 1980 and 1984 the volume increased by 29.6 per cent from 14.2 million to 18.4 million tonnes (see Table 3.6). There is no identifiable source refinery (or refineries) for gas oil exports: they may have originated anywhere in the Soviet Union. Export parcels are assembled by rail and river barge from a large number of inland refineries, but it is thought that more is exported from the Baltic ports than from the Black Sea. Shipments are typically 38,000 tonnes, but some is moved directly to destinations in North West Europe such as Hamburg and Rotterdam from inland refineries and railway terminals in much smaller parcels, some as small as 6,000 tonnes.

The quality of 'Russian gas oil', as Soviet exports of this product are known to oil traders, is different for the Baltic and the Black Sea. Russian gas oil exported from the Baltic is usually of good quality and is sufficiently reliable to be traded to a precise specification (see Table 10.3), while gas oil exported from the Black Sea is of a poorer, and unreliable, quality. In particular, the sulphur content of Black Sea gas oil is higher (0.3–0.5 per cent by weight) and has been rising recently.

Table 10.3: Characteristics of Russian Gas Oil Exported from the Baltic.

Sulphur (% weight)	<0.3
Pour Point (°C)	<10
Diesel Index	>53
Density (at 20 °C)	<0.850

Source: Interviews

Russian gas oil from the Baltic is ideally suited to most European inland markets. It can be blended to form both heating and automotive gas oil and its specifications are often better than those set for many markets. For example, its diesel index exceeds the minimum standard set for automotive gas oil in all European countries. These facts, combined with the availability of very large quantities from the Soviet Union, have helped to make Russian gas oil the linchpin of the North West European gas oil market, and have led to the development of an active forward market in Russian gas oil, which acts as a pricing barometer for other less liquid markets. The operation of this unique market is examined in more detail in the next chapter.

Fuel oil exports from the Soviet Union to the West have increased substantially since 1980, both in absolute terms and as a share of total products exports. In 1980, the Soviet Union exported just over 4 million tonnes of fuel oil to the OECD (17 per cent of products exports); by 1984 this had increased by 67 per cent to just under 7 million tonnes (21 per cent of products exports). Fuel oil is exported from both Baltic and Black Sea ports. Baltic exports are usually in 20,000-tonne parcels, while Black Sea exports are usually in parcels of 50,000 tonnes. Exports from the Black Sea are shipped virtually continually, while those from the northern port of Klaipeda dry up almost completely in the winter months as the Baltic ices up.

Once again there are quality differences between the product exported from the Baltic and that exported from the Black Sea, although these are not so marked as in the case of gas oil. Most of the fuel oil currently exported (about 90 per cent) is a grade known as 'F10', although other grades such as 'F5' are sometimes available. F10 exports from the Baltic are guaranteed to meet higher quality specifications than exports from the Black Sea. For example, the maximum sulphur content permitted in the specification of the Baltic contracts is 2.0 per cent, while that for Black Sea contracts is 2.5 per cent. On average, though, the quality achieved for F10 delivered from either source exceeds the standards indicated by contracts, and F10 is normally a very high quality residual fuel oil containing a high proportion of gas oil (see Table 10.4). It is usually straight-run material and makes an ideal visbreaker feedstock. However, cargoes are occasionally contaminated with cracked material and end-users are wary of buying cargoes without guarantees of origin. When it contains cracked material it can only be used for burning and its value is accordingly lower. Unreliable quality is thus a problem for purchasers of F10 from both the Baltic and the Black Sea.

The high average quality of F10 compared with SEB atmospheric residue suggests either that it is usually cut at lower temperatures (approximately 200 °C) or that it contains significant amounts of back-blended gas oil or possibly kerosine.

Soviet fuel oil exports compete in both the Mediterranean and North West European markets for refinery feedstocks. In the Mediterranean, F10 cargoes also provide the main source of fuel oil imports, as inland

Table 10.4: Average Outturn Characteristics of F10 compared with SEB Residual Fuel Oil and Gas Oil.

	F10	*SEB Residual Fuel Oil 350+ °C*	*Gas Oil 180–350 °C*
Sulphur (% weight)	1.6–2.0	2.6	0.57
Viscosity[a]	80–100	191	3.69
Specific Gravity (at 15 °C)	0.930–0.945	0.952	0.840

Note: (a) Viscosity is given in centistokes at 50 °C for F10 and fuel oil and at 20 °C for gas oil.

Source: Interviews

markets in southern Europe have no use for the low-sulphur fuel oil produced in North African refineries. Its main competitor is Iraqi atmospheric residue.

Light distillates, including naphtha, gasoline, kerosine and, more recently, LPG, are also exported to the West. Of these the most important in terms of volume are naphtha and gasoline. Between 1980 and 1982 the total volume of these light distillates exported to the West increased from 4.4 million to 6.8 million tonnes. In 1984, however, this volume fell to 5.6 million tonnes.

Soviet naphtha exports represent a fairly good quality general purpose product which meets the open specifications on the North West European markets. It is traded as a petrochemical feedstock (for ethylene crackers) or a gasoline blending component (for catalytic reformers). Its quality is reliable.

Soviet gasoline is a heavy, low-octane, high-lead product of variable quality, very much at the poor end of the quality spectrum. It is closer to, say, Nigerian domestic grades than to any grade used in the European market. Soviet kerosine is also of poor and unreliable quality. All this reflects difficulties facing the Soviet refining system in trying to manufacture distillate fuels meeting the higher octane and lower flash point standards used in Europe. Both are exported only in small quantities.

From the evidence presented above it can be seen that the average quality of the *main* grades of Soviet export oil products is high and often exceeds the standards required by end-users. Witness the low sulphur content and high diesel index of gas oil, and the high gas oil content of F10. There are problems of reliability with fuel oil; but gasoline and kerosine, which are both of poor and unreliable quality, can be ignored because the volumes exported are small. Thus it seems that the Soviet export agency, *Soyuznefteksport*, is sensitive to world market requirements and has responded to changing specifications in its major West European markets.

(*c*) *Fluctuations in Soviet Oil Exports*. We have seen in Chapter 3 that Soviet crude oil exports to the West have a marked seasonal pattern around an upward trend (see Figure 3.2). The first quarter is generally the lowest, the second and third are higher, and exports fall back again in the fourth quarter. It is interesting to note that the seasonally adjusted pattern of crude oil exports reveals a number of major episodes in which crude oil exports deviated sharply from their expected trend. The first of these was in the second and third quarters of 1981, the second in 1Q84, the third in 1Q85, and the last in 4Q85. Furthermore, with the exception of 1Q84, the level of exports during all these episodes lay well below the expected trend. In other words, once seasonal variations are taken into account, the underlying pattern of Soviet crude oil exports during the period 1980–85 is a steady rise interrupted by occasional 'catastrophic' collapses in export volumes. As a result, assuming that the market anticipates the trend correctly, all the remaining uncertainty associated with crude oil exports is probably on the downside.

Furthermore, there is also seasonality in fuel oil exports and the cyclical pattern is fairly regular. By contrast, seasonal variations in gas oil exports, though less marked, are also less regular. All Soviet oil exports are subject to occasional collapses and/or surges, which are often independent of seasonal movements and difficult for the market to anticipate.

10.3 The Markets for Soviet Oil

The market for Soviet oil in the West involves two stages. First, there is what might be called the 'primary' market because this is where Soviet oil exports are sold in the first place. The Soviet export agencies (the primary suppliers) usually sell most export oil to a set of buyers (contract holders or primary buyers) with whom the Soviets have contractual arrangements. Very little oil is sold 'spot' on a cargo-by-cargo basis, and even these sales are usually made to existing contract holders. The primary market is therefore a term market and its size for each type of oil will be in direct proportion to the volume exported to the West by the Soviet Union. The persistence of term contracts for Soviet oil exports during a period in which almost every other supplier was obliged to move to spot contracting is an unusual feature of this market which is discussed below. And next, there is a 'secondary' market, in which some of the oil acquired directly by contract holders (or primary buyers) is sold to others who, for either trading or end-use reasons, wish to purchase Soviet crude oil or products. The secondary market involves three types of contract: spot, physical forward and 'paper' forward sales. The size of these secondary markets does not necessarily bear any relation to the volume of each type of oil exported by the Soviet Union. The physical volumes involved cannot be larger than the amounts exported but in some cases the same parcel is bought and sold several times in forward transactions. There is a small overlap between primary and secondary markets because the Soviet agencies (the primary suppliers) now sell some oil spot or forward. The frequency of these spot/forward sales, which were rare in the past, seems to have increased in 1985–6.

A rough indication of the relative sizes of the primary and secondary markets for each export stream can be obtained by comparing the approximate numbers of shipments for each stream of oil exported to the West with the numbers of spot transactions reported by a market reporting agency such as *Petroleum Argus*. The average number of shipments is estimated on the basis of the total quantity of oil imported by OECD countries divided by the typical parcel sizes given above.

It can be seen that the size of the secondary market for crude oil is very small in relation to the primary shipments, about one-tenth of the total volume exported (see Table 10.5). By comparison the secondary

Table 10.5: Relative Sizes of Primary and Secondary Markets. 1984. Average Numbers of Transactions per Month.

Export Stream	Estimated Primary Shipments	Reported Secondary Transactions	Ratio
Crude Oil	100	8–10	0.08–0.1
Gas Oil	40	40–50	1.00–1.25
Fuel Oil	21	15–20	0.71–0.95

markets for fuel oil and gas oil are much larger. *Argus* reports of fuel oil deals represent about three-quarters of the total volume exported and those for gas oil actually exceed the export volume. It seems that not only is less retained by the holders of term contracts for gas oil and fuel oil, but also some cargoes are bought and sold several times before they reach the ultimate end-user.

(*a*) *Contracts*. The first, and most important, factor that needs to be taken into account when trying to explain the structure of the markets for Soviet oil exports is the nature of the term contracts themselves. It seems that most term contracts are cast in the same general mould: the buyer agrees to lift oil at a predetermined price as and when cargoes are nominated by the seller. This is the reverse of almost every other type of contract in the world oil market: nominations are usually made at the discretion of the buyer. Negotiations take place annually, usually during the fourth quarter, and contracts are usually agreed for annual volumes, but often specify quarterly or 'seasonal' volumes. Various contractual arrangements exist. For example, oil products exported from the Soviet Union may be lifted either under an annual f.o.b. or c.i.f. contract at prices based on *Platt's* quotations on the date of loading, or under a 'framework' contract, which commits the buyer to lift a specified annual quantity at prices that are 'negotiated' monthly. Some products are also sold 'spot' outside annual contractual arrangements, but usually to the existing contract holders at the prices agreed for the term contracts. Soviet oil products are hardly ever sold spot *directly* to a company not holding a term or framework contract. In addition some oil products traded on international markets are lifted under oil-for-services or barter arrangements or as the result of locational exchanges whereby Western companies supply, say, Vietnam, in return for Soviet oil in North West Europe or the Mediterranean. Many of these 'exchange' contracts have recently been concluded with Japanese trading houses such as Mitsubishi, C. Itoh or Toyamenko.

However, it seems that contract holders do not always expect the volumes to be fulfilled, although the volumes specified do change from year to year and seem to bear some relation to Soviet export plans. A supply contract with the Soviet Union is thus usually regarded more as an 'entry ticket' for future business than as a document with which to monitor performance. The exception to this rule is Finland, which has a complex countertrade agreement for the supply of crude oil and products and so expects contract volumes to be fulfilled.

(*b*) *Term Contract Holders*. The second factor relevant to an analysis of the structure of Soviet export market is the identity of primary buyers. The type of term contract holder differs from one primary market to the next and this can affect the relative size of the secondary market.

As far as crude oil is concerned, it appears that the majority of contract holders are refiners (end-users). Such companies appear to be less inclined to resell the crude oil on the spot market, either because of responsive contract prices, c.i.f. delivery terms, and (for some) distinct locational and quality advantages or because of destination restrictions imposed by the contract. As a result the secondary market for SEB is rather smaller than the volumes sold into the primary market might suggest.

In the case of products exports the majority of contract holders appear to be trading companies. For each product there appear to be between fifteen and twenty companies that specialize in dealing with the Soviets, but some specialize in fuel oil, others in gas oil, and others in naphtha. Many of these have long-standing relationships. Such companies are not usually end-users, although some are active in the blending market and others also own refineries or rent processing capacity. Nevertheless, many of these companies onsell Soviet products obtained under term contracts to end-users, either directly or through the spot market. Since these secondary transactions often involve multiple sales of the same cargo, either on a physical basis, as in the case of gas oil in the Mediterranean, or as forward paper contracts, as in the case of gas oil in North West Europe, the secondary market for exports of some Soviet products is rather larger than the size of the primary market might suggest.

(*c*) *Differences in the Sizes of Secondary Markets: a Possible Explanation*. Part of the reason for the differences in the relative sizes of the primary and secondary markets for crude oil, F10 and gas oil lies in differences in the identity of contract holders (refiners or traders) and in characteristics of the oil exported by the Soviet Union in each of the primary markets. Bringing together information about the main characteristics of Soviet crude oil and products described in Section 10.2 and data on the relative sizes of the primary and secondary markets presented in Table 10.5 reveals interesting relationships (see Table 10.6).

As regards trading characteristics, F10 is at one end of the spectrum because its quality, though good, is unreliable. Gas oil is at the other end: the size and quality of each parcel is predictable and the delivery arrangements are uniform. Crude oil lies somewhere between these two extremes: it is of fairly predictable quality but has variable parcel sizes and delivery terms. In this ranking, F10 is a non-standardized and gas oil a standardized commodity, and crude oil displays features of both, depending on the criterion used.

Non-standardized commodities create opportunities for traders who are prepared to take on the quality risk and use their skills to exploit a market niche. Indeed this has always been one of the main reasons for the existence of trading companies in the oil business. This is clearly an important factor in explaining the identity of the primary buyers, and the primary/secondary structure of the market. In the case of Soviet fuel oil, we find that the primary buyers are traders and not refiners. The latter wish to buy straight-run fuel oil as a feedstock for their

Table 10.6: Trading Characteristics of Soviet Oil and Structure of Major Export Markets.

	Crude Oil	F10	Gas Oil[a]
Quality of Commodity	Good	Good	Good
Reliability of Quality	Good	Poor	Good
Regular Seasonal Pattern	Significant	Very significant	Not very significant
Irregular Fluctuations in Quantity	Occasional (−)	Occasional (±)	Frequent (±)
Size of Parcel and Delivery Arrangements	Variable	Variable	Uniform
Contract Holders	Refiners	Traders	Traders
Nature of Secondary Market	Spot	Spot	Spot/forward
Relative Size of the Secondary Market	Small	Larger	Much larger

Note: (a) Baltic exports as traded on the forward market for Russian gas oil in North West Europe.

upgrading plant but if they bought directly from the Soviet agencies they would run the risk of receiving parcels that are not straight-run material. They buy instead from traders at a premium. The trader takes the risk in his direct dealings with the Soviet export agency, onsells the straight-run cargoes at a slightly higher price to refiners, and disposes of the poor-quality cargoes at a discount to blenders or power utilities who use them as burning fuels. It is thus easy to explain the dominance of traders among primary buyers and the existence of a secondary market. This secondary market will, however, involve spot transactions only. It is difficult to enter into term commitments with secondary buyers because of uncertainty about primary supplies (due to both seasonality and some accidental fluctuations). It is also difficult to extend transactions forward because a prerequisite for a forward market is that the commodity is standardized.

Standardized commodities do not present the same trading opportunities since quality risks cannot exist by definition. However, they create a different set of opportunities, provided that sufficient volumes are available: the possibility of developing a forward (or futures) market in which the price and the delivery date are the only negotiable items. In the world oil market standardized commodities are rare and it is therefore not surprising that the small number of crude varieties that can be packaged in standard parcels of reliable quality – WTI, Brent and more recently Dubai – have given rise to the emergence of particular forward or futures markets. Russian gas oil also provides such an opportunity. This has attracted traders in the primary market and led to the development of an active and 'economically efficient' forward physical market which is studied in detail in the next chapter. Thus, rather paradoxically, there is a secondary market for Soviet F10 because this export product is non-standardized and a secondary market for Russian gas oil because it *is* standardized. But the nature of the markets is different: the first is spot and the second both spot and forward, a characteristic which explains its larger relative size given that forward dealings involve chains of paper contracts for each physical parcel.

But what about crude oil? If standardization of the commodity were the only factor explaining the relative sizes of secondary markets, we would expect crude oil to have at least as large a secondary market as F10. As shown in Table 10.5, however, this is certainly not the case. The reason is simply that the imperfect standardization of the crude oil parcel exported by the Soviet Union does not create major problems for the refiner. SEB is of good and reliable quality. Parcel size and delivery arrangements are not uniform and supply volumes are uncertain, but this need not cause major inconvenience to end-users because SEB has several close substitutes available today in large quantities in slack oil markets. Thus, the primary buyers of Soviet crude oil are refiners rather than traders, and refiners absorb a large proportion of their purchases in their own plant. The secondary market is therefore relatively small.

The characteristics of commodities do not provide a complete explanation of why markets develop in particular ways. They do create opportunities for traders but these would not be fully realized if the primary sellers had a strong preference for direct deals with end-users, either for political reasons (which sometimes lie behind the familiar 'destination clause' of certain OPEC oil sales contracts) or for economic reasons (to save the intermediaries' fee). Why then has the Soviet Union chosen to market oil products through traders?

In the case of fuel oil, the answer seems straightforward. Assuming that refiners are less willing than traders to take the quality risk, the Soviet Union may have no choice but to market F10 through traders. But this answer does not apply to gas oil, for which there is no quality risk and which displays less seasonality than either F10 or crude oil. Other factors must therefore be at work.

In today's market conditions buyers have an almost absolute preference for spot contracts. It seems that *Soyuznefteksport* prefers term contracts because they do not involve the additional costs associated with recurrent contracting: collecting market information and identifying the best best buyer for each contract, both of which are significant in a relatively opaque market such as oil. Furthermore, supply uncertainties and difficulties (e.g. the shortage of storage capacity at the terminals) weaken the position of *Soyuznefteksport* in both spot and term markets. The ability to defer sales in the spot market and the reliability of supplies in the term market are crucial to bargaining power.

In these circumstances, *Soyuznefteksport* can only improve its position if it is able to find a way of reducing the costs imposed by buyers' preferences for spot contracts and its weak bargaining position due to problems of supply. One solution is to find a third party who can engage in spot sales at lower costs and mitigate the effects of the unreliability of supplies from the Soviet Union by means of access to other varieties of crude oil and products. This third party is found in either oil traders or oil brokers. Both incur lower costs in collecting market information and identifying buyers because of knowledge acquired dealing with oil from other sources as well and because of economies of scale; and traders can live more easily with uncertain supplies than end-users because of their greater access to immediate market information. They know how to find the best buyer quickly if they are landed with additional volumes, and the cheapest seller of an alternative crude or product if they face a shortfall. They are prepared to take the specific quantity or quality risk if the price is right.[1]

We now have all the elements that explain the distinctive contractual structure of the export market for Soviet oil products, in which *Soyuznefteksport* sells to oil traders on a term contract that specifies price but not volume, and the traders then onsell to end-users on spot contracts. These arrangements enable the Soviet Union to diversify away from specific price risks and establish its oil exports on the same competitive footing as other suppliers in the world oil market. But, in

---

[1] Brokers and traders have different methods of and motives for doing business. A broker's role is to find the best price for a particular contract and introduce the buyer to the seller. In return he takes a fixed commission on the deal, if it is successful. His incentive to get the highest price derives from his desire to increase the volume of his business, and hence his profit from commissions, and his comparative advantage derives from economies of scale.

A trader's role is quite different. He takes an uncovered position, either long or short depending on his expectations. In the case of a long position, he buys the oil from the seller and then tries to find a buyer. As a result he is exposed to the risk that the price will fall while he owns the oil. However, he also faces the possibility that the price will rise, which will allow him to make a speculative gain. His objective is therefore to maximize his profits (net of costs) by buying and selling oil in the face of price uncertainty. His advantages also derive from economies of scale in collecting market information, but his risks are much greater than those of the broker so he will require a bigger margin (commission) from the seller to take his oil.

Thus there is nothing to choose between the services of a broker and a trader as far as collecting market information and identifying the best buyer for a given contract are concerned; in fact the broker is cheaper. However, the broker does nothing to alleviate the weak bargaining position that may result from the uncertain supply schedule for Soviet oil exports while the trader may.

order to achieve this reduction in price risk, it will need to pay a premium to traders to compensate them for the risks that they now carry.

10.4 Prices

Crude oil is mainly sold c.i.f. at contract prices which are renegotiated at intervals determined by market conditions. Until recently, different term prices were set for exports from the Black Sea and the Baltic. The term pricing history for SEB from 1980 to 1985 is shown in Table 10.7. It can be seen that the term price differential between the Black Sea and the Baltic disappeared in early 1984 and has not re-emerged. Prior to February 1984 this differential fluctuated between 10 and 20 cents per barrel, with the Black Sea price usually, but not always, below the Baltic price. Term pricing almost collapsed in 1986 as spot prices on the world market became very volatile and some buyers put pressure on the Soviet Union to concede netback pricing for crude oil. According to Press reports some buyers, notably the Japanese trading houses, were successful, but others continued to lift at term prices.[2]

In the recent past, it seems that term prices have been fairly responsive to changes in spot market prices. This is clearly demonstrated by Figure 10.1, which compares the term price set by *Soyuznefteksport* for SEB from the Baltic with monthly average spot market prices for the same crude as reported by the *OPEC Bulletin*. It can be seen that from the middle of 1982 onwards the term price is rarely far out of line with the spot price, although there is usually a small delay between spot price changes and term price adjustments. In addition, the figure shows that term prices have tended, on average, to be set slightly below spot prices.

It is possible to get a further idea of just how responsive term prices for SEB were by comparing them with term prices set by the British National Oil Corporation (BNOC) for its main competitor in the North Sea market, the Flotta blend. That Flotta and SEB are close substitutes is demonstrated by Figure 10.2, which shows the spot and term price differentials between the two crudes. On average, spot SEB trades slightly above spot Flotta, which is to be expected since SEB is sold c.i.f. and Flotta f.o.b., but apart from this the two prices move closely together. Quite a different picture emerges when the respective term prices are compared. Before 1982 there were some very large fluctuations in the wake of the price rises of 1979–80; but from 1982 onwards SEB term prices were usually below Flotta term prices. The reason for

---

[2] *Petroleum Argus*, 9 June 1986, p. 5.

Table 10.7: Term Prices of Soviet Export Blend. 1980–85. Dollars per Barrel.

	c.i.f. North West Europe	*c.i.f. Mediterranean*
1980		
Jan 1	33.20	32.36
Feb 1	34.50	34.14
Mar		
Apr		
May		
Jun		
Jul		
Aug		
Sep		
Oct		
Nov		
Dec		
1981		
Jan		
Feb 1	38.90	38.70
Mar		
Apr		
May		
Jun 1	35.85	35.65
Jul		
Aug		
Sep		
Oct 1	34.75	34.60
Nov		
Dec 1	35.50	35.35
1982		
Jan 1	35.10	35.00
Feb		
Mar 1	29.10	29.00
Apr 1	30.10	30.00
May 1	30.60	30.50
Jun 1	31.30	31.20
Jul		
Aug		
Sep 1	32.10	32.00
Oct 1	32.30	32.20
Nov		
Dec		

	c.i.f. North West Europe	c.i.f. Mediterranean
1983		
Jan 1	31.60	31.50
Feb 1	29.25	29.15
Mar 1	28.10	28.00
Apr		
May 1	28.50	28.60
Jun		
Jul 1	29.00	29.10
Aug 15	29.50	29.50
Sep		
Oct		
Nov 1	29.00	29.00
Dec 1	28.60	28.50
1984		
Jan		
Feb		
Mar 1	29.00	29.00
Apr		
May		
Jun		
Jul 27	27.50	27.50
Aug		
Sep 1	27.75	27.75
Oct 1	28.00	28.00
Nov		
Dec		
1985		
Jan		
Feb		
Mar		
Apr		
May 1	27.00	27.00
Jun		
Jul 1	25.50	25.50
Aug 1	26.00	26.00
Aug 21	26.25	26.25
Sep 1	26.50	26.50
Sep 16	26.90	26.90
Oct		
Nov 1	27.60	27.60
Dec 1	28.00	28.00

Source: *PIW*

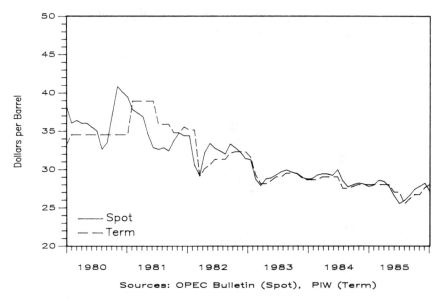

Figure 10.1 Monthly Average Prices of Soviet Export Blend (Baltic). 1980–85.

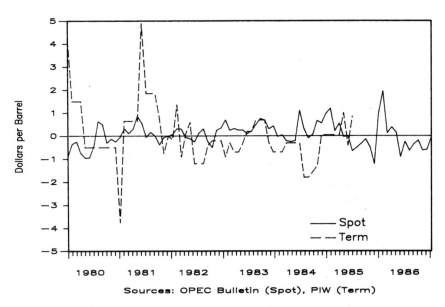

Figure 10.2 Soviet Export Blend (Baltic)/Flotta Monthly Average Spot and Term Price Differentials. 1980–86.

this is that Flotta term prices were far less responsive to spot price movements than SEB term prices, and there were a number of periods of large spot price movements during which the Flotta term price remained unchanged.

Products are usually also sold c.i.f., but on the basis of pricing formulae related to *Platt's* quotations, adjusted for quality, freight and insurance. Prices are usually calculated as of the date of the bill of lading, which is also taken to be the date of delivery, and between twenty and thirty days' credit are given. Any taxes and duties levied outside the Soviet Union are, of course, the responsibility of the buyer. Quality premiums, like term crude oil prices, are adjusted at intervals determined by market conditions. At present they are made monthly, but with increased price volatility there is pressure from *Soyuznefteksport* for fortnightly revisions. Freight adjustments reflect deliveries to destinations other than those specified by the price formula. Two-port discharges usually attract a penalty and f.o.b. liftings will be given a discount.

The exact structure of the pricing formula is different for each product and each market and there are probably small variations for each customer, but the general principle is always the same. The prices charged are market-related prices close to the average achieved in the markets for each export stream on the day the oil is lifted:

(a) Gas oil (North West Europe) – the mean of the means of *Platt's* cargoes c.i.f. ARA and *Platt's* barges f.o.b. Rotterdam;
(b) Gas oil (Mediterranean) – the mean of the means of *Platt's* cargoes c.i.f. Italy and *Platt's* cargoes f.o.b. Genoa;
(c) Fuel oil (North West Europe) – the mean of the means of *Platt's* high-sulphur cargoes c.i.f. ARA and *Platt's* high-sulphur barges f.o.b. Rotterdam;
(d) Fuel oil (Mediterranean) – the mean of the means of *Platt's* high-sulphur cargoes c.i.f. Italy and *Platt's* high-sulphur cargoes f.o.b. Genoa.

Typical values derived from these formulae for gas oil and fuel oil in North West Europe and the Mediterranean are illustrated in Figures 10.3 and 10.4 respectively. It can be seen that over the period 1980–86 North West European prices have moved from, on average, a discount under to a premium over Mediterranean prices, but otherwise prices for each export channel move closely together.

The sizes of the premiums set by *Soyuznefteksport* for gas oil and fuel oil are much more difficult to establish as there are no systematic records available in the public domain, simply the comments of traders. In the case of gas oil it appears that the premium is usually

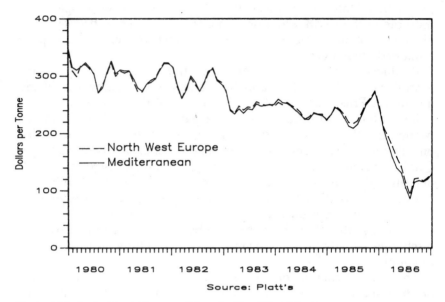

Figure 10.3 Soviet Term Contract Prices for Gas Oil. 1980–86.

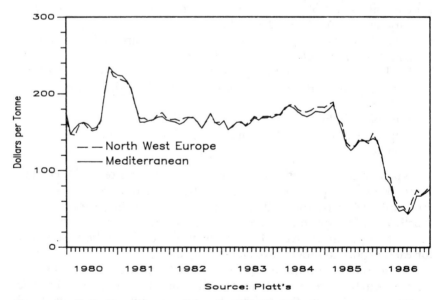

Figure 10.4 Soviet Term Contract Prices for Fuel Oil. 1980–86.

quite small, between $1 and $3 per tonne for example in North West Europe, which is intended to reflect the value of the lower average specific gravity of Russian gas oil from the Baltic.

In the case of fuel oil, the premium can be much higher as it reflects the value of straight-run fuel to refiners. A rough guide to the size of this premium can be gained from the spot market premium reported by *Argus* for Soviet fuel oil exports (F10) in North West Europe over the last three years. This is shown in Figure 10.5. It can be seen that the spot premium has varied between almost nothing and about $25 per tonne. According to traders, the premium set by *Soyuznefteksport* for liftings under term contracts usually reflects current spot market valuations, but it changes less frequently.

In the past these formulae were usually established without extensive negotiations and were generally regarded as reasonable by Western buyers. In general, the Soviets appear to have been more concerned to get the right procedures established to ensure offtake rather than to extract the last cent on each barrel sold. Recently, however, low oil prices and the reluctance of some traders to take on term contracts in a period of great uncertainty have forced the Soviets into the market with a much keener attitude to pricing. With a new management team in *Soyuznefteksport* and an even more pressing requirement for hard currency, more direct Soviet involvement in pricing decisions is to be expected.

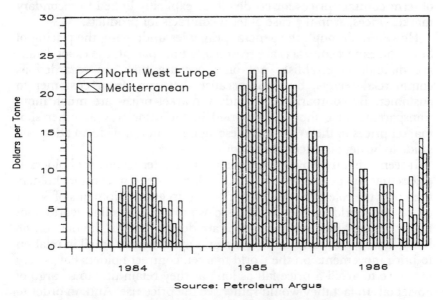

Figure 10.5 Monthly Average Assessment of F10 Premium. 1984–6.

10.5 Soviet Export Behaviour

Two widespread views about Soviet oil export behaviour are worth noting and assessing. First, the observed increase in the average volume of oil exported by the Soviet Union in the 1980s, which has given it a much larger share of a declining world oil market, has led to accusations that the Soviet Union has been systematically undercutting world oil prices. Secondly, the frequent and large variations in the volume of Soviet oil exports, which the market cannot anticipate for lack of information and understanding, have led to suggestions that oil exports are deliberately manipulated to achieve some kind of revenue objective.

(a) *Pricing Behaviour*. As we have seen above, the Soviet oil export market involves two stages (primary and secondary) and therefore two sets of prices. Both sets have a role to play.

As far as the Soviet Union is concerned, it is the primary market prices that matter since these will determine oil export revenues; while as far as the term contract holders are concerned, it is the difference between the primary and secondary market prices that matters since these will determine the value of the contract. In practice, the two markets are very closely related since primary market prices are either very responsive to changes in the secondary spot markets, as in the case of term contract prices for crude oil, or explicitly linked to secondary market prices, as in the case of term contracts for products.

However, although the general principles underlying the pricing of Soviet oil export contracts are reasonably transparent, the exact details are difficult to establish, not only because they are regarded as commercial secrets, but also because they vary from customer to customer. By comparison, secondary market prices are much more transparent, since they are reported in the same way as other spot market prices in the West, but these alone do not provide an adequate guide to Soviet oil pricing behaviour.

It seems that the Soviet Union sells its oil to term contract holders at prices that will guarantee that it is lifted. But the term contract holders then play the role of middlemen, placing irregular shipments of Soviet oil on the world market at prices close to the prevailing world spot market price. Since contract prices are determined on the date of the bill of lading, and since trading margins are generally small in relation to price movements on the world market, contract holders have every incentive to avoid a price fall as long as they retain title to a cargo of Soviet oil. In fact they would rather see the price rise. And, in order to minimize the risk of a price fall, contract holders will try to sell forward without disturbing the market as soon as they have been nominated a cargo. It is unlikely that these contractual arrangements would persist if contract holders made a loss because the secondary (spot) market price for Soviet oil always fell as soon as a cargo was loaded.

However, it is necessary for the Soviet Union to offer contract holders some incentive to sign term contracts since both the quantity supplied and the timing of shipments remain at the discretion of the Soviet export agency. As a result primary market prices should tend to be at a discount to secondary market prices. As we have seen, the form of the contracts provides several means of creating an incentive: first, the general price level may be set at a discount to competing sources of supply; secondly, quality adjustments may understate the value of a particular cargo; thirdly, freight adjustments for c.i.f. deliveries in Soviet vessels to certain destinations may overstate the actual savings; and, lastly, credit terms may be better than those obtained elsewhere.

In the case of crude oil (see Section 10.4) it appears that term prices for SEB over the last five-to-six years have tended, on average, to be set slightly below spot prices for the same crude oil. However, the average size of discount is not large, of the order of only 50 cents per barrel, and the size of the discount has tended to fall over time. Such a pattern of differentials between term and spot prices is not unique to SEB.

In the case of products, the pricing formulae are such that the differentials between primary and secondary market prices are also small, as they are all based on a trading range, either between cargoes and barges in North West Europe or between c.i.f. and f.o.b. cargoes in the Mediterranean. These are typically between $1 and $3 per tonne, although they can rise to as much as $10 per tonne in exceptional circumstances. However, there is no fixed relationship between the pairs of prices used in the pricing formulae since, for example, there are episodes during which Rotterdam barges trade at a premium to North West European cargoes and vice versa. The contract holder must not only be alert to the arbitrage opportunities for each cargo of Soviet oil, but must also be sufficiently flexible to take advantage of the changing secondary market prices. The only clear source of incentive is the thirty days' credit offered on term product contracts which is worth between $1 and $2 per tonne. This compares with two working days' credit usually offered on a spot products deal. In addition quality and freight adjustments can be used to create trading incentives if required. And the evidence from interviews with traders and market reports suggests that these are often used to good effect by the Soviet export agency.

Finally, EEC import duties provide an additional source of incentive in the North West European gas oil market. Strictly speaking, imports of Russian gas oil into the EEC are subject to an import tax of 3.5 per

cent of landed value as it is classed as a 'finished product' and comes
from a country which has no trade agreement with the EEC exempting
it from EEC import taxes (as is the case with some Middle East oil-
exporting countries). Soviet crude oil, naphtha and straight-run fuel oil
escape duty because they are classed as 'feedstocks' destined for further
processing. As a result buyers try to find ways to avoid paying duty
since this can yield a significant extra margin on the contract. They are
not always successful so it cannot be regarded as a guaranteed margin
but it does play an important role in this market. These duty
'loopholes' are described in more detail in Chapter 11 below.

Overall, it seems that the terms of Soviet oil export contracts do allow
for a small regular discount on world spot market prices which, taken
out of context, could be interpreted as systematic undercutting of world
market prices. In addition, the fact that the Soviet export agency can
also increase the size of the discount by adjusting the other price
variables under its control also contributes to an impression of undercutting at certain times. However, given the quantity and timing
disadvantages inherent in the contracts, and given the fact that there is
no incentive for contract holders to pass on any discount to end-users, it
seems unlikely that lower prices in the primary market will be
transmitted to the secondary market where Soviet oil exports compete
directly with other sources of supply. And unless this does happen
Soviet oil exports cannot truly be described as undercutting the world
market.

(b) The Manipulation of Export Volumes. Soviet oil export contracts give
the seller complete freedom to decide on both the timing and the
quantity of oil supplied to a given customer. A common explanation for
the wide discretion enjoyed by the Soviet Union over volume in the
contracts is that the Soviet export agency wishes to control the volume
exported in the short term in order to respond to changes in world
market prices, or to influence those prices.

Our analysis of the trading characteristics of Soviet oil export
commodities suggests that the Soviet Union needs this contractual
flexibility given that variations in export volumes in the short term are
the result of unpredictable supply factors. If this is correct, there should
be no prima-facie case for arguing that contractual flexibility is for the
purpose of market manipulation.

We examined the relationship between the non-seasonal variations
in Soviet exports of crude, gas oil and fuel oil and changes in the
primary market price for each export stream. In no case is there a
systematic relationship between changes in export volumes and
changes in prices (current or lagged) in the short term. Of course one

can always find occasional episodes during which prices and volumes appear to be related but this is not sufficient to establish a relationship. Let us add that the absence of short-term volume responses to price changes does not contradict the findings of Part II of this book about year-to-year planned adjustments of export volumes to balance-of-payments problems. We are concerned here with day-to-day intervention on the market which is a very different phenomenon.

To conclude, it seems that the Soviet export agency does not adjust oil export volumes in the short term in response to price changes, but it certainly adjusts prices of sales to contract holders in order to dispose immediately of the variable quantities of oil that happen to be available for export. The Soviet Union is in effect a price taker in the world oil market. However, price takers have a modicum of power over prices when markets are in disequilibrium. By changing their offer price for the sole purpose of disposing of their own supplies, they set new competitive price levels for other suppliers. They exercise this influence unwittingly, and by the same token provide ammunition to those who believe that they are manipulating the market consciously.

11 THE FORWARD MARKET FOR RUSSIAN GAS OIL

11.1 Introduction

The Soviet Union is not an active player on the world oil market. Despite the scale of its oil exports, the Soviet Union has remained aloof from the market, selling much of its oil to trading intermediaries under term contracts. Such intermediaries then onsell cargoes of Soviet oil, either directly to end-users or to each other, depending on the particular trading opportunities that present themselves at the time. It is at this point that the export market for Soviet oil interacts with the world oil market, and consequently may influence the behaviour of world market prices.

As we have seen in Chapter 10 above, the characteristics of the types of oil exported by the Soviet Union differ sufficiently to ensure that each grade is traded in a separate market. Furthermore, the contractual arrangements are such that the sizes of the secondary markets in crude oil, naphtha, gas oil and fuel oil bear no relation to the volumes actually exported by the Soviet Union, and it is the size of the secondary market in each product that will determine the impact of Soviet oil exports on the world market.

The largest secondary market is for gas oil delivered into North West Europe. This market is also important for an entirely different reason. Over the last three-to-four years the secondary market for Soviet gas oil exports has evolved a new dimension. It has become a forward market dealing in paper claims to future deliveries of Soviet gas oil cargoes. As in other paper markets, such as Brent, the total level of trading is much greater than the underlying volume of gas oil exports might suggest. As a result of the increased trading activity associated with Soviet gas oil exports, the market in 'Russian gas oil' as it is known to oil traders, has acquired a barometric role for players in other associated, but less active, markets.

During the last few years a number of informal forward paper markets have evolved in both crude oil and products. At the same time, the New York Mercantile Exchange has been successful in establishing an 'energy futures complex' based on crude oil and a number of refined products. All have become important pricing indicators for the world oil market because they provide a continuous means of price discovery in an otherwise thin spot market for oil; and all have also attracted criticism on the grounds that they are vehicles for speculation, responsible for increasing price volatility, and that their prices do not always reflect the underlying fundamental position.

The purpose of this chapter is therefore to examine the structure, role and performance of the forward market for Russian gas oil, in order to establish whether the charge of speculation is justified. It will describe the main features of the market, its operation, size and structure, the identity and motives of the participants, the behaviour of prices, and the relationship between the forward market and other markets for gas oil in North West Europe. Finally, the results will be compared with those obtained from the Institute's similar studies of the forward market for Brent (Mabro et al, 1986; Bacon, 1986).

11.2 The Main Features of the Market

The Russian gas oil market in North West Europe is an informal forward commodity market trading standard cargo lots of 18–25,000 tonnes of Russian gas oil for delivery c.i.f. ARA. Forward trading is conducted on the basis of half-month delivery ranges and takes place over a four-to-eight week horizon, i.e. one-to-three forward periods ahead. The forward contract specifies Russian gas oil (substitute grades are not acceptable without special arrangements) delivered c.i.f. ARA during a half-month period to meet fairly precise product quality specifications. Russian gas oil traded must have a sulphur content of less than 0.3 per cent by weight, a pour point of $-15\,°C$, a cloud filter pour point of $-12\,°C$ and a specific gravity of 0.836 (at 15 °C). A typical example of a Russian gas oil contract is reproduced in full in Appendix 5.

As with its counterpart in the crude oil market, the Brent market, trading in Russian gas oil takes place directly between participants, and not through an exchange as on a futures market. Consequently, contracts for each forward trading period cannot be discharged until that forward period is reached; and the market cannot be fully cleared until the end of each trading period when the backlog of forward 'paper' contracts between participants has been matched to the actual number of 'wet' cargoes of Russian gas oil available from term contract holders during the period.

Since there are usually more paper contracts made than there are spot cargoes available, each cargo will pass through several hands in the process of clearing the market, thus creating a sequence of contracts linking the original 'wet' seller to the ultimate 'wet' purchaser. Such a sequence of contracts is known as a 'daisy chain'. It is a rather haphazard way of clearing a market, and the process is open to abuse, as was seen in the Brent market during January and February 1986 and April 1987.

The convention in the Russian gas oil market is that two clear working days' notice are required for nomination of the arrival of a wet cargo against a forward paper contract. This is a much shorter period than the fifteen days required in the Brent market and, since the market deals in c.i.f. cargoes, traders can recycle cargoes arriving at the end of one period for use at the beginning of the next if the economics are profitable. In this way one cargo may be used to 'wet' chains for two adjacent periods.

As we have seen above (Chapter 10) gas oil is sold by the Soviet Union on term contracts to between fifteen and twenty traders and major oil companies. Some of these have contracts for delivery from Baltic ports, some from Black Sea ports and some from both. Most of the oil is delivered c.i.f. in Soviet flag vessels, although a few long-standing customers are allowed to lift f.o.b. on their own ships. Although export volumes are subject to large, irregular fluctuations, shipments to North West Europe are regarded as sufficiently reliable to support a forward market of this type. This is not the case in the Mediterranean, where the market remains strictly physical.

Shipments are typically 38,000 tonnes compared with a forward contract of 18–25,000 tonnes. Parcels are therefore usually divided into two contracts of approximately 19,000 tonnes. However, traders often use the contractual tolerance to compensate for losses or to capitalize on gains. Thus, if a contract is sold forward at a profit, the full 25,000 tonnes will be delivered to the buyer and, conversely, if it is sold at a loss, only the minimum quantity will be delivered.

The existence of a forward market therefore allows companies supplying or purchasing Russian gas oil cargoes in North West Europe to hedge against adverse price movements before the cargo is delivered, or to speculate on the outcome of prices in the future. In practice it is difficult to distinguish between the two motives in relation to a particular deal as both may be present, but it is useful to remember that a hedger can be simply defined as an agent who moves towards greater certainty as a result of his actions, while a speculator moves towards a position of greater uncertainty.

There are certain features of the term contracts held by traders that are likely to encourage the development of a forward market for hedging purposes, and therefore for speculative purposes also, since hedgers cannot perform in the absence of speculators. These are price uncertainty and volume uncertainty.

Price uncertainty arises because, although the contract price is derived from a formula (based on *Platt's* prices), the actual price paid by the trader will not necessarily reflect the value of the cargo on arrival at its destination. These will be different for a number of reasons: the formula is an average of *Platt's* barges and cargoes, the basing date is bill of lading and not arrival c.i.f. ARA, and the freight rate charged by the Soviet shipping fleet for deliveries to other destinations may be different from the market rate.

Volume uncertainty arises because, although the total volume of gas oil available from the Soviet Union is regarded as sufficiently reliable to support a forward market, the timing of cargoes available to an individual contract holder is not. Thus a holder of a Russian contract may wish to enter into a contract to supply, say, a barge customer, without being entirely sure of having a cargo to meet the obligation. In these circumstances the forward market offers a relatively secure source of supply should the cargo not materialize in the required date range, and a reasonable hedge if it does.

Forward trading is a relatively recent phenomenon in the evolution of world oil markets. It is, however, well suited to the oil business, and those markets that have acquired a forward dimension have expanded rapidly.

The main attraction of forward markets lies in the combination of traditional physical trading practices and novel (at least for oil) commodity trading techniques. Despite the enthusiasm of futures markets merchants for paper trading as an anonymous medium for hedging and speculating, oil trading remains primarily a physical business, in which reputations matter and profits depend on taking risks. Nevertheless, oil traders have found that they need a medium for forward dealing and it is characteristic of the business that they have developed their own styles of trading instead of relying on institutions created by others. In oil, forward markets allow traders to hedge their physical positions and speculate on the future price while retaining both their right to discriminate between partners and their preference for physical delivery.

One consequence of the development of forward markets has been to concentrate trading activity into a small number of highly visible markets: Brent and Dubai in the international crude oil market, and Russian gas oil in the North West European products market. As a result, these markets have assumed the role of pricing barometers, closely watched by physical and forward traders alike. Yet, despite their contribution to improved price transparency in the oil industry, there are many who distrust forward markets, arguing that they have increased price volatility and that the speculative actions of a few players can move the market against the trend.

The Russian gas oil market is no exception. Not all traders are prepared to play 'Russian roulette' and several companies with direct access to cargoes of Russian gas oil prefer to keep their business strictly physical. Nevertheless the market is active and regarded by many as the most important indicator of spot market trends in Western Europe.

11.3 Market Size and Term Structure

(*a*) *Data Sources and Preparation*. There is no formal exchange for trading Russian gas oil. All transactions are completed privately between companies participating in the market and so information must be obtained by direct sampling. There are various specialist oil market reporting agencies that supply this information. The best known of these are *Platt's* and *Petroleum Argus*. *Petroleum Argus* have kindly agreed to make their detailed records available on a confidential basis for the purposes of this study.

Argus may not be absolutely comprehensive in its coverage, but it is believed to be the more rigorous in recording information about deals of different maturities in the forward market for Russian gas oil. *Argus* hold such records from about the middle of 1984, and this determined the start of the time period covered by our analysis. Using the *Argus* records we have been able to create a substantial data base of Russian gas oil deals for both spot and forward contracts on the North West European c.i.f. cargo market, covering a period of two years from July 1984 to June 1986.

The data base contains just over 2,200 trading records. Each record specifies the date on which the deal was done, the delivery month, the delivery period or dates for forward deals, the price or differerential at which the deal was done, the names of the buyer and seller (if known), and the location (usually ARA) agreed for delivery. Other non-EEC gas oil deals recorded by *Argus* that do not meet the requirements of the spot and forward markets for Russian gas oil in North West Europe were excluded.

The information held on the data base was used to construct a series of average prices for spot and forward deals of different maturities reported in each half-month trading period. In addition, we know how many deals were reported in each period and which companies bought and sold the contracts. As some of this information is confidential we have used these results simply to describe the main statistical features of the Russian gas oil market in North West Europe and to test ideas about the way in which it functions. We have not included any specific details about particular transactions, and companies will not be named when the analysis is concerned with individual conduct, but they will appear in lists referring to groups of participants in the Russian gas oil market.

(*b*) *Market Size and the Pattern of Trading*. Over the period from July 1984 to June 1986 *Argus* recorded 2,207 deals that conformed to the specifications of the forward market for Russian gas oil. This gives an average of forty-six deals per half-month trading period, or between four and five deals per working day. As each deal represents between 18,000 and 25,000 tonnes (i.e. an average of 21,500 tonnes), this would imply a turnover of between 86,000 and 108,000 tonnes per day or almost 2 million tonnes per month, which represents about half the inland gas oil market in a major consuming country such as West Germany or the equivalent of one Brent cargo.

In order to examine the pattern of trading in more detail, the 2,000 or so deals in the Russian gas oil data base were sorted on the basis of maturity and aggregated on the basis of half-month trading periods. Table 11.1 shows for each trading period how many contracts were agreed for the current (spot) period and the subsequent forward periods.

In general, trading appears to be concentrated on the spot, first forward, and second forward periods, with relatively few deals made for the third and fourth forward periods. Over 90 per cent of the deals recorded by *Argus* were for these first three periods, and only three deals were recorded for forward periods beyond the fourth; these were included with the fourth-period deals for the purpose of analysis. The changing composition of trading in each half-month period is illustrated by Figure 11.1.

One consequence of the informal nature of the market is that there exists at any moment a 'stock' or 'population' of undischarged contracts for a range of future delivery periods. New contracts, like births, add to the population, and discharged contracts, like deaths, subtract from the population. As the contracts have different maturities, it is also possible to calculate the average 'forwardness' of 'life expectancy' of new contracts, the 'backwardness' or 'age' of discharged contracts, and the age and life expectancy of the existing population of contracts.

New contracts, or in a different terminology, deals *in* the period, are the total number of deals made during the current period (the horizontal sum of entries in Table 11.1). Discharged contracts, or deals *for* the period, are the total number of deals made for the current period in this and all previous periods (the diagonal sum of entries in Table 11.1). Undischarged contracts, or deals *at* period end, are the sum of all deals outstanding for the next period and each subsequent

Table 11.1: Deals Done in Each Trading Period for Forward Periods. July 1984–
June 1986.

	Current (Spot)	First Period	Second Period	Third Period	Fourth Period	Total Number
1984:13	5	9	2	0	0	16
1984:14	11	22	9	2	0	44
1984:15	13	25	10	0	0	48
1984:16	12	8	9	0	0	29
1984:17	7	11	8	1	0	27
1984:18	12	9	14	0	0	35
1984:19	8	9	5	0	0	22
1984:20	9	21	37	0	0	67
1984:21	13	18	17	0	0	48
1984:22	12	16	0	6	5	39
1984:23	8	0	1	8	0	17
1984:24	4	0	4	1	0	9
1985: 1	8	11	15	0	0	34
1985: 2	12	30	11	0	0	53
1985: 3	16	23	7	0	0	46
1985: 4	4	14	10	0	0	28
1985: 5	4	20	11	0	0	35
1985: 6	10	13	7	0	0	30
1985: 7	7	10	1	0	0	18
1985: 8	12	12	2	0	0	26
1985: 9	20	9	4	0	0	33
1985:10	10	12	4	0	0	26
1985:11	19	29	12	0	0	60
1985:12	17	20	5	0	0	42
1985:13	10	3	0	5	0	18
1985:14	10	3	15	5	0	33
1985:15	11	16	19	17	1	64
1985:16	13	9	17	11	0	50
1985:17	14	7	14	1	0	36
1985:18	5	12	8	1	1	27
1985:19	17	23	20	11	0	71
1985:20	16	31	17	10	0	74
1985:21	32	26	37	0	0	95
1985:22	24	61	15	20	1	121
1985:23	11	11	37	14	3	76
1985:24	6	23	13	9	0	51
1986: 1	17	17	26	5	1	66
1986: 2	18	69	32	3	0	122
1986: 3	16	25	25	2	2	70
1986: 4	8	13	3	0	1	25
1986: 5	13	16	13	0	1	43
1986: 6	5	8	3	1	0	17
1986: 7	29	11	11	0	1	52
1986: 8	11	12	10	4	0	37
1986: 9	11	16	12	1	3	43
1986:10	11	16	4	7	2	40

	Current (Spot)	First Period	Second Period	Third Period	Fourth Period	Total Number
1986:11	19	25	27	10	1	82
1986:12	12	27	13	8	2	62
Total	592	831	596	163	25	2,207
Average	12	17	12	3	<1	46

Source: *Petroleum Argus*

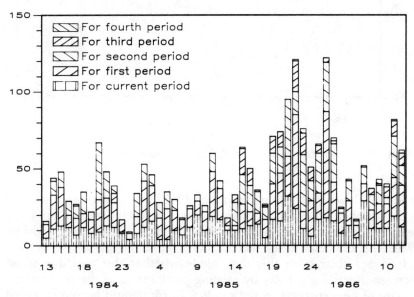

Figure 11.1 Composition of Russian Gas Oil Deals In Each Period. July 1984–June 1986.

forward period (the triangular sum of entries in Table 11.1). Each of these measures provides a different view of the changing pattern of activity on the market, and must be interpreted accordingly.

The number of new deals in each period reflects the general level of interest in the market, either from existing participants who wish to trade more or less for various reasons or from new participants who decide to enter the market. It has been argued elsewhere that the wider the spread of views about future prices in a forward market of this type, the greater the number of deals (Bacon, 1986, p. 14).

It can be seen from the data in Table 11.1 (see Figure 11.2) that the number of new deals *in each half-month* fluctuated considerably over the period under examination. For most of the time the number of deals fluctuated between a low of 10–25 deals per trading period and a high

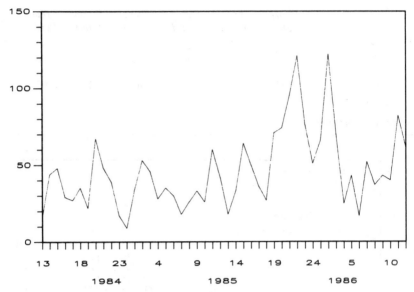

Figure 11.2 New Deals In Each Period. July 1984–June 1986.

of 50–70. However, the fourth quarter of 1985 saw an explosive increase in the number of new deals, pushing the peak level of trading up to 121 deals in the second half of November (1985:22). This continued into 1986, with 122 deals in the second half of January (1986:2).

It is not clear from this data alone whether this was due to an increase in trading activity by existing participants or the result of the activity of new entrants to the market, but it should be remembered that this was a period of great uncertainty in the world oil market when a rising price trend reversed, leading to the price collapse in early 1986, and so it is likely that it represents a sudden change in perceptions by existing participants. This question is examined further below.

The number of deals made *for a given period* is a direct consequence of previous decisions to enter into contracts for particular delivery periods. It is likely to reflect a number of different factors, such as earlier views about the likely range of spot prices in the delivery period including estimates of the likely number of cargoes to be supplied by the Soviet Union or the level of demand for gas oil in North West Europe.

In practical terms, it represents the number of contracts that must be discharged before the market can be cleared and will, together with the actual number of 'wet' cargoes made available to the market, partly determine the length and complexity of the 'daisy chains' established for that period (see Section 11.4). It also provides the basis from which profits and losses incurred by participants from trading are calculated.

Inspection of the data in Table 11.1 (see Figure 11.3) reveals that the number of deals made *for* each period also fluctuated considerably. Although the data also show the same explosion in trading for the fourth quarter of 1985, the actual pattern differs in a number of respects from that established for deals *in* the period, the most notable being the pronounced drop in deals for the last period in each year. In general there seems to be a lag of about one period between changes in the level of trading activity *in* a given period and changes in the number of deals accumulated *for* a given period. This reflects the short trading horizon in the market.

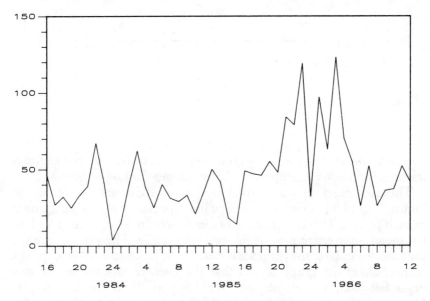

Figure 11.3 Deals For the Period. August 1984–June 1986.

The number of deals outstanding *at the end of each period* is a measure of the 'market overhang'. This can be interpreted as a measure of the total liquidity of the market at any time.

Inspection of the data in Table 11.1 (see Figures 11.2 and 11.4) also shows a rough correlation between the patterns of deals in the period and deals outstanding at the end of each period, reflecting the short average trading horizons observed above. However, during the second quarter of 1985, the market overhang fell more quickly than the level of trading, indicating a temporary shift to even shorter trading horizons.

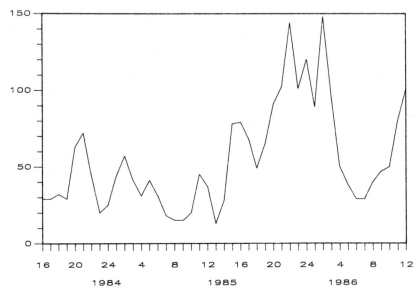

Figure 11.4 Deals At Period End. August 1984–June 1986.

During the fourth quarter of 1985 and the first quarter of 1986, however, the market overhang grew even more rapidly than the level of trading, indicating a temporary shift to longer trading horizons.

These changes in the market trading horizon are confirmed by Figure 11.5 which shows the average life expectancy of new deals made in each period. This is a measure of the 'forwardness' of trading, or how far ahead on average new deals are being made. The precise method used to calculate the index is described by Bacon, 1986, p. 18. Inspection of the graph shows that the average forwardness of new deals fell from a high of just over 1.5 periods in the first half of December 1984 (1984:23) to a low of 0.5 periods in the first half of May 1985 (1985:9), before rising again to highs of 1.7 periods in the second half of July 1985 (1985:15) and 1.8 periods in the first half of December 1985 (1985:23). However, there is no evidence of a correlation between the average forwardness of new deals and the number of new deals in each period as was found for the Brent market (Bacon, 1986, p. 25).

In the case of the Brent market there was also a very strong correlation between the number of deals for a given trading period and the average age of expiring deals (Bacon, 1986, p. 46). It was argued that these two results, which indicated that increases in trading activity tended to extend the trading horizon, suggested speculative motives for changes in the level of trading since price uncertainty (and therefore the

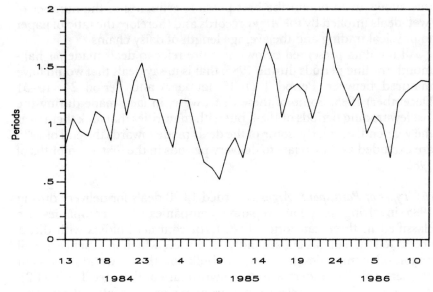

Figure 11.5 Forwardness In the Period. July 1984–June 1986.

scope for speculative gain) is clearly greater the further forward one trades. It is significant that no such results were found for the Russian gas oil market. Changes in trading activity were not correlated with changes in the average trading horizon whichever measure was used, indicating, perhaps, that speculation does not provide the main motive for trading on the forward market for Russian gas oil.

11.4 Market Composition

(*a*) *The Data*. The information provided by *Argus* on Russian gas oil trading includes not only the dates on which deals were struck, the maturities of the deals and the prices agreed, but also the names of the companies that bought and sold the contracts. The identities of the buyers and sellers were given to us on a confidential basis, as was the case for the Institute's earlier Brent market study (Mabro et al, 1986), so we cannot publish a detailed description of the trading activity of individual companies. However, it is possible to use the company names to process the trading records and hence to construct a detailed picture of the distribution of activity among the companies.

We concentrate on trading for one year only, 1985, since there is no reason to suppose that this will be unrepresentative. We present the data in terms of deals *for* the period rather than deals *in* the period as this allows us to obtain the best possible estimates of the number of 'wet' deals implied by the *Argus* records and therefore the ratio of paper to physical trading and the average length of daisy chains.

All the data presented below therefore refer to deals made *for* half-month trading periods during 1985, that is to say deals that would have matured between Period 1 (1–15 January) and Period 24 (16–31 December) 1985. Some of these deals were, in fact, made during the last few trading periods of 1984, but with maturities that took them over the year end. Similarly, some of the deals made towards the end of 1985 are excluded as they relate to delivery periods in the first few months of 1986.

(*b*) *Types of Participant*. *Argus* recorded 1,050 deals for delivery during 1985 involving sixty-four separate companies. The companies are classified in three categories: first, term contract holders with direct access to Russian gas oil; secondly, end-users which in practice are all major oil companies that buy in bulk for their own downstream markets; thirdly, traders with no downstream outlets (see Table 11.2). The companies themselves range from major international oil companies, such as BP, Esso, Shell and Texaco, with large downstream markets to service, to specialist Russian gas oil trading companies, such as Transol and Vanol.

Argus recorded more than sixty-four names, but since a number of companies operate under more than one name, or have several subsidiaries operating in the market, the deals made by a company or its subsidiaries have been added together. As *Argus* do not always

---

Table 11.2: Companies Participating in the Russian Gas Oil Market. 1985.

(*a*) *Term Contract Holders*

Apex, Avant, BP, Coastal, Gatoil, Koch, Langham Hill, Mabanaft, Neopetrol, Neste, Pegasus, Phibro, Scanoil, Shell, Thyssen, Tradax, Transol, Vanol, Vitol.

(*b*) *End-users*

CFP (Total), Elf-Aquitaine, Esso, Mobil, Norsk Hydro, Petrofina, Statoil, Texaco.

(*c*) *Trading Companies*

AOT, Astra, Attock, Britoil, Cedar, Clipper, Dutch State Mines, Edda, Gill & Duffus, Gotco, IOC, IPCO, LED, Marc Rich, Marubeni, Mebro, Merx Handel, Metallgesellschaft, Mitsubishi, Mitsui, Norwegian Oil, Nova, Oroleum, Petra, Petrodutch, PJA, Propetrol, Rossill, Standard Energy, Tinon, Transoil, Transpetrol, Tricon, Turbo, Voest Alpine, Willco.

Sources: *Petroleum Argus*, Interviews

succeed in identifying the parties to a deal, some sellers and buyers are described as 'unknown'. Only 191 parties (ninety-eight sellers and ninety-three buyers) were not identified in deals made for delivery during 1985; a success rate of 91 per cent. The success rate fluctuated over the year between 70 and 100 per cent, but was usually just over 90 per cent.

(*c*) *Distribution of Activity among Participants.* How is trading activity distributed among the sixty-four companies identified above? Table 11.3 ranks the top companies (without identifying them) in order of total activity, that is the sum of sells and buys made by each company. Since each deal involves a seller and a buyer, the total market activity is twice the number of deals recorded for delivery in 1985.

As on the Brent market, the most striking feature is the concentration of trading activity in the hands of a small number of companies.

Table 11.3: Top Twenty-five Companies Participating in the Russian Gas Oil Market in Order of Total Activity (excluding Unknowns). 1985.

Rank	Total Deals
1	206
2	153
3	151
4	138
5	137
6	132
7	86
8	78
9	62
10	60
11	53
12	52
13	44
14	38
15	37
16	36
17	34
18	33
19	29
20	27
21	27
22	25
23	22
24	21
25	19

Source: *Petroleum Argus*

The top ten companies alone account for 63 per cent of the identified activity during 1985, and the top thirty companies account for over 92 per cent. The picture is virtually identical on both the buying and selling sides of the market (see Table 11.4).

Table 11.4: Number of Sells and Buys by Top Ten and Top Thirty Companies in the Russian Gas Oil Market and Percentage Shares. 1985.

	Sells	*% Share*	*Buys*	*% Share*
Top Ten	602	63.2	601	62.8
Top Thirty	877	92.1	891	93.1
Total Identified	952	(100.0)	957	(100.0)

Source: *Petroleum Argus*

More formal methods can be used to measure the degree of concentration in the market. These include the Herfindahl index and the Gini coefficent. Both provide a means of quantifying the inequality of distribution of activity among companies participating in the Russian gas oil market.

The Gini coefficient is a measure of relative inequality which takes values between 0 and 1; the closer the value to unity, the greater the inequality, and hence the concentration of trading activity. The value obtained for the Gini coefficient indicates a very unequal distribution of activity among the companies participating in the Russian gas oil market (see Table 11.5). It is interesting to note, however, that the value is lower than that obtained using data for the Brent market in 1984, suggesting that the Brent market was rather more concentrated.

The Herfindahl index takes into account the number of companies in the market and their shares. It can be converted, by taking its inverse, into the number of equal-sized companies that would yield the same degree of market concentration as the actual distribution of companies with unequal shares.

Table 11.5: Gini Coefficients for Trading in Russian Gas Oil, 1985, and Brent, 1984.

	Russian Gas Oil	*Brent*
Total Activity	1,909	4,605
Number of Companies	64	108
Average Activity	30	43
Gini Coefficient	0.64	0.72

In the case of the Russian gas oil market, an H-index of 0.0507 was obtained, which is equivalent to having approximately twenty equal-sized firms in a market that actually involves sixty-four. Although this represents a reasonable degree of concentration in the market, it is not low enough to suggest the existence of a monopoly or an oligopoly.

Not all the companies identified above were continually involved in trading Russian gas oil. Table 11.6 shows the number of companies involved in selling, buying and trading for each half-month period during 1985, together with the average number of deals made by the active companies.

It can be seen that the total number of companies involved in trading for any one period during 1985 fluctuated between a low of ten in Period 15 (1–15 August) and a high of thirty-four in Period 23 (1–15 December). The average for the year was twenty-three.

Table 11.6: Trading in Russian Gas Oil. 1985.

Period	Total Deals	Number of Companies			Average Number of Deals per Company
		Sellers	Buyers	Total	
1	15	7	9	13	1.2
2	40	18	18	23	1.7
3	62	24	23	28	2.2
4	38	21	20	26	1.5
5	25	12	10	15	1.7
6	40	15	17	18	2.2
7	31	15	11	19	1.6
8	29	16	15	23	1.3
9	32	16	14	21	1.5
10	21	14	12	20	1.1
11	34	15	16	19	1.8
12	50	17	20	23	2.2
13	42	20	19	26	1.6
14	18	11	10	16	1.1
15	14	9	7	10	1.4
16	49	21	18	26	1.9
17	47	21	19	27	1.7
18	46	20	20	25	1.8
19	55	20	23	29	1.9
20	48	17	17	21	2.3
21	84	23	27	33	2.5
22	79	25	25	33	2.4
23	119	27	28	34	3.5
24	32	15	14	18	1.8

Source: *Petroleum Argus*

In addition, the number of companies on the selling side varied between seven in Period 1 and twenty-seven in Period 23; and the number on the buying side between seven in Period 15 and twenty-eight in Period 23. It should be remembered that some companies both buy and sell for a given period, so the total number of companies involved for any period is less than the sum of the companies buying and selling.

In general the numbers of companies on the selling and buying sides of the market for each period appear to be approximately the same.

The number of companies involved in the market for a given period and the total number of deals made for a period move approximately together, suggesting that changes in the level of trading may be associated with entries and exits from the market. However, the average number of deals made by active companies for each period also fluctuates during the year, varying between a low of 1.1 in Period 10 and a high of 3.5 in Period 23. The average for the year is 1.9.

This result tends to suggest that fluctuations in the total number of deals made for each period cannot be explained simply in terms of increases in the number of companies involved in the market: if this were the case then the average number of deals per company would be approximately constant.

Since there also appears to be a better correlation between the number of deals made for each period and the average number of deals per participant (they peak in the same periods), it seems reasonable to argue that changes in the level of dealing for periods during 1985 were more due to changing activity on the part of each participant than to changes in the number of participants, although it appears that increased levels of activity by existing participants also tend to attract new entrants into the market.

The companies have been broken into four groups depending on the frequency with which they trade: first, companies present in the market more than 75 per cent of the time (very active companies); secondly, companies present between 50 and 75 per cent of the time (active); thirdly, companies present between 25 and 50 per cent of the time (less active); and finally, companies present less than 25 per cent of the time (occasional). The numbers of companies falling into each group are summarized in Table 11.7.

It can be seen that the market is characterized by a hard core of eleven very active companies that are present in at least nineteen of the twenty-four trading periods in 1985. These companies account for 58 per cent of the identified trading activity in the year. In addition there are a further eight active companies present in at least half the trading periods which account for a further 14 per cent of the activity. The

Table 11.7: Classification of Companies by Regularity of their Trading Activity.

Category	Number
Very Active	11
Active	8
Less Active	15
Occasional	30
Total	64

remaining forty-five companies are present in less than half the trading periods and account for 28 per cent of the activity, the vast majority of these being only occasional traders.

Furthermore, most of the very active companies also tended to do more deals on average than the other participants for each trading period in which they were involved. The very active companies usually averaged at least three deals per period and many averaged more than four. The highest averaged almost nine. By comparison the active companies tended to average two deals for each period, and the less active and occasional traders only between one and two.

The trading motives of companies in each of the three categories identified previously (term contract holders, end-users and traders) correspond to those of the long-hedgers, short-hedgers and speculators in a forward or futures market. In practice, it is not always possible to distinguish motives so easily, since a company may both hedge and speculate. However, on average one would expect a term contract holder, who is by definition net long, to be a long-hedger in the forward market; an end-user, who is net short, to be a short-hedger; and a trader, who is net balanced, to be a speculator. Some companies may, of course, combine these functions in which case their overall position – net seller, net buyer or balanced – is what matters.

Table 11.8 shows the holders of Russian gas oil contracts amongst the top thirty companies. It is particularly striking that nine out of the ten most active companies are known to have had supply contracts with the Soviet Union during 1985, and that fifteen of the nineteen known contract holders are to be found in the top twenty-five most active companies. The overriding impression is of a market dominated by companies with access to physical cargoes of Russian gas oil. Such companies would therefore be in a position to hedge their availabilities in the forward market.

(d) Hedgers and Speculators. The detailed information on the trading activity of individual companies participating in the Russian gas oil

Table 11.8: Holders of Russian Contracts among the Top Twenty-five Participants in the Russian Gas Oil Market.

Rank	Russian Contract?
1	Yes
2	Yes
3	Yes
4	Yes
5	Yes
6	Yes
7	Yes
8	Yes
9	Yes
10	No
11	Yes
12	No
13	No
14	No
15	Yes
16	No
17	Yes
18	Yes
19	Yes
20	No
21	Yes
22	No
23	No
24	No
25	No

market can also be used to assess the net position of companies for each half-month trading period during 1985. This is the difference between the total number of sells and buys made by each company for each period. On average some companies tend to be net sellers, some net buyers and some in balance. Table 11.9 shows the ten largest net sellers and buyers for the year.

Both the net sellers and the net buyers include companies with Russian contracts, suggesting perhaps that some of the term contract holders may also be end-users using the forward market to augment their supplies of Russian cargoes. One reason for this may be the unpredictability of Russian contract quantities for individual companies. Thus a company with a term contract might sell in the barge market, having hedged its position in the forward cargo market, and then not receive a cargo in the right date range to meet the barge commitment. In these circumstances the company would need to take

Table 11.9: Top Net Sellers and Buyers in the Russian Gas Oil Market.

Rank	Net Sellers Russian Contract?	Deals	Net Buyers Russian Contract?	Deals
1	Yes	33	No	34
2	Yes	19	Yes	26
3	No	16	Yes	25
4	No	14	Yes	24
5	Yes	11	No	13
6	No	10	No	6
7	Yes	8	Yes	6
8	Yes	8	Yes	5
9	No	5	No	4

Source: *Petroleum Argus*

delivery of the forward cargo from another more fortunate company in order to meet its obligations in the barge market.

The sum of the net sales (or purchases) made for a given period gives the net transfer of contracts from sellers to buyers when the market clears for the period. This provides a rough measure of the number of 'wet' contracts made available to the market, assuming that the *Argus* coverage of the market is representative and not biased towards either sellers or buyers. The ratio of total sells or buys to net deals will give a rough measure of the average length of a daisy chain for the period (see Table 11.10).

It can be seen that the number of net deals for each period fluctuates between a low of five in Period 15 (1–15 August) and a high of twenty-nine in Periods 21–23 (1–15 November to 1–15 December). The total for the year is 379, giving an average of sixteen per half-month trading period. Given that the median size of a forward Russian gas oil contract is 21,500 tonnes (18–25,000 range), this would represent 688,000 tonnes per month or just over 8 mtpa of Russian gas oil passing through the forward market in North West Europe. This is approximately half the total exports of gas oil from the Soviet Union to OECD Europe in 1985.

As far as daisy chains are concerned, the ratio of total to net deals varies between a low of 1.4 in Period 1 (1–15 January) to a high of 4.4 in Period 6 (16–31 March), typically taking values between two and three. The average for 1985 is 2.8. *Argus* suggest that daisy chains in the Russian gas oil market are usually around five and rarely more than eight deals long, which is not inconsistent with this result since, as we argued in the case of Brent, perceptions tend to focus on the mode

Table 11.10: Number of Deals, Net Transfers and Average Length of Daisy Chains on the Russian Gas Oil Market by Trading Period.

Period Number	Total Deals	Net Deals	Ratio Total/Net
1	15	11	1.4
2	40	19	2.1
3	62	18	3.4
4	38	14	2.7
5	25	9	2.8
6	40	9	4.4
7	31	13	2.4
8	29	15	1.9
9	32	13	2.5
10	21	14	1.5
11	34	13	2.6
12	50	14	3.6
13	42	19	2.2
14	18	12	1.5
15	14	5	2.8
16	49	19	2.5
17	47	21	2.2
18	46	14	3.2
19	55	16	3.4
20	48	14	3.4
21	84	29	2.8
22	79	29	2.7
23	119	29	4.1
24	32	10	3.2
Total	1,050	379	2.8

Source: *Petroleum Argus*

rather than the mean and thus may overstate the value (Mabro et al, 1986, p. 198).

An average daisy chain in the Russian gas oil market will therefore involve three-to-four players:

Net Seller – Trader – Net Buyer

or:

Net Seller – Trader – Trader – Net Buyer

indicating that the number of purely speculative players is small in relation to the number of net sellers and net buyers. By comparison, daisy chains in the Brent market were much longer, averaging between nine and sixteen in 1984, and much more in 1985. As a result, one would expect that the forward market for Russian gas oil would be less likely to experience the clearing problems that arose in the Brent market in the first quarter of 1986 and the second quarter of 1987.

11.5 Price Behaviour and Market Efficiency

Trading on a forward market generates a spectrum of prices. On any day there will be a number of different prices, each relating to a specific forward trading period. As a result it is never possible to say what the market price is without referring to the period for which the deal is being made.

The prices themselves reflect a variety of influences depending on the type of deal that is being struck. Prices for the current delivery period, that is to say 'spot' prices, will reflect the price at which participants are prepared to buy and sell wet cargoes of Russian gas oil for delivery c.i.f. ARA. This price will be influenced mainly by the fundamentals of supply and demand for gas oil in the ARA range, although it will also be affected by technical factors such as arbitrage opportunities between the non-EEC market and the EEC cargo and barge markets in North West Europe, and the actual number of Russian gas oil cargoes available to wet the backlog of paper contracts for that period.

Prices for the different forward periods, that is to say prices for the next two half-month trading periods, will reflect the prices at which participants are prepared to buy and sell paper contracts for delivery during these periods. These prices will be influenced more by price expectations than by the current fundamentals of supply and demand for gas oil. Such expectations can be formed in a number of different ways, ranging from a simple extrapolation of the current level or trend in prices to a sophisticated assessment of future price levels based on a wide range of relevant market information.

One of the more interesting questions raised by forward markets is the relationship between prices struck for deals of different maturities, in particular between spot and forward prices. This can take several forms, and the nature of the relationship can help to reveal the way in which the market is being used by the various participants.

Although the Russian gas oil market is an active market by most product trading standards, it is not sufficiently active to generate a continuous series of prices for deals of different maturities on a daily basis. As a result, it is necessary to aggregate deals over a longer period. Furthermore, since forward deals relate to delivery at any point during a specified half-month trading period, there is uncertainty about the exact maturity of any deal at any moment. For this reason we decided to aggregate prices on the basis of trading periods rather than weeks or months. The exact procedure has already been described above in Section 11.3 and the price data are shown in Table 11.11.

It can be seen from the data in Table 11.11 that continuous (or almost continuous) period average price series could be obtained only for the spot, first forward and second forward trading periods. Deals for the third and fourth forward trading periods were still too infrequent to yield continuous series. The analysis that follows will therefore focus on the relationship between these first three price series.

Table 11.11: Spot and Forward Prices on the Russian Gas Oil Market. July 1984–December 1985. Dollars per Tonne.

Period	Spot	One-period Forward	Two-period Forward
1984:13	227.30	229.71	231.87
1984:14	222.37	222.75	221.04
1984:15	217.71	223.84	224.45
1984:16	230.00	231.37	236.72
1984:17	230.10	232.02	233.25
1984:18	237.12	239.63	242.82
1984:19	244.21	243.86	243.55
1984:20	225.90	231.75	228.61
1984:21	231.58	234.53	237.54
1984:22	231.72	229.07	n.a.
1984:23	225.05	226.75[a]	226.00
1984:24	218.25	216.75[a]	222.31
1985: 1	220.70	225.21	221.58
1985: 2	236.42	231.30	226.42
1985: 3	239.09	234.03	236.57
1985: 4	250.68	239.81	234.60
1985: 5	238.67	233.15	229.85
1985: 6	237.37	233.81	231.95
1985: 7	234.17	232.92	228.50
1985: 8	230.76	227.18	226.00
1985: 9	219.84	218.31	213.06
1985:10	217.56	216.14	215.68
1985:11	215.44	213.64	210.43
1985:12	218.04	214.72	215.75
1985:13	219.90	217.66	217.15[a]
1985:14	219.18	218.66	219.16
1985:15	227.02	227.79	225.23
1985:16	243.55	237.06	235.81
1985:17	248.66	245.50	246.56
1985:18	249.35	247.68	245.90
1985:19	258.57	256.09	256.87
1985:20	260.64	257.50	257.23
1985:21	267.42	266.73	265.16
1985:22	279.34	275.48	276.60

Period	Spot	One-period Forward	Two-period Forward
1985:23	258.06	253.72	249.88
1985:24	237.66	239.72	237.34
1986: 1	239.16	230.67	228.94
1986: 2	211.91	193.71	182.41
1986: 3	195.82	179.49	169.87
1986: 4	191.11	187.56	175.16
1986: 5	185.82	163.78	152.50
1986: 6	183.30	163.89	151.83
1986: 7	144.00	145.47	141.10
1986: 8	154.19	137.90	133.87
1986: 9	158.84	144.07	137.33
1986:10	134.29	133.32	132.37
1986:11	121.40	118.61	117.86
1986:12	113.57	114.84	114.80

Note: (a) These figures are estimated from contemporary exchanges.
Source: *Petroleum Argus*

Figure 11.6 shows period average Russian gas oil prices for current (spot), first forward and second forward period deals from mid-1984 to the end of 1985. It can be seen that the three series move very closely together, fluctuating around an average of about $230 per tonne until mid-1985. In the second half of 1985, however, there is a very steep increase in prices from a low point of $215 per tonne in 1985:11 to a high point of $280 per tonne in 1985:22. After this point prices then fall away steeply, reaching $114 per tonne by the end of the sample period.

In some periods forward prices are below spot prices (this is known as 'backwardation' in commodity markets); and in some periods forward prices are above spot prices (this is known as 'contango'). The difference between spot prices and the first forward and second forward period prices (spot minus forward) is shown in Figure 11.7. It can be seen that, on average, the market was in contango (spot below forward) in the second half of 1984, and in backwardation (spot above forward) in 1985 and 1986. This general pattern was repeated in other oil markets such as the Brent forward market during the same period (Bacon, 1986).

Since forward prices tend to reflect expectations of future prices, price differentials between spot and forward periods should reflect expectations of future price movements. Thus, if the first and second period prices are successively lower (higher) than the spot price, it is reasonable to argue that the market as a whole expects a decline (increase) in spot prices in the future. In the case of the Brent market it has been found that 'almost without exception if the one month

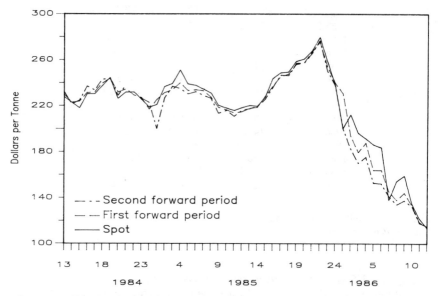

Figure 11.6 Russian Gas Oil Prices (Cargoes c.i.f. ARA). July 1984–June 1986.

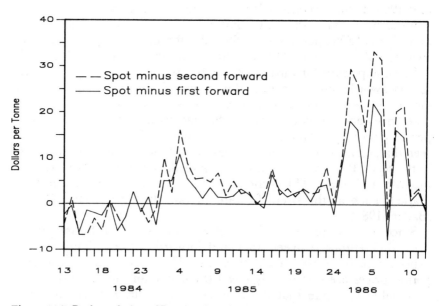

Figure 11.7 Backwardation of Russian Gas Oil Prices. July 1984–June 1986.

forward price is set below (above) the current price, then the two month price will be even more below (above) the current price . . . There is no notable occasion on which (say) the one month price was below the current price and the two month price was nearer to the current price (indicating the expectation of a fall in price followed by a partial recovery).' This 'suggests very strongly that expectations [in the Brent market] were very much formed on an extrapolative basis.' (Bacon, 1986, p. 29.)

It is interesting to observe that this is not the case in the Russian gas oil market; there are many occasions on which the second period price is closer to the spot price than the first period price (see Figure 11.7). As a result it seems reasonable to suggest that expectations in the Russian gas oil market are formed in a different fashion.

In a forward market, in which buyers and sellers are able and willing to hedge against adverse price movements by selling and buying forward contracts, it is possible to argue that the spot price expected for the next period will be related to the forward price established now:

$$PE_t(t + 1) = a + P_t(t + 1) \tag{11.1}$$

where $PE_t(t + 1)$ is the spot price expected at time t to be ruling at time $t + 1$. With a forecasting regime that makes random, rather than systematic, errors this can be replaced by the equation:

$$P_{t+1}(t + 1) = a + P_t(t + 1) + u_t \tag{11.2}$$

where $E(u_t) = 0$ and u_t is a random variable.

If the market is being used solely for hedging purposes, and if participants can forecast correctly on average, then the regression of the spot price for period $t + 1$ on the forward price for the same period established in period t should yield a coefficient b which is not significantly different from unity:

$$P_t(t) = a + bP_{t-1}(t) \tag{11.3}$$

However, such a test may fail if forecasts are biased or if participants do not, in fact, attempt to arbitrage between spot and forward markets.

Furthermore, the forward price established in period $t-1$, should, according to the 'efficient markets hypothesis' of Fama, 1970, encapsulate *all* systematic knowledge available at time $t-1$ concerning the future spot price in period t. Any new information about the future spot price should cause participants to change their pattern of trading, and the forward price should react accordingly. Hence the forward price should be the best (and sufficient) predictor of the future spot price, and no other currently available price series should be able to improve on the predictive power of the current forward price for the future spot price.

Of course, the forward price does not have to be a very accurate predictor of the spot price: it just has to be the best available at the time. This can be tested by adding other relevant price series to the regression of spot prices in period t against the forward price in period $t-1$. Two sets of prices in particular should not be able to improve on the performance of the lagged forward price: current or earlier spot prices, and forward prices set in earlier periods for the same terminal date, for example:

$$P_t(t) = a + bP_{t-1}(t) + cP_{t-1}(t-1) \qquad (11.4)$$

or:

$$P_t(t) = a + bP_{t-1}(t) + cP_{t-2}(t) \qquad (11.5)$$

The results presented below are based on a data set of thirty-six observations running from the first half of July 1984 (1984:13) to the second half of December 1985 (1985:24). Three price series were used, representing the average prices established in each half-month trading period for spot deals, first forward period deals and second forward period deals respectively. The price data are presented in Table 11.11.

It is important to note two features of the data set. First, there was a steep fall in spot prices starting in the first half of December 1985 (1985:23) and continuing to the end of the sample, which does not appear to have been captured in the forward prices set in earlier periods; this corresponds to sharp falls in other markets such as Brent. Such a large and unexpected fall in prices is likely to bias the results of any regression and it proved necessary to exclude these observations from some tests.

Secondly, it was necessary to estimate forward prices in some periods from contemporary deals such as exchanges. This was done for the one-period forward price in 1984:23 and 1984:24 and for the two-period forward price in 1985:13. There was no suitable basis for estimation in 1984:22 for second period forward prices, so it was necessary to use a shorter run of data for tests involving the two-period forward price.

In order to establish whether or not the forward price is in fact the best predictor of the future spot price, three basic equations were estimated using an ordinary least squares system:

$$P_t(t) = a + bP_{t-1}(t) \tag{11.6}$$

$$P_t(t) = a + bP_{t-1}(t-1) \tag{11.7}$$

$$P_t(t) = a + bP_{t-1}(t) + cP_{t-1}(t-1) \tag{11.8}$$

The results are summarized below.

Table 11.12 shows the results of regressions using the data set with the price fall removed (1984:15–1985:22) for each of the three equations specified above. Two observations are 'lost' at the start of the period to allow for lags of up to two periods.

Table 11.12: Regressions of Spot Prices on Lagged Forward and Lagged Spot Prices. August 1984–November 1985 (32 Observations). Dollars per Tonne.

Equation Number	Constant	$P_{t-1}(t)$	$P_{t-1}(t-1)$	R^2	DWS	SEE	d_L	d_U	Durbin's h-statistic
11.6	−20.22 (0.84)	1.10 (10.60)		0.79	1.38	7.43	1.16	1.28	
11.7	3.27 (0.13)		0.99 (9.48)	0.75	1.82	8.10	1.16	1.28	0.64 (<1.645)
11.8	−19.17 (0.78)	0.97 (2.36)	0.12 (0.31)	0.79	1.46	7.55	1.10	1.35	0.71 (<1.645)

It can be seen that both the lagged forward price (in equation 11.6) and the lagged spot price (in equation 11.7) yield significant results with good explanatory power.

In both cases the coefficient b of the independent variable is not significantly different from unity. However, the lagged forward price is, on average, a better predictor of the future spot price than the lagged spot price; the correlation coefficient R^2 is higher and the standard error SEE is lower. Furthermore, when both price series are included in the same regression (equation 11.8), the lagged forward price is chosen in preference to the lagged spot price. In fact the coefficient of the lagged spot price is not significantly different from zero, whereas the coefficient of the lagged forward price is not significantly different from unity. In other words the introduction of the lagged spot price to the regression does not add anything to the explanatory power of the equation.

A similar result is obtained (see Table 11.13) by regressing the spot price against the spot price of two periods before and the forward price prevailing two periods before:

$$P_t(t) = a + bP_{t-2}(t) + cP_{t-2}(t-2) \tag{11.9}$$

Table 11.13: Regressions of Spot Prices on One- and Two-period Lagged Forward and Spot Prices. January–November 1985 (22 Observations). Dollars per Tonne.

Equation Number	Constant	$P_{t-1}(t)$	$P_{t-2}(t)$	$P_{t-1}(t-1)$	$P_{t-2}(t-2)$	R^2	DWS	SEE	d_L	d_U
11.9	−23.07		1.59		−0.45	0.70	1.10	10.32	0.91	1.28
	(0.59)		(2.81)		(0.85)					
11.10	−5.95	1.51	−0.47			0.91	1.93	5.72	0.91	1.28
	(0.27)	(6.73)	(1.82)							
11.11	−8.51	2.26	−0.50	−0.70		0.92	1.88	5.45	0.83	1.41
	(0.41)	(4.60)	(2.04)	(1.70)						

Once again, the forward price is the better predictor of the future spot price, in this case two periods ahead rather than one. However, it should be noted that the data sample used for this regression is smaller than that used in Table 11.12. There are only twenty-three observations, as it was not possible to obtain a complete series of second forward period prices.

Further evidence is obtained if the forecasting power of the one-period and two-period forward prices are compared over the same shorter sample period:

$$P_t(t) = a + bP_{t-1}(t) + cP_{t-2}(t) \qquad (11.10)$$

In this case the one-period forward price is preferred to the two-period forward price (see Table 11.13), as a predictor of the future spot price, since it reflects not only all the information available two periods before, but also any relevant information that has arisen since the two-period forward price was settled.

An alternative approach is to add both one- and two-period forward prices to the lagged spot price:

$$P_t(t) = a + bP_{t-1}(t-1) + cP_{t-1}(t) + dP_{t-2}(t) \qquad (11.11)$$

which also yields a similar result (see Table 11.13), with the lagged one-period forward price being the dominant variable.

The results obtained from these regressions provide an interesting contrast to those obtained for the Brent market by Mabro et al, 1986 (Annex 4). In the case of Brent, the results showed that the lagged *spot* price was the dominant forecasting variable in all cases, thus rejecting the efficient markets hypothesis in its weak form. The evidence from the forward market for Russian gas oil in North West Europe, however, does not reject the efficient markets hypothesis, since the lagged *forward* price was found to be the dominant forecasting variable.

It was argued that the Brent market data reject the efficient markets hypothesis because the market was being used for purposes other than physical arbitrage and hedging. These included, for example, short-term speculation by traders who were not interested in taking delivery of Brent cargoes. The effect was to create a market that was 'dominated by deals that are made with considerations other than expectations of what the price will actually turn out to be in the delivery period.' (Mabro et al, 1986, p. 292.)

In view of the fact that the Russian gas oil market data do not reject the efficient markets hypothesis, it is reasonable to argue the opposite. Thus the results presented above suggest that the market is used primarily for physical arbitrage and hedging, and that speculators do not play a major role in setting prices.

11.6 Price Relationships and Market Share

Russian gas oil plays a barometric role in the North West European gas oil market. It has achieved this position primarily because it is a forward market. Participants in other related markets are likely to use forward markets as an indicator of market trends for two reasons: first, because the level of activity is generally higher in a forward market than in spot markets, and secondly, because forward trading acts as a focus for price expectations and is therefore thought to be a good guide to market sentiment.

There is no objective means of measuring the total level of activity in any spot market in which transactions are not formally recorded. However, it is possible to make a rough estimate of relative levels of activity in the various markets for gas oil if one assumes that reporting agencies such as *Argus* manage to sample the market in an unbiased fashion.

The simplest method of estimating the market share of Russian gas oil in the North West European gas oil market is to count the number of deals of each type reported by *Argus* in a representative period such as 1985.

Argus record daily deals for non-EEC (Russian) gas oil cargoes c.i.f. ARA, EEC gas oil cargoes, and gas oil barges f.o.b. Rotterdam.

During 1985 *Argus* recorded a total of 1,327 gas oil deals in North West Europe. 1,097 of these were Russian gas oil deals, mostly paper deals for forward periods. On this basis Russian gas oil trading represents 83 per cent of North West European gas oil trading. The results are shown for each month in 1985 in Table 11.14. The lowest estimate is 67 per cent in February and the highest 95 per cent in December. This estimate was confirmed by a Russian gas oil trader, who expressed the view that Russian gas oil represents about 80 per cent of the North West European gas oil trading, and clearly demonstrates that Russian gas oil plays a dominant role in the North West European products market.

Table 11.14:   Russian Gas Oil Deals as a Share of Reported Gas Oil Deals in North West Europe. 1985.

Month	Russian Gas Oil	Other Gas Oil	Total Gas Oil	% Share
Jan	105	37	142	74
Feb	70	35	105	67
Mar	64	18	82	78
Apr	54	17	71	76
May	57	14	71	80
Jun	88	20	108	81
Jul	55	18	73	75
Aug	121	24	145	83
Sep	56	9	65	86
Oct	100	14	114	88
Nov	203	17	220	92
Dec	124	7	131	95
Total	1,097	230	1,327	83

Source: *Petroleum Argus*

The ARA range is the locus of three closely linked markets for gas oil: the Rhine barge market, the EEC-qualified cargo market and the non-EEC-qualified cargo market. The three markets are distinguished by the sizes of parcels traded and whether or not import duty is payable.

The barge market deals in small parcels, usually in the range of 1,000–6,000 tonnes, suitable for inland delivery. These are sold f.o.b. and are usually EEC qualified. It is this commodity that is traded on the London gas oil futures market (the International Petroleum Exchange), although it should be noted that the parcel size on the London market is smaller: only 100 tonnes.

The cargo market deals in large parcels, usually 20–60,000 tonnes delivered c.i.f. North West Europe. It is divided into an EEC-qualified market (in which no import duty is payable) and a non-EEC-qualified market (in which EEC import duty is levied).

As explained above (Chapter 10) EEC duty is levied at a rate of 3.5 per cent of the c.i.f. value of cargoes imported from non-member countries. However, as a result of various trade agreements between the EEC and countries in North Africa and the Middle East, duty is only payable in reality on oil imported from a limited number of countries. The Soviet Union is one of these.

Although Russian gas oil imports are not exempt from EEC duties, importers can still avoid paying import duty if the gas oil is either in transit for a non-EEC country such as Sweden or Switzerland, can be offset against duty credits associated with other oil movements by the same company, or imported for further processing and thus classified as a 'feedstock' rather than a 'finished product'. In the Netherlands, Belgium and West Germany the customs authorities allow importers to 'stabilize' non-EEC qualified gas oil by washing it with caustic soda and sulphuric acid, thus avoiding import duty. The cost of this process is estimated to be around $3 per tonne, which compared in 1985 with import duties of $7–8 per tonne. Recently, however, lower oil prices have reduced this operation to break-even.

During 1986, however, traders have been discouraged from using this method of avoiding duty by a spectacular failure in the stabilization process in February, which left customers with heating oil that would not burn! Since then, buyers have been reluctant to accept 'stabilized' material and there are rumours that the customs authorities are reconsidering whether to allow this loophole to persist. In addition, prices have fallen so much that the economics of the stabilization process are frequently no better than break-even. Nevertheless, despite these difficulties, arbitrage continues between the three gas oil markets in much the same way as it always has done, and the Russian gas oil market is still regarded as a useful indicator of price trends.

How effective the Russian gas oil market is as an indicator of spot market trends in the EEC cargo market and Rotterdam barge market will depend on, first, the degree of correlation between the spot price of Russian gas oil and spot prices in the other cargo and barge markets, and, secondly, the extent to which price expectations in all markets are channelled through the forward market for Russian gas oil.

The question of price correlation is investigated below using simple regression analysis. The data used are period average spot prices for gas oil in the North West European cargo and barge markets as reported by *Platt's*, together with spot prices for Russian gas oil from the *Argus* data base. The periods used are consistent with those in the forward market for Russian gas oil and were calculated from daily *Platt's* quotations. Averages were calculated for the high and low ends of the range quoted by *Platt's* for cargoes c.i.f. ARA and barges f.o.b.

Rotterdam. According to *Platt's*, the low end of the cargo trading range is usually non-EEC gas oil. We have taken the three representative series to be as follows:

(a) *PR* (non-EEC cargoes): spot Russian gas oil (*Argus*);
(b) *PC* (EEC cargoes): cargoes high (*Platt's*);
(c) *PB* (Rotterdam barges): barges high (*Platt's*).

Inspection of the *Platt's* price data shows that prices in the three markets move very closely together. This is confirmed by the results of our regression analysis which are given in Table 11.15. The highest correlation ($\bar{R}^2 = 0.995$) is between the prices in the two EEC-qualified markets for gas oil, *PC* and *PB*. But the correlation between the two cargo markets, non-EEC-qualified, *PR*, and EEC-qualified, *PC*, is not much lower ($\bar{R}^2 = 0.990$), and the correlation between the prices in the EEC barge market, *PB*, and the non-EEC cargo market, *PR*, is slightly lower still ($\bar{R}^2 = 0.987$). However, it is hardly possible to distinguish between the three results in any objective sense.

Table 11.15: Correlation Matrix for Spot Gas Oil Prices in North West Europe. Period Average Observations. 1984:15–1986:12.

($\bar{R}^2$)	PR	PC	PB
PR	1.0000	0.9901	0.9874
PC		1.0000	0.9950
PB			1.0000

The question of price expectations in the Russian gas oil market has already been examined in Section 11.5, where it was found that, during the period under examination, forward prices for Russian gas oil were, in general, a better predictor of future spot prices than previously established spot prices. It was argued that this suggests that the prime function of the market is for physical arbitrage and hedging rather than speculation. This result supports the idea that the Russian gas oil market provides an effective channel for price expectations in that market.

Given the high degree of correlation between the three spot markets for gas oil in North West Europe (which suggests that the price risks of using the forward market for hedging other types of gas oil are fairly low), it is reasonable to suggest that the forward market may also provide an effective channel for price expectations in other related gas oil markets. If this is the case, then the same tests can be applied in order to see whether or not the forward price of *Russian* gas oil is a

better predictor of the future spot prices of EEC cargoes and Rotterdam barges.

In view of the serious statistical difficulties posed by the collapse in
oil prices at the end of 1985 and the beginning of 1986 we restrict this
analysis to the sub-period identified in Section 11.3 (1984:15–1985:22).
As before, three sets of equations were estimated and the results are
shown in Table 11.16.

Table 11.16: Regressions of Spot Cargo and Barge Prices on Lagged Forward
Russian Gas Oil Prices and Lagged Spot Cargo and Barge Prices.
August 1984–November 1985 (32 Observations). Dollars per Tonne.

Dependent Variable	Constant	$PR_{t-1}(t)$	$PC_{t-1}(t-1)$	$PB_{t-1}(t-1)$	R^2	DWS	SEE	d_L	d_U
$PC_t(t)$	−26.74 (1.11)	1.10 (2.84)	0.04 (0.12)		0.82	1.54	7.24	1.10	1.35
$PB_t(t)$	−8.22 (0.37)	0.87 (2.65)		0.17 (0.53)	0.80	1.62	6.85	1.10	1.35

In both cases the results were the same as those obtained for the
Russian gas oil market. The one-period lagged forward price for
Russian gas oil proved to be a better predictor of the future spot price
for EEC cargoes, *PC*, and Rotterdam barges, *PB*, than the lagged spot
price in either market. Thus it would seem that the forward market for
Russian gas oil does in fact act as an effective barometer for other
related markets in the ARA range since it provides the best available
guide to market trends for all types of gas oil.

11.7 Conclusion

The results of our analysis provide a number of possible insights into
the operation of the Russian gas oil market when compared with that of
the Brent market. In the preceding sections we have examined a
number of different aspects of the Russian gas oil market: its size,
growth and pattern of trading, the nature and motives of participants
and the behaviour of prices. In each case there were important
differences between the Russian gas oil market and the Brent market
which highlight the different functions of the two markets.

First, there is size. The Russian gas oil market is much smaller than
the Brent market. The total reported daily turnover is approximately
equivalent to only one Brent cargo, while the reported turnover in the
Brent market during the same period was between ten and fifteen

cargoes per day. Furthermore, apart from a number of short episodes during which trading levels increased sharply before falling back again, the size of the Russian gas oil market has remained fairly constant during most of the period under study.

Secondly, there is the pattern of trading. Trading horizons in the Russian gas oil market are much shorter than those in the Brent market. Each forward trading period is for half a month rather than a full month, and the majority of trading is concentrated in the first forward period (at most one month ahead) with hardly any deals extending beyond the fourth forward period (at most two-and-a-half months ahead). In the case of the Brent market, the average forwardness was found to be between one and two months ahead, and deals were often made four or five months forward. Also there is no evidence that speculative motives might provide an explanation for changes in the pattern of trading on the Russian gas oil market as was found in the case of Brent.

Thirdly, there is the nature of the participants. The Russian gas oil market is dominated by companies known to hold term contracts for Russian gas oil from the Soviet export agency. In the case of the Brent market, over half the trading activity was accounted for by companies that neither owned North Sea production nor wished to take delivery of it.

Fourthly, there are the motives of the participants. The majority of the t: ling activity in the Russian gas oil market is accounted for by companies with access to physical cargoes of Russian gas oil. Such companies are in a position to hedge, either as sellers against the expectation of future supplies from the Soviet Union, or as buyers against a forward commitment to supply Russian gas oil to an end-user, and both would expect to make or take delivery. In the case of the Brent market, not only was the majority of the trading activity accounted for by trading companies with little interest in the physical commodity, but also those who did own production used the market mainly to establish an arm's length price for UK tax purposes. Thus the prime interest of the pure trading companies was to speculate rather than to hedge, and the prime interest of the primary suppliers was the price at which the deal was struck (in relation to their perception of the price at which internal transfers would be taxed) rather than the actual outcome in the month.

Fifthly, there is the ratio of paper deals to wet deals, which provides a rough indication of the level of speculative activity in relation to hedging. In the case of the Russian gas oil market this was found to be very low, on average two-to-three paper deals for every wet cargo put onto the market. In the case of the Brent market this was found to be very high, ranging from nine to sixteen paper deals for every wet cargo in 1984, and much more in 1985.

Finally, there is the behaviour of prices. In the case of Russian gas oil, the forward price was found to be the best predictor of future spot prices, also suggesting that the primary function of the market is for hedging. In the case of Brent, the forward price performed worse than the current spot price as a predictor of future spot prices, suggesting that the Brent market was used primarily for purposes other than hedging.

Given that, on the basis of the evidence presented above, the main function of the forward market for Russian gas oil appears to be to provide a hedging mechanism for holders of Russian gas oil term contracts, and given that this function appears to be discharged efficiently, it is interesting to ask why the Russian gas oil market has not attracted a greater level of interest from non-contract holders, either as a hedging instrument for other grades of gas oil traded on the Rotterdam spot market or for general speculative purposes as has happened in the case of Brent.

The lack of growth in the Russian gas oil market is all the more curious since it is clearly used as a pricing barometer by traders in other markets, and apparently provides the best predictor of future prices in the associated EEC-qualified cargo and barge markets in North West Europe. In the case of a formal futures market, such a high degree of correlation with other markets for similar commodities (in other words a small basis risk) would tend to encourage new entrants into the market to hedge their positions in the associated commodities and so increase the overall level of activity. More activity would tend to attract speculators, thus further increasing the size of the market.

The main difference between the Russian gas oil market and a formal futures market is the way it is organized. In a formal futures market, the exchange becomes a party to every deal and there are elaborate rules to maintain liquidity and ensure deliverability. In an informal forward market such as the Russian gas oil market, deals are still made directly between participants, and liquidity and deliverability are the collective responsibility of the participants, who retain the right to choose with whom they deal. As a result, the barriers to entry for a new participant can be formidable and may well deter new players.

Of course, the same rules apply to Brent market, which is another informal forward market. However, it seems likely that the grounds for discrimination may well be different. In the Brent market, the size of the parcel makes the credit-worthiness and track record of the trading partner the most important attribute. Liquidity and deliverability are not usually regarded as a problem since there is almost always a Brent producer prepared to supply a cargo or take an offsetting position (at a price). In the Russian gas oil market, the underlying uncertainty over the exact timing of availabilities from the Soviet Union probably makes access to a physical cargo the most important attribute for a trading partner. In these circumstances it is not surprising that the Russian gas oil market remains largely confined to those with term contracts for the supply of Russian gas oil, and that playing the Russian gas oil market is known as 'Russian roulette' by those outside this rather small group of trading companies.

PART IV

APPENDICES

APPENDIX 1
SEASONALITY OF SOVIET EXPORTS OF REFINED PRODUCTS

A1.1 Gas Oil

Statistical analysis of the seasonality of gas oil exports yields the results shown in Table A1.1. A dummy variable was used to test for a 'structural' change between 4Q81 and 1Q82. As this is significant, the test supports the idea that there was a step change in the average level of gas oil exports between 1981 and 1982. It can be seen that the coefficient is fairly small (880,400 tonnes) compared with the average level of exports in the period from 1980 to end 1981.

Table A1.1: Regression Statistics for Seasonality of Gas Oil Exports. 1980–85 (24 Observations). Thousand Tonnes per Quarter.

Variable	Coefficient	Standard Error	t-statistic
Constant	2,678.8	357.94	7.48
Dummy	880.4	309.99	2.84
Second Quarter	584.7	413.31	1.41
Third Quarter	1,238.5	413.31	3.00
Fourth Quarter	1,304.8	413.31	3.16
$R^2 = 0.53$,	$SEE = 715.88$,	$DWS = 1.81$	

The average level of gas oil exports in the period from 1Q82 to 4Q85 is estimated at 3.6 million tonnes, but only the third and fourth quarters return significant seasonal factors. The average level in these last two quarters of the year is 1.2–1.3 million tonnes above the average level for the first quarter.

In addition the deseasonalized pattern is very unstable, as indicated by the relatively poor explanatory power of the regression ($R^2 = 0.53$), with frequent deviations above and below the expected mean level. These occurred in all years except 1982. The general pattern is thus one of irregular and unpredictable fluctuations in export volumes with both upside and downside uncertainties.

A1.2 Fuel Oil

Within the year fuel oil exports show a distinct seasonal pattern. Exports are lowest in the first quarter, rise in the second and third quarters, and fall away

Table A1.2: Regression Statistics for Seasonality of Fuel Oil Exports. 1980–85 (24 Observations). Thousand Tonnes per Quarter.

Variable	Coefficient	Standard Error	t-statistic
Constant	90.3	195.63	0.46
Dummy	877.1	169.42	5.18
Second Quarter	1,005.8	225.90	4.45
Third Quarter	1,480.2	225.90	6.55
Fourth Quarter	914.3	225.90	4.04

$R^2 = 0.79$, $SEE = 391.27$, $DWS = 2.32$

again in the fourth. This is confirmed by statistical analysis which yields the results shown in Table A1.2.

Once again the dummy variable was used to test for a 'structural' change of the type outlined above between 4Q81 and 1Q82. Since this is significant, our test supports the idea that there was a quantum increase of 877,100 tonnes in the average level of fuel oil exports between 1981 and 1982.

From 1982 onwards there is a statistically significant seasonal pattern around a flat trend. The average level of fuel oil exports in the first quarter is 967,400 tonnes and the seasonal variation in the subsequent quarters lies in the range of 914,300 tonnes (fourth quarter) to 1.5 million tonnes (third quarter). The underlying trend appears to be resonably stable, given the good explanatory power of the regression ($R^2 = 0.79$), and there are only a few episodes where actual export volumes deviate substantially from those predicted by the regression. These occurred in 1Q–3Q81, which pre-dates the apparent change in export patterns, in 4Q82, and in 1Q–2Q85. It is interesting to note that these major fluctuations were both above and below the trend and tended to be associated with the winter quarters, suggesting, perhaps, that variations in Soviet weather patterns may be responsible.

A1.3 Light Distillates

Within the year, light-distillate exports show no regular seasonal pattern. This is confirmed by statistical analysis which yields the results as shown in Table A1.3.

None of the seasonal factors is significant. However, as with the regressions for gas oil and fuel oil, the best results are obtained using the dummy variable to capture the apparent structural change which seems to have occurred in all products exports between 1981 and 1982. This variable is also significant in the case of Soviet light-distillate exports, indicating an increase of 432,500 tonnes in the average level of exports between the two periods. The average level of light-distillate exports in the period from 1982 onwards is therefore about 1.5 million tonnes per quarter. In addition, the overall explanatory power of the regression is not very good ($R^2 = 0.60$), which suggests that there are frequent unexplained fluctuations around the trend.

Table A1.3: Regression Statistics for Seasonality of Light-distillate Exports. 1980–85 (24 Observations). Thousand Tonnes per Quarter.

Variable	Coefficient	Standard Error	t-statistic
Constant	1,103.2	100.12	11.02
Dummy	432.5	86.71	4.99
Second Quarter	107.8	115.61	0.93
Third Quarter	−43.7	115.61	−0.38
Fourth Quarter	148.7	115.61	1.29

$R^2 = 0.60$, $SEE = 200.25$, $DWS = 0.968$

APPENDIX 2
DETAILS OF THE SOVIET REFINERY SYSTEM

Table A2.1: Soviet Refineries by Region. 1986 Capacities in Thousand Barrels per Day and Dates of Commissioning.

	Capacity	Date of Commissioning
Caucasus/Caspian [1]		
Baku	820	1930s
Batumi	120	1930
Groznyi	480	1887
Gurev [2]	100	1945–7
Krasnodar/Tuapse	120	1909
Krasnovodsk	240	1942–3
Central		
Gorkii	480	1958
Moscow	240	1934–8
Ryazan	300	1960
Yaroslavl	480	1961
Volga–Urals [3]		
Kuibyshev [4]	720	1945
Nizhnekamsk	240	1979
Orsk [5]	240	1936
Perm	480	1957–8
Salavat/Ishimbai	240	1934–6
Saratov	300	1934
Syzran [6]	200	1942
Ufa	920	1936–8
Volgograd	240	1957
North West		
Kirishi	360	1966
Mazheikiai	240	1980
Mozyr	240	1975
Novopolotsk	400	1963
Ukhta	120	1947–9
Ukraine		
Drogobych	60	pre-1917
Kherson [7]	180	1930s
Kremenchug	300	1966
Lisichansk	360	1976

	Capacity	Date of Commissioning
Nadvornaya	120	1950s
Odessa	120	1930s
Central Asia/Kazakhstan		
Alty-Aryk[8]	40	1908
Chimkent	120	1985
Fergana[9]	140	1958–9
Pavlodar	360	1978
Siberia		
Achinsk	120	1982
Angarsk	600	1960–61
Omsk	600	1955
Far East[10]		
Khabarovsk	180	1935
Komsomolsk	60	1942

1. Wilson and Sagers list Tbilisi amongst the refineries in this region, Wilson describes it as 'small, old and obsolete', Sagers does not mention it, and it is not marked as a refinery on the map published by the UK Ministry of Defence. We have therefore assumed it is either inoperable or no longer in existence.
2. Wilson and OCS give capacity of Gurev in 1982 as 60,000 b/d. However, Sagers gives 1960 capacity as 100,000 b/d and throughput in 1980 as 120,000 b/d. Wilson says it was 'enlarged' in 1971. The discrepancy may possibly be due to older plant now being inoperable.
3. Krasnokamsk refinery, near Perm, is listed by both Wilson and OCS. Sagers states that it was listed in a primary source in 1969 but not in a more recent one in 1976. He assumes that it must have been dismantled in the early 1970s.
4. The older Kuibyshev refinery has a capacity of 120,000 b/d and was built in 1945. Novo-Kuibyshev, built around 1950, has a capacity of 600,000 b/d.
5. 240,000 b/d is the capacity given for Orsk in both Wilson and OCS data. Sagers gives a 1960 capacity of 40,000 b/d and estimates throughput in 1980 to have been 80,000 b/d. Wilson states that Orsk is amongst the least efficient of Soviet refineries and that it is running well under capacity.
6. Syzran capacity, according to Wilson and OCS, is 120,000 b/d. However, Sagers gives the capacity as at least 10 mtpa (200,000 b/d), based on primary source reports of three CDUs being built there, of 3, 5 and 2 mtpa respectively.
7. Wilson gives the date of building of Kherson as 1960; Sagers says that the refinery originated in the pre-war period and was restored after 1945.
8. Alty-Aryk is included in Sagers' refinery list but not in those of Wilson or OCS. It appears to be near to, but distinct from, Fergana in Central Asia.
9. Wilson and OCS give Fergana's capacity as 80,000 b/d, Sagers, however, gives a 1960 capacity of 100,000 b/d and states that the refinery was expanded in 1972. He estimates throughput in 1980 to be around 140,000 b/d at 'full capacity'. He cites a primary source giving a capacity of 120,000 b/d in 1964.
10. Sagers and Wilson differ significantly in their estimates of capacities for the Far East refineries. Wilson gives their capacities as 180,000 and 60,000 b/d respectively (agreeing with OCS). Sagers, on the other hand, says that Komsomolsk is 'somewhat larger' than Khabarovsk and gives total throughput in 1980 as only 100,000 b/d for the two refineries. We have put Wilson/OCS numbers in the tables but these may overstate the capacity at Khabarovsk.

Table A2.2: Age Distribution of Soviet Refinery Capacity by Region.[1] Thousand Barrels per Day.

	Pre-1945	1945–59	1960–69	1970–79	1980–85	Total
Caucasus/Caspian						
Baku[2]	200	220	–	240	160	820
Batumi	80	40	–	–	–	120
Groznyi[3]	240	–	120	120	–	480
Gurev	–	100	–	–	–	100
Krasnodar/Tuapse	20	60	40[e]	–	–	120
Krasnovodsk	140	–	100	–	–	240
	680	420	260	360	160	1,880
Central						
Gorkii	–	80	160	240	–	480
Moscow	60	–	60	120	–	240
Ryazan	–	–	180	120	–	300
Yaroslavl	–	–	480	–	–	480
	60	80	880	480	–	1,500
Volga–Urals						
Kuibyshev	–	360	240[e]	120[e]	–	720
Nizhnekamsk	–	–	–	240	–	240
Orsk	40	200	–	–	–	240
Perm	–	140	280	60	–	480
Salavat/Ishimbai	40	100	40[e]	60[e]	–	240
Saratov	80	100	120	–	–	300
Syzran	40	100	60	–	–	200
Ufa	40	320	440	120	–	920
Volgograd[4]	–	100	140[e]	–	–	240
	240	1,420	1,320	600	–	3,580
North West						
Kirishi[5]	–	–	240	120	–	360
Mazheikiai	–	–	–	–	240	240
Mozyr	–	–	–	240	–	240
Novopolotsk	–	–	160	240	–	400
Ukhta	–	120	–	–	–	120
	–	120	400	600	240	1,360
Ukraine						
Drogobych[6]	20	–	40	–	–	60
Kherson	20	–	120	40	–	180
Kremenchug[7]	–	–	180	120	–	300
Lisichansk	–	–	–	240	120	360
Nadvornaya	–	20	100	–	–	120
Odessa	20	100	–	–	–	120
	60	120	440	400	120	1,140

	Pre-1945	1945–59	1960–69	1970–79	1980–85	Total
Central Asia/Kazakhstan						
Alty-Aryk	20	20	–	–	–	40
Chimkent	–	–	–	–	120	120
Fergana	–	80	–	60	–	140
Pavlodar	–	–	–	120	240	360
	20	100	–	180	360	660
Siberia						
Achinsk	–	–	–	–	120	120
Angarsk	–	–	300	260	40	600
Omsk	–	320	120	160	–	600
	–	320	420	420	160	1,320
Far East						
Khabarovsk	20	160ᵉ	–	–	–	180
Komsomolsk	20	–	–	40ᵉ	–	60
	40	160	–	40	–	240

1. These data have been assembled from information published in Sagers, 1984, and in Wilson, 1983. In some cases, where the 1980 capacity is greater than that in 1960 but no reference is found to an expansion, we have estimated the timing of the expansion of plant. Such figures are identified as estimates.
2. At the beginning of the 1980s Baku had four separate plants. Two of these were very old (pre-1917) and were apparently to have been demolished in the early 1980s (Sagers). The other two were expanded in 1976 and 1981 respectively, but Sagers says that older sections of these plants were also to be razed.

   Total capacity in 1983, according to Wilson and OCS, was 820,000 b/d. Wilson disaggregates this total between the two newer plants as follows:

Novo-Baku	360,000 b/d	(built in 1953)
Baku '22nd Congress'	460,000 b/d	(built in the 1930s)

   Sagers reports capacity at Novo-Baku in 1964 to have been around 6 mtpa (120,000 b/d). Wilson refers to a 1972 plan calling for a doubling of capacity there and says that this was accomplished in 1977 with the commissioning of a new CDU to process Mangyshlak crude from Kazakhstan. According to Sagers the capacity of this new plant was 120,000 b/d. Wilson states that a further CDU was brought on stream in 1979, bringing the refinery's capacity to 18 mtpa (360,000 b/d).

   Both Wilson and Sagers report the commissioning of a new 6–8 million tonne unit at Baku '22nd Congress' in 1981.

   No other expansion at '22nd Congress' is mentioned by either source. Since 300,000 b/d seems too large for a pre-war refinery, we have estimated 200,000 b/d to be pre-war, with 100,000 b/d added in 1945–59 to bring 1960 capacity to the 420,000 b/d given by Sagers.

   It is possible that Wilson's figure of 460,000 b/d includes old plant that has now been razed or is mothballed.
3. Sagers gives capacity at Groznyi in 1960 as 240,000 b/d, and throughput in 1970 as 360,000 b/d. He and Wilson agree that a new 120,000 b/d unit was opened at the

Groznyi 'Lenin' plant in 1979, bringing capacity to 480,000 b/d. Since all three plants at Groznyi date from before World War II (one from 1897!), we have assumed that 240,000 b/d capacity is pre-war.

4. No mention is made in either source of an expansion at Volgograd. However, they both agree on current capacity of 240,000 b/d and Sagers gives 1960 capacity of 100,000 b/d. We have assumed the extra capacity was added in the 1960s.

5. Sagers says that the third CDU at Kirishi was added in 1971; Wilson gives this date as 1980. They agree that current capacity is 360,000 b/d.

6. According to Sagers the original plant dates from before the Revolution and was 'restored and expanded' after World War II. An additional 40,000 b/d is therefore assumed to have been added in the 1960s to reconcile Sagers' 1960 figure of 20,000 b/d with Wilson's and OCS's 60,000 b/d in 1983.

7. Sagers reports that Kremenchug had three 60,000 b/d units by 1970 and that a fourth was added in 1972.

   Wilson and OCS report 1983 capacity as 300,000 b/d and Wilson says that the refinery was expanded in 1978 with the opening of a crude pipeline from Lisichansk.

Table A2.3: Capacity, Throughput and Utilization Rates of Individual Refineries. 1980. Thousand Barrels per Day.

	Capacity	*Throughput*	*Utilization (%)*
Caucasus/Caspian			
Baku	600	500	83
Batumi	120	100	83
Groznyi	480	300	63
Gurev	100	120	120
Krasnodar/Tuapse	120	100	83
Krasnovodsk	240	160	67
Central			
Gorkii	480	500	104
Moscow	240	200	83
Ryazan	300	400	133
Yaroslavl[1]	480	220	46
Volga–Urals[2]			
Kuibyshev	720	685	95
Nizhnekamsk	240	160	67
Orsk	240	80	33
Perm	480	220	46
Salavat/Ishimbai	240	200	83
Saratov	300	120	40
Syzran	200	240	120
Ufa	920	725	79
Volgograd	240	200	83
North West			
Kirishi	360	400	111
Mazheikiai	120	140	117
Mozyr	240	240	100

	Capacity	Throughput	Utilization (%)
Novopolotsk	400	460	115
Ukhta[3]	120	40	33
Ukraine			
Drogobych	60	40	67
Kherson	180	120	67
Kremenchug	300	320	107
Lisichansk	240	300	125
Nadvornaya[4]	120	60	50
Odessa	120	60	50
Central Asia/Kazakhstan			
Alty-Aryk	40	40	100
Chimkent	n/a	n/a	n/a
Fergana	140	140	100
Pavlodar	120	160	133
Siberia			
Achinsk	n/a	n/a	n/a
Angarsk	560	460	82
Omsk	600	520	87
Far East			
Khabarovsk[5]	180	40	22
Komsomolsk	60	60	100

1. Sagers sees no increase in the capacity of Yaroslavl after 1974 and his throughput estimate of 220,000 b/d in 1980 is therefore unchanged from his figure for 1974. Wilson and OCS give a much higher capacity of 480,000 b/d.
2. The utilization rates appear to vary considerably from refinery to refinery in this region. Orsk, Perm and Saratov are apparently the most underused and those are certainly amongst the older refineries. However, Syzran is of comparable age, having had no new plant since 1970, and is fully utilized, according to Sagers' figures. Although the throughput for the region is probably quite accurate *in toto*, it is possible that his methodology for determining refinery-by-refinery throughput has led to apparent discrepancies in utilization between refineries which do not occur in practice.
3. Ukhta alone out of the five refineries in the North West region is not in close proximity to a large market. It is situated north of Moscow in the Komi ASSR where it refines local crude from the Komi field.
4. Lvov/Nadvornaya refines local crude from the declining West Ukrainian field. It is not in the pipeline network.
5. This apparently low utilization rate at Khabarovsk is due to the discrepancy between Sagers' estimate of capacity (40,000 b/d) and those of Wilson and OCS (180,000 b/d).

APPENDIX 3
THE SOVIET REFINERY MODEL

A3.1 The Model

A small linear programming model developed by High and Watt Associates for use on an IBM PC was kindly made available to us for analysis of the Soviet refining system.

The small size of the model allowed quick analysis and easy manipulation; on the other hand certain simplifying assumptions had to be made which must be taken into account in any deductions made from the analysis.

The main simplifying assumption made in constructing the model was that the refining system operates as one single refinery, in both technical and economic terms.

In practice the forty refinery complexes, many separated by huge distances, will each attempt to match output with local demand patterns which may differ significantly from region to region. Small amounts of excess product from inland regions may be too far from the ports to make them worth exporting. In these cases there will be an incentive to consume whatever the refinery produces locally. In winter particularly, the transportation of fuel oil over long distances is difficult because of its high viscosity, and this factor may inhibit its substitution by natural gas in areas where refinery output contains a high percentage of residue.

The assumption of a single refinery also fails to take into consideration the disparities in terms of age and efficiency of plant in different parts of the country. We have seen that the proportion of primary capacity that is more than twenty-five years old varies from 9 per cent in the North West to over 80 per cent in the Far East (see Section 4.2). Similarly, upgrading capacity comprises only 5 per cent of distillation capacity in the Far East compared with 15 per cent in the Caucasus/Caspian and Central Asia/Kazakhstan. Soviet refineries are, on average, believed to run less efficiently than those in Western Europe or the USA and this has been taken into account; however, overall technical efficiency may still be overestimated.

Products exports will be affected by some regional factors as well as by global factors. There may be no economic incentive for inland refineries to produce gas oil or F10 for export; refineries near the Black Sea or the Baltic, on the other hand, may run proportionately more crude than their local demand requires.

The other main assumptions relate to the qualities of crude and products. Soviet Export Blend is used as the only crude because no other detailed assays are available. This is less of an approximation now that it would have been in

1980 since all but five refineries are linked to the transcontinental pipeline system. Soviet Export Blend is a mixture of Siberian and Volga–Urals crudes, which are similar in composition, although Siberian crude is less sulphurous and slightly lighter (Campbell, 1976). Small amounts of other crudes are refined locally, including Ukrainian and Azerbaidzhanian crudes (light and low sulphur), Sakhalin from the Far East (exported in small quantities to Japan) and Mangyshlak crude from the north-east corner of the Caspian Sea, a sulphurous and waxy crude which has to be refined in specially built distillation units.

Since these local crudes make up less than 14 per cent of total production, the error involved in ignoring them is likely to be small. Only one or two quality specifications were set for each product. Specifications on exports are, of course, well documented but restrictions on internally consumed production are less well known. In the past consumers have tended to take whatever was produced rather than demand that specific standards be met (Sagers and Tretyakova, 1985); it appears, however, that quality controls are now adhered to more strictly. It is likely that specifications may vary regionally and also seasonally, since products require different qualities to perform well in cold weather. For simplicity, however, only one grade of each product has been included in the model.

A3.2 Method

Crude throughput and final demand for years up to 1985 were derived from the annual oil balance (see Chapter 2).

Total demand was split into main product streams using data from Campbell, 1983, Sagers and Tretyakova, 1985, and OCS. Since products exports to other CMEA countries are not sold at West European market prices and are of the same specifications as those used in the Soviet Union, the fixed demand in the model included exports to the CMEA. Export streams for Western markets were allowed for gasoline, naphtha, gas oil and F10.

In the modelling of past years for which certain data were known, crude throughput and internal demand were entered as fixed variables while export volumes were left unbounded. Since exports to the West were known for these years, the more uncertain demand levels and product specifications were varied until the export volumes generated were close to the actual figures.

This method allowed us to investigate the limits on individual product demands and specifications.

Once calibration of the historic data was completed, the effects on exports of varying crude throughput, plant capacities, demand and product qualities were investigated.

Details of the model data for 1980 are given below:

(*a*) *Crude*. The assay was based on that of Soviet Export Blend, but a slightly deeper cut (1 per cent) for gas oil was allowed (see Chapter 10 for the assay for Soviet Export Blend). Throughput was fixed at 451 mtpa or 9.1 mb/d.

(*b*) *Capacities*. For simplicity, all cracking was treated as catalytic cracking and no coking was included, since the capacity in 1980 was relatively small and the technology is complicated to model.

Cracking Process	*'000 b/d*
Crude Distillation	10,800
Catalytic Reforming	700
Catalytic Cracking	400
Visbreaking	80
Desulphurization[1]	2,000

(*c*) *Demand*[2]

	mtpa
Gasoline/LPG	66
Naphtha	12
Kerosine	31
Gas Oil	97
Residue[3]	191
Total[4]	397

(*d*) *Product Qualities*

Gasoline (one grade)[5]	5% minimum RON 93
	95% minimum RON 73
	Maximum RVP[6] 12.5
Kerosine	Maximum naphtha content 30%
	Straight-run cuts only
Gas Oil (one grade)	Maximum sulphur 0.3% weight[7]
	Pour point $-15\,°C$

[1] Since no accurate capacity for desulphurization was known, a large upper limit of 2 mb/d was set and the model allowed to use as much as it required under different assumptions.

[2] The fixed element of demand includes exports to the CMEA. An initial breakdown into individual products was estimated from data given by Campbell, 1983; Sagers and Tretyakova, 1985; and OCS. These figures appeared to give the best fit for 1980.

[3] This includes *mazut*, bitumen and lubricants.

[4] From the annual oil balance, Soviet final demand was 392 million tonnes, of which 9 million was supplied from gas refineries. Fixed demand on the oil refining system was therefore 383 million tonnes for domestic Soviet consumption plus 14 million for the CMEA countries.

[5] The quality of domestic gasoline was not known accurately and was varied frequently during calibration. These figures appeared to be the best quality attainable given the other constraints on the model. Exported gasoline is of poor quality and it was assumed that no specific export grade is made.

[6] Reid vapour pressure – a measure of the volatility of motor gasoline.

[7] This figure was reduced to 0.2 per cent for years after 1983.

| F10 | Maximum sulphur 2% weight
Maximum viscosity 100
centistokes at 50 °C
Straight-run cuts only |
| Other Residue | No quality restrictions |

APPENDIX 4
DEFINITIONS OF VARIABLES AND DATA SOURCES

Variable	Definition	Sources
CO	Crude oil exports to the OECD countries (excluding Finland) in million tonnes	OECD/IEA, *Quarterly Oil and Gas Statistics*
RP	Refined products exports to the OECD countries (excluding Finland)	OECD/IEA, *Quarterly Oil and Gas Statistics*
PI	Average oil price index (1980 = 100) of major fuel-exporting countries (annual)	IMF, *Primary Commodities: Market Developments and Outlook*
PO	Official prices of Arabian Light (quarterly)	IMF, *International Financial Statistics*
TOT	Terms-of-trade index (1980 = 100) computed as a ratio of the oil price index to an import price index, constructed as the weighted average of the US wheat price index and the unit value index of manufactured exports of developed market economies	(a) UNCTAD, *Handbook of International Trade and Development Statistics* (b) IMF, *International Financial Statistics* (c) IMF, *Primary Commodities: Market Developments and Outlook*
TBR	Trade balance with MDCs (excluding Finland) in million foreign trade roubles	
TBU	Trade balance with MDCs (excluding Finland) in million US dollars converted at official rates	(a) *VTSS* yearbook and monthly bulletin (b) WIIW (ed), 1985
TBC	Trade balance with MDCs (excluding Finland) divided by exports to the same area in the corresponding year	
TTBR TTBU TTBC	Trade balances with *all* non-Socialist countries in units as above	As for *TBR*, *TBU*, and *TBC*

RPCM   Refined products exports to   PlanEcon, 1986
         the CMEA–6 in million tonnes

APPENDIX 5
TYPICAL RUSSIAN GAS OIL CONTRACT

1. SELLER

....
....
....
....

2. BUYER

....
....
....
....

3. PRODUCT

Russian Gasoil

4. QUANTITY

20,000 Metric Tons $+/-$ 10 percent in sellers option.

5. QUALITY

Normal Russian Export Grade Gasoil having a pour point of max -10 degrees C. and a sulphur content of max 0.30 weight percent.

6. DELIVERY

In one lot as full or part cargo CIF one safe berth/port Antwerp, Rotterdam or Amsterdam buyers option during the period (15 day range) in sellers option. Sellers to give 2 working days notice of vessels delivery basis Rotterdam. Notice to be given within 17:00 hours London time.

7. PRICE

U.S. . . . . Dollars per metric ton CIF one safe berth/port Antwerp, Rotterdam or Amsterdam on Non-EEC basis.

8. PAYMENT

In U.S. dollars net cash by telegraphic transfer with value latest 2 days after discharge or 4 days after NOR tendered in disport (whichever first) against sellers telex invoice and their telexed letter of indemnity for missing documents. Such documents to follow soonest. Payment shall be covered by a letter of credit opened (from a bank and in a form acceptable to sellers) promptly upon receipt of nomination.

If after two working days notice no discharge port has been declared N.O.R. will be deemed to have been tendered and accepted for payment purposes provided vessel is anchored safely within area of discharge (respectively Amsterdam/Rotterdam/Antwerp).

If due date falls on Saturday or bank holiday other than Monday then value previous banking day to apply, if due date falls on Sunday or Monday bank holiday the value following banking day to apply.

9. DETERMINATION OF QUANTITY/QUALITY

As ascertained at loadport. In the event of a part cargo delivery with no separate bill of lading or unsegregated, possible outturn gains/losses shall be ascertained in disport(s) by an independent inspector and pro rated amongst receivers. Costs of the inspection to be shared 50/50 between buyer and seller.

10. LAYTIME

36 hours shinc (pro rata in case of part cargo) plus 6 hours NOR.

11. DEMURRAGE

As per charter party or AFRA applicable to size of delivery vessel in the event of Russian Tonnage.

12. OTHER TERMS AND CONDITIONS

(A) I. This contract shall be governed and interpreted by English law.
    II. Jurisdiction: Each party expressly submits to the jurisdiction of the London High Court.
(B)   Sellers to provide certificate of insurance covering at least Ingostrakh terms and conditions including leakage and/or shortage in excess of 0.5 percent for minimum 105 percent invoice value. Buyers to follow Ingostrakh requirements and rules for outturn inspection for insurance purposes. A combination of Ingostrakh and other first class insurance certificate acceptable or a first class Western insurance certificate covering 110 percent of cargo value with minimum terms/cover as Ingostrakh's certificate.
(C)   Otherwise this contract shall be governed by INCO terms 1980 with later amendments to apply.

BIBLIOGRAPHY

API, *Basic Petroleum Data Book: Petroleum Industry Statistics*, various issues, American Petroleum Institute, Washington DC.

Arrow, K. J., 1959, 'Toward a theory of price adjustment' in Abramovitz, M. and others, *The Allocation of Economic Resources: Essays in Honor of Bernard Francis Haley*, Stanford University Press.

Bacon, R., 1986, *The Brent Market: an Analysis of Recent Developments*, OIES Working Paper WPM8, Oxford Institute for Energy Studies.

Balkay, B., 1984, 'Intra-CMEA cooperation in fuels and energy in the light of recent developments in the world economy' in Nyiri, K. (ed), *Inter-CMEA Cooperation in Energy and New Trends in the World Economy*, Hungarian Council for World Economy, Budapest.

Balkay, B., 1985, *Some Macroeconomic Aspects of the CMEA Countries' Mineral Economy*, Forschungsbericht Nr 105, The Vienna Institute for Comparative Economic Studies.

Bergson, A. and Levine, H. S. (eds), 1983, *The Soviet Economy: Toward the Year 2000*, George Allen & Unwin, London.

Bethkenhagen, J., 1985, 'The impact of energy on East–West trade: retrospect and prospects' in Saunders, C. T. (ed), *East–West Trade and Finance in the World Economy: A New Look for the 1980s*, Macmillan Press for the Vienna Institute for Comparative Economic Studies, London.

BIS, *Annual Report*, various issues, Bank for International Settlements, Basle.

BP Statistical Review of World Energy, various issues, The British Petroleum Company plc, London.

Burkett, J., Portes, R., and Winter, D., 1981, *Macroeconomic Adjustment and Foreign Trade of Centrally Planned Economies*, NBER Working Paper No. 736, National Bureau of Economic Research, Cambridge, Massachusetts.

Campbell, R. W., 1968, *The Economics of Soviet Oil and Gas*, The Johns Hopkins University Press for Resources for the Future, Baltimore.

Campbell, R. W., 1976, *Trends in the Soviet Oil and Gas Industry*, The Johns Hopkins University Press for Resources for the Future, Baltimore and London.

Campbell, R. W., 1983, 'Energy' in Bergson and Levine (eds), 1983.

Charemza, W. and Gronicki, M., 1987 forthcoming, *Plans and Disequilibria in Centrally Planned Economies: Empirical Investigation for Poland*, North-Holland, Amsterdam.

Chassard, C. and Halliwell, M., 1986, *The NYMEX Crude Oil Futures Market: an Analysis of its Performance*, OIES Working Paper WPM9, Oxford Institute for Energy Studies.

CIA, *Handbook of Economic Statistics*, various issues, Directorate of Intelligence, Central Intelligence Agency, US Government Printing Office, Washington DC.

CIA, *International Energy Statistical Review*, various issues, Directorate of Intelligence, Central Intelligence Agency, US Government Printing Office, Washington DC.

CIA, 1977a, *Prospects for Soviet Oil Production*, Central Intelligence Agency, Washington DC.

CIA, 1977b, *Prospects for Soviet Oil Production: A Supplemental Analysis*, Central Intelligence Agency, Washington DC.

CIA, 1985, *USSR Energy Atlas*, US Government Printing Office, Washington DC.

Davidson, J. E. H., Hendry, D. F., Srba, F. and Yeo, S., 1978, 'Econometric modelling of the aggregate time-series relationship between consumers' expenditure and income in the United Kingdom', *The Economic Journal*, Vol. 88, December, pp. 661–692, Blackwell, Oxford.

Deger, S., 1985, 'Soviet arms sales to developing countries: the economic forces' in Cassen, R. (ed), *Soviet Interests in the Third World*, Sage Publications for the Royal Institute of International Affairs, London.

Dienes, L. and Shabad, T., 1979, *The Soviet Energy System: Resource Use and Policies*, V. H. Winston & Sons, Washington DC.

Dietz, R., 1985, 'Advantages and disadvantages in Soviet trade with Eastern Europe: the pricing dimension' in *East European Economies: Slow Growth in the 1980's*, Vol. 2, Selected papers submitted to the Joint Economic Committee, Congress of the United States, US Government Printing Office, Washington DC.

Economist Intelligence Unit, *Quarterly Energy Review: USSR & Eastern Europe*, various issues, The Economist Publications Ltd, London.

Estrada, J. H., 1984, 'The importance of the natural gas industry in the Soviet economy' in NATO, 1984.

Fama, E. F., 1970, 'Efficient capital markets: a review of theory and empirical work', *Journal of Finance*, Vol. XXV, No. 2, May, pp. 383–417, American Finance Association, New York.

FAO Production Yearbook, various issues, Statistics Division, Economic and Social Policy Department, Food and Agriculture Organization of the United Nations, Rome.

FAO Trade Yearbook, various issues, Statistics Division, Economic and Social Policy Department, Food and Agriculture Organization of the United Nations, Rome.

Gold, various issues, Consolidated Gold Fields PLC, London.

Goldman, M. I., 1980, *The Enigma of Soviet Petroleum*, George Allen & Unwin, London.

Goldman, M. I., 1983, 'The changing role of raw material exports and Soviet foreign trade' in Jensen et al, 1983.

Gustafson, T., 1983, 'Soviet energy policy' in JEC, 1983, Part 1.

Gustafson, T., 1985a, 'The origins of the Soviet oil crisis, 1970–85', *Soviet*

Economy, Vol. 1, No. 2, April–June, pp. 103–135, V. H. Winston & Sons, Washington DC.

Gustafson, T., 1985b, 'Soviet adaptation to technological pressures: the case of the oil and gas sector, 1975–85' in NATO, 1985.

Hannigan, J. B. and McMillan, C. H., 1984, 'The Soviet Union and world trade in oil and gas' in Kostecki (ed), 1984.

Hanson, P., 1981, Trade and Technology in Soviet–Western Relations, Macmillan, London

Hanson, P., 1982, 'The Soviet system as a recipient of foreign technology' in Amann, R. and Cooper, J. M. (eds), *Industrial Innovation in the Soviet Union*, Yale University Press, New Haven and London.

Hendry, D. F., 1979, 'Predictive failure and econometric modelling in macroeconomics: the transactions demand for money' in Ormerod, P. (ed), *Economic Modelling: Current Issues and Problems in Macroeconomic Modelling in the UK and the US*, Heinemann, London.

Hewett, E. A., 1983a, 'Soviet primary product exports to CMEA and the West' in Jensen et al, 1983.

Hewett, E. A., 1983b, 'Foreign economic relations' in Bergson and Levine (eds), 1983.

Hewett, E. A., 1984a, *Energy, Economics, and Foreign Policy in the Soviet Union*, The Brookings Institution, Washington DC.

Hewett, E. A., 1984b, 'Soviet economic relations with the CMEA countries' in NATO, 1984.

Hewett, E. A., 1987 forthcoming, 'Soviet oil' in Mabro, R. (ed), *The 1986 Oil Price Crisis: Economic Effects and Policy Responses*, Oxford University Press for the Oxford Institute for Energy Studies.

Holzman, F. D., 1968, 'Soviet central planning and its impact on foreign trade behavior and adjustment mechanisms' in Brown, A. A. and Neuberger, E. (eds), *International Trade and Central Planning: An Analysis of Economic Interactions*, University of California Press, Berkeley and Los Angeles.

IMF, *International Financial Statistics*, various issues, Bureau of Statistics, International Monetary Fund, Washington DC.

IMF, *Primary Commodities: Market Developments and Outlook*, Commodities Division of the Research Department, International Monetary Fund, Washington DC.

JEC, 1983, *Soviet Economy in the 1980's: Problems and Prospects*, Parts 1 and 2, Selected papers submitted to the Joint Economic Committee, Congress of the United States, US Government Printing Office, Washington DC.

Jensen, R. G., Shabad, T., and Wright, A. W. (eds), 1983, *Soviet Natural Resources in the World Economy*, The University of Chicago Press.

Kanet, R. E., 1983, 'Soviet and East European arms transfers to the Third World: strategic, political, and economic factors' in NATO, 1983.

Kaser, M. C., 1983a, 'External relations of Comecon countries: gold sales and prospects' in NATO, 1983.

Kaser, M. C., 1983b, 'The Soviet gold-mining industry' in Jensen et al, 1983.

Kaser, M. C., 1984, 'The Soviet impact on world trade in gold and platinum' in Kostecki (ed), 1984.

Kostecki, M. M., 1984, 'The Soviet Union in international grain markets' in Kostecki, M. M. (ed), *The Soviet Impact on Commodity Markets*, Macmillan, London.

Leggett, R., 1983, 'Soviet investment policy in the 11th five-year plan' in JEC, 1983, Part 1.

Mabro, R., Bacon, R., Chadwick, M., Halliwell, M. and Long, D., 1986, *The Market for North Sea Crude Oil*, Oxford University Press for the Oxford Institute for Energy Studies.

Marrese, M. and Vanous, J., 1983, *Soviet Subsidization of Trade with Eastern Europe: A Soviet Perspective*, Research Series No. 52, Institute of International Studies, University of California, Berkeley.

Narodnoe khozyaistvo SSSR: statisticheskii ezhegodnik (National Economy of the USSR: Statistical Yearbook), various issues, TsSU SSSR (Central Statistical Office of the USSR), Moscow.

NATO, 1983, *External Economic Relations of CMEA Countries: Their Significance and Impact in a Global Perspective*, Colloquium, Economics and Information Directorate, NATO, Brussels.

NATO, 1984, *The Soviet Economy after Brezhnev*, Colloquium, Economics and Information Directorate, NATO, Brussels.

NATO, 1985, *Adaptability to New Technologies of the USSR and East European Countries*, Colloquium, Economics and Information Directorate, NATO, Brussels.

Neuberger, E. and Tyson, L. D'A. (eds), 1980, *The Impact of International Economic Disturbances on the Soviet Union and Eastern Europe: Transmission and Response*, Pergamon Press, New York.

OECD, *Financial Market Trends*, various issues, Organisation for Economic Co-operation and Development, Paris.

OECD, *Foreign Trade by Commodities, Series C*, various issues, Department of Economics and Statistics, Organisation for Economic Co-operation and Development, Paris.

OECD/IEA, *Quarterly Oil and Gas Statistics*, various issues, Organisation for Economic Co-operation and Development/ International Energy Agency, Paris.

Oil & Gas Journal, various issues, PennWell Publishing Co., Tulsa, Oklahoma.

OPEC Annual Statistical Bulletin, various issues, The Secretariat, Organization of the Petroleum Exporting Countries, Vienna.

OPEC Bulletin, various issues, Organization of the Petroleum Exporting Countries, Vienna.

Petroleum Economist, various issues, Petroleum Press Bureau Ltd, London.

Petroleum Intelligence Weekly, various issues, Petroleum & Energy Intelligence Weekly, Inc., New York.

PlanEcon, 1986, *Soviet and East European Energy Databank*, PlanEcon, Inc., Washington DC.

Platt's Oilgram Price Report, various issues, McGraw-Hill, Inc., New York.

Platt's Oil Price Handbook and Oilmanac, various issues, McGraw-Hill, Inc., New York.

Portes, R. D., 1980, 'Internal and external balance in a centrally planned economy' in Neuberger and Tyson (eds), 1980.

Portes, R. D., 1983, Background Paper in *Deficits and Détente*, Report of an International Conference on the Balance of Trade in the Comecon Countries, The Twentieth Century Fund, New York.

Roberts, S. J., 1984, *Who Makes the Oil Price? An Analysis of Oil Price Movements 1978–1982*, OIES Working Paper WPM4, Oxford Institute for Energy Studies.

Sagers, M. J., 1984, *Refinery Throughput in the USSR*, CIR Staff Paper No. 2, USSR Input–Output Branch, Center for International Research, Bureau of the Census, US Department of Commerce, Washington DC.

Sagers, M. J. and Tretyakova, A. F., 1985, *Restructuring the Soviet Petroleum Refining Industry*, CIR Staff Paper No. 4, Soviet Economic Studies Branch, Center for International Research, Bureau of the Census, US Department of Commerce, Washington DC.

Sagers, M. J. and Tretyakova, A. F., 1986, 'Constraints in gas for oil substitution in the USSR: the oil refining industry and gas storage', *Soviet Economy*, Vol. 2, No. 1, V. H. Winston & Sons, Washington DC.

Stern, J. P., 1983, 'CMEA oil acquisition policy in the Middle East and the Gulf: the search for economic and political strategies' in JEC, 1983, Part 1.

Stern, J. P., 1984, *International Gas Trade in Europe: The Policies of Exporting and Importing Countries*, British Institutes' Joint Energy Policy Programme, Energy Paper No. 8, Heinemann, London.

Treml, V. G., 1983, 'Soviet dependence on foreign trade' in NATO, 1983.

Tretyakova, A. and Heinemeier, M., 1986, *Cost Estimates for the Soviet Oil Industry: 1970 to 1990*, CIR Staff Paper No. 20, Center for International Research, Bureau of the Census, US Department of Commerce, Washington DC.

UNCTAD, *Handbook of International Trade and Development Statistics*, various issues, United Nations Conference on Trade and Development, Geneva.

UNECE, *Economic Bulletin for Europe: The Journal of the United Nations Economic Commission for Europe*, various issues, Pergamon Press for the United Nations, Oxford.

UNECE, *Economic Survey of Europe*, various issues, United Nations, New York.

VTSS yearbook, *Vneshnyaya torgovlya SSSR: statisticheskii obzor* (Foreign Trade of the USSR: Statistical Abstract), various issues, Ministry of Foreign Trade, Moscow.

VTSS monthly bulletin, various issues, Ministry of Foreign Trade, Moscow (see above).

Weekly Petroleum Argus, various issues, Petroleum Argus Ltd, London.

WIIW (ed), 1985, *Comecon Foreign Trade Data 1984*, Macmillan Press for the Vienna Institute for Comparative Economic Studies, London.

WIIW (ed), 1986, *CMEA Selected Economic Indicators 1986*, Die Erste Österreichische Spar-Casse – Bank (First Austrian Bank), Vienna.

Wilson, D., 1983, *The Demand for Energy in the Soviet Union*, Croom Helm, London.

Wilson, D., 1986, 'Serious implications in oil shortfall in the USSR', *Petroleum Review*, Vol. 40, No. 468, January, pp. 18–19, The Institute of Petroleum, London.

Wolf, T. A., 1982, 'Soviet market power and pricing behaviour in Western export markets', *Soviet Studies*, Vol. XXXIV, No. 4, October, pp. 529–546, University of Glasgow Press.

Wolf, T. A., 1983, 'Changes in the pattern of Soviet trade with the CMEA and the "non-Socialist" countries' in NATO, 1983.

Yuasa, T., 1985, 'The Soviet crude oil production hit the ceiling – delicate effects on oil exports', *Energy in Japan*, No. 76, September, pp. 23–30, The Institute of Energy Economics, Tokyo.

Zoeter, J. P., 1983, 'USSR: hard currency trade and payments' in JEC, 1983, Part 2.